THE RETURN
OF THE AUTHOR

Rethinking Theory

GENERAL EDITOR

Gary Saul Morson

CONSULTING EDITORS

Robert Alter
Frederick Crews
John M. Ellis
Caryl Emerson

The Return
of the Author

Eugen Simion

Edited with an introduction by
James W. Newcomb

Translated from Romanian by
James W. Newcomb and Lidia Vianu

Northwestern University Press
Evanston, Illinois

Northwestern University Press
Evanston, Illinois 60208–4210

Library of Congress Cataloging-in-Publication Data

Simion, Eugen.
    [Întoarcerea autorului. English]
    The return of the author / Eugen Simion ; edited with an
introduction by James W. Newcomb ; translated from Romanian by
James W. Newcomb and Lidia Vianu.
        p.   cm.—(Rethinking theory)
    Not all the original essays are included.
    Includes bibliographical references.
    ISBN 0-8101-1272-8. — ISBN 0-8101-1273-6 (pbk.)
    1. French literature—20th century—History and criticism.
I. Newcomb, James W.   II. Title.   III. Series.
PQ305.S4913   1996
801'.95'0904—dc20   96-14373
                                                                         CIP

Contents

II. The Author's Life of the Author

Introduction

Eugen Simion's title *The Return of the Author* (*Întoarcerea Autorului*) represents a good deal more than just an assertion of the reappearance of the author, that figure who, for a number of reasons, seems to have been temporarily absent from the field of criticism. This title and the work it represents arrive not merely in a setting unreceptive to the author's return, but indeed in a world where the presumption implicit in suggesting such a return borders on a simplistic, if not perverse, nostalgia for a dead past.

For the contemporary reader of criticism, the demise of the author as an object of study and esteem or even as a concept is well known and in a good many circles generally taken as no longer arguable. If Roland Barthes in "The Death of the Author" (1968) did not sufficiently finish off discussion of the idea of the author, Michel Foucault's "What Is an Author?" (1969) certainly managed to relegate the author to a mere "projection" lacking substance beyond the convenience the word *author* might offer to critics writing about texts. With the ascendancy of structuralist and then poststructuralist criticism in America, many minds rested assured that consideration of an author in critical discourse was moot, transcending intentionality, character, or any other issue centered upon the idea of a being who creates a work.

Nor has the author fared much better, as one might reasonably expect, in critical standpoints grounded more centrally in the politics of empowerment. Whether the discourse examines and champions groups identified by gender, ethnic origin, or other characteristics, the Foucauldian strictures continue to relegate the author to the role of being a convenient marker by which a group may identify the extent of its inclusion or exclusion from dominant positions in the creation or the study of literature. Usually, the individual who is an author can only be subsumed into the group regardless of whether the group is dominant or seeking to be so. In those infrequent instances where an author does receive consideration as an individual, the critical stance otherwise employed most often is more or less held in suspension rather than expanded to incorporate or include the living being of an author.

The history of the author's banishment from critical transactions stretches back much further, however, than just the past few decades, for the critical positions prevailing, in America at least, before the rise of the poststructuralists also relegated the author to a position on the fringes of critical discourse. Latter-day pronouncements by mostly French thinkers on the superfluity of the author

1

thus fell on fertile ground in America, where the formalisms familiar to an earlier generation of critics had dominated. Whether these earlier formalisms drew their inspiration from the New Criticism of the Cleanth Brooks and Robert Penn Warren variety or the Cambridge method of I. A. Richards, American critics of this earlier generation had accepted as indisputable that the author was at best a peripheral figure of little interest in the business of criticism. Discussions of the author could only suggest those nineteenth-century critics who, with only mild discomfort at the disparity between widely held tastes and the overriding strictures of morality, dismissed Lord Byron because he was, after all, "a rake and a rogue." The "text itself" was the only legitimate focus to the mind of mid-century American critics.

To be sure, arguments for chasing the author from the critical engagement with a work differed in the two generations of criticism. With the advent of the New Criticism, the Anglo-American formalisms centered attention on what were taken to be eternal and unchanging works. Eternal verities having universal truth as their hallmark characterized the works worthy of esteem and critical notice. History and historical issues, of course, could not affect the fixed and transcendent character of these "great" works studied by the critics; because an author, in his or her finitude and mortal condition, was a historical figure, accounts of the writer as a person were curiosities if not just unnecessary asides. In no serious critical discussion could the author or the author's life bear greatly on the judgments leading to an understanding of the universals furnishing criticism its justification.

While New Criticism rejected the author on theoretical grounds, in practical application this approach represented a modern turning away from the biographism of the nineteenth century, where the moral standing of an author served as a measure of the quality inherent in the author's works. If the inadequacies of biographical criticism as practiced in the nineteenth century have so paled into ill-defined memories in our own time as to make us forget why biographism was discarded as a defensible foundation for commenting on a work, more recent critical pronouncements are sufficient to remind us that the biography of a writer stands as a bit of exotica, a diverting recreation perhaps, but by no means a central feature in an assessment of that writer's works. So even as the New Criticism was running its course, the author's lack of standing, in American criticism at any rate, created conditions receptive to an outright dismissal of authorial agency in the creation of the work.

The agenda common in our time to all species of formalism removes a work from the world producing and receiving it in order to concentrate on the "text itself." To be sure, not all species of criticism are formalistic, and other paradigms exist. If the reader at least has come to play a role in constituting the literary work in the eyes of American criticism, through the instigation of continental critics such as Wolfgang Iser and Hans Robert Jauss, the ascendant formalisms still, and not without reason, fear the concept of the author.

Given the presuppositions of a formalistic view of literature, the author is indeed menacing, for granting the author admittance to the literary equation opens the way to determining a text, to centering it and asserting a unity parallel to the supposed unity of the consciousness that produced it. For the formalist, to acknowledge the existence of the author is tantamount to granting that person the authority to fix the meaning of the text. While earlier formalisms though rejecting the author, imputed a unity to texts, more recent theorists deny such unity as well. Deconstructionists, too, share the ahistorical cast of earlier formalisms and, as is becoming increasingly clear, must share the critical dead-end of past formalisms, where the solipsism created theoretically finally shows itself.

Hence, for the better part of our century, the author has been safely ignored, with some discomfort by the earlier formalisms but without apology by the critical stances superseding them. Poststructuralists, particularly Foucault and the later Barthes, rejected the notion of presumably unified works that defied history with transcendental truths and posited instead texts constituted anew by each rereading. Still, the author posited by poststructuralist argument—indeed, a paradoxical positing—had to be banished as a consequence of his or her removal from readings subsequent to the initial impulse first giving being to the text.

While the two critical positions brought disparate premises to the question of what little might be said of an author, their grounding was shaped in both cases by the rationalistic spirit characterizing their argument. In either case the author is argued out of the critic's field of view, in the earlier formalisms because the author was not germane to the critic's central concern and in the more recent case because the amorphous and ever-changing text quite logically must reside beyond a relationship with the author. Remaining faithful to the ultimately rationalistic principles underlying the newer formalisms, such criticism, quite consistently, locks out the author from its discourse.

In broad terms, this then was the critical landscape in the west when Eugen Simion published *The Return of the Author* in Bucharest in 1981 during perhaps the darkest period in modern Romanian history. At that time Nicolae Ceauşescu had implemented what he learned on his infamous 1971 Asian trip to North Korea, where Kim Il Sung had taught him the finer points of converting what had been a simple authoritarian state ruled by a decidedly nationalistic regime into a thoroughgoing totalitarian reign of terror complete with a cult of personality. In the Romania of the now completely despotic Ceauşescu, a country where the very act of speaking to a foreigner required a trip to the dreaded Securitate for a report and a lengthy interrogation, intellectual life was all but stifled and forced to move underground or migrate. And so Simion's book languished virtually unread outside his country. These circumstances do not mean that in the interim the widespread acceptance of the author's demise went unchallenged in the west, but voices issuing the challenge (e.g., such critics as Philippe Lejeune in *Poétique*) were by no means common.

Nor is it at all clear that Simion would have gained much of a hearing in the decade subsequent to the publication of his book. As critics in America rallied around the postmodernists who accepted the death of the author as an article of faith, Simion's voice undoubtedly stood scant chance of attracting a disinterested audience. For one thing, he wrote as an intelligent and perceptive mind intent on presenting his case with clarity, declining to employ the critical jargon of mainstream critical discourse. Another obstacle to finding an audience among thinkers in the west was the central European habit of moving in leisurely fashion through his subject, neither availing himself of the rigors of academic form, nor presuming the precision of scientific investigation—eschewing, as he terms it at one point, "methodological terrorism." Then too, Eugen Simion is not given to the fulmination so characteristic of contemporary criticism, preferring instead to argue his case with presentations of the evidence for readers to see and judge. Instead of a polemic, Simion simply lays out what he sees and then wonders on paper how what he has seen stands so strikingly at odds with the author's death notices witnessed in our time.

With Ceauşescu's overthrow at the end of 1990, the opportunity for contacts with scholars and critics outside of Romania opened again, and what in 1981 had been a single voice asking only that the question of the author at least be opened for discussion joined the still small but growing band of thinkers skeptical not necessarily of the whole of contemporary critical thought but of some of the critical pieties canonized as transcending further discussion.

In the years since Simion published, the increased emphasis on the permutations of class, and more particularly ethnicity and gender, as they inform expressive discourse suggests that a more sympathetic reception of the author in criticism is likely. With the reshaping of canons to remedy exclusions based on gender or ethnicity, it would seem that the author and the conditions of the author's existence would have risen to a new prominence. Still, with his reluctance to assent to the rationalistically derived conclusions of the poststructuralists, Simion can expect a less than warm welcome from more contemporary western critics (both those drawing on Gramscian premises and those proceeding from Althusserian groundings), who so often seem to place but a limited faith in empirical evidence.

If this brief account of the critical setting in America broadly covers that location where *The Return of the Author* would assert itself now, the critical atmosphere differs not so greatly from the intellectual audience for which it was originally written. The Romanian habit of referring to Bucharest as "the Paris of the East" on its surface seems redolent of middle-American boosterism, but a long history of Franco-Romanian connections in architecture, fashion, and intellectual life stretching over the last century or two lends credence to the phrase. In the years just after Simion returned to Bucharest, having taught in Paris, he reacted to developments in France he felt he could not accept. In particular, his book was an attempt to distance himself from the *Tel Quel* group.

This distance also provides something of a contradiction, for if Barthes is one of the founding fathers of the critical stance finding its voice in *Tel Quel*, he is also someone Simion wants to see as at odds with the direction in which *Tel Quel* as journal and as publisher was taking the idea of the author. Throughout *The Return of the Author* Simion refers to the *nouvelle critique* or the *newer critics* to underscore his opposition to the critical position refusing to acknowledge the author. Occasionally, as if to remind the reader of their association with formalist criticism, he will call these same critics the *neo-rhetoricians* or the *rhetorical critics*. If Simion cannot shake these critics loose from their position, he can at the very least show that one of the most distinguished names associated with the author's death is not so wholly committed to the *Tel Quel* agenda.

To efface the author altogether strikes Simion as antihuman, a not surprising response from a person who has lived so much of his life in close proximity to concentration camps and gulags, institutions sharing the common goal of destroying all particles of the human, the individual. In a very important sense, Simion feels the need to assert the presence of the human in the literary product, for without human presence, for Simion, literature as valued product is barely defensible.

Fully aware of the theoretical underpinnings of those determined to eliminate the author, Simion nonetheless is unable to dismiss entirely the person behind the work. If the cry in our century has not been just the lone voice, but hordes of onlookers crying out *le roi est nu*, Simion was willing to stand as the lone individual who quietly points out that the emperor *does* have some clothes on despite what the crowd calls out. Not just an unfounded assertion, Simion's observation is backed by the investigation presented here, which declines to allow theoretical requirements to contort what experience has demonstrated to be otherwise. Given a choice between a theoretical necessity requiring blinders and what his own eyes present to him, Simion is likely to respond, "Well, . . ."

Nor is Simion able to subscribe wholly to the critical positions with foundations grounded in historical, political, and cultural discourses increasingly shaping the center of American critical thought. These discourses, whether Gramscian, Althusserian, or occasionally arising from more indigenous sources, usually manifest a distrust of empiricism that too often extends to presentations of empirical evidence, and it would take a special kind of arrogance to ask a Romanian intellectual, a person who has lived under political fictions of obscene dimension, to ignore the empirical altogether for the sake of a theory, whether that theory be political or critical or of some other kind.

It remained for Simion, an outsider not altogether outside, to doubt the doubters, to look for himself to see whether the emperor indeed had no clothes.

Simion's contribution to this skepticism, his doubt that the author is defunct, takes the form of examining the course of this idea in our century. Beginning with Marcel Proust's vendetta against the biographism of Charles Augustin Sainte-Beuve and moving on through the pronouncements of Roland Barthes, Simion is ever asking what we are to make of the curious state of affairs wherein the most vehement denials of the existence of an author invariably are attended not only by an exceptional degree of self-referentiality, not just as the person whose name happens to sit on a title page, but by a self-referentiality to that concept of author at the same time so thoroughly denounced.

Simion divides *The Return of the Author* into two parts. The first of these, twenty-four brief chapters, constitutes his argument (*demonstration* is perhaps a more apt description) that, despite protests to the contrary, the presence of the author is inescapable. The second part of the book, where Jean-Paul Sartre, André Malraux, Eugène Ionesco, and Roland Barthes are examined more closely, is something of an application of the argument Simion lays down in the first part. This latter part then is not just an exposition showing that the author is present despite disclaimers to the contrary, but is itself a demonstration of how the critic approaches a writer's work without ignoring the person who is the writer.

Given the theoretical environment in which Simion asserts the author's presence, it is perhaps surprising that he begins with Marcel Proust, who antedates the rise of the formalisms that thrust aside the author on theoretical grounds. A theoretical argument for the reintroduction of the author into critical discourse could be justified easily by beginning with either the American New Critics or the poststructuralists, but beginning with Proust warrants explanation. Not only does Simion begin with Proust, but in the Romanian version of the work he entitled the first part of the book "Contre Saint Proust" to indicate his questioning of Proust's *Contre Sainte-Beuve* and also to signify how the Proustian denial of the author's presence provides a precedent for later writers who would reject the author as a term in the critical enterprise. Though Proust's motivations for rejecting the author, or to be precise the author as represented in Sainte-Beuve's biographism, rest more on a personal antipathy than on a theoretical foundation, subsequent writers were quick to articulate theoretically coherent premises to justify the author's dismissal. While Proust, whose *Remembrance of Things Past* is arguably the most intensely autobiographical of fictional works in our century, seems an unlikely starting point for discussions of the author's disappearance, his vehemence in rejecting even the possibility of biographical criticism rests, as Simion demonstrates in his first six chapters, on a relationship to Sainte-Beuve that represents more than a mere difference of critical standpoints. It is worth noting, as well, that Barthes's initial battles with the French intellectual establishment attack an entrenched historical approach not so greatly removed from the Sainte-Beuve serving as Proust's target.

The "Sainte-Beuve complex" identified in Proust establishes a twofold pattern Simion finds repeated over and over in other writers. It would be a mistake, however, to think that Simion is citing a lesser-known collection of Proust's essays as the seminal influence on subsequent critics. Still, Proust, with firm demarcations, will distinguish between the self that writes and the person who lives an everyday life, and even firmer is his desire that the disjunction not be abrogated. Drawing on the posthumously published *Contre Sainte-Beuve*, Simion sees in Proust's railings another element in the pattern: the reaction against the authority figure residing not just in the concept of the author but in the prying critic as well. Without pushing into the practice of psychobiography, Simion presents us with speculations as to how authority customarily resting in the father, that traditional rival against whom the son would create his own manner of being in the world, is easily transferred to the critic who practices biographism and, by extension, to the very idea of an author.

With Proust as the model, Simion in the remaining eighteen chapters of part I goes on to examine Stéphane Mallarmé, Paul Valéry, Sartre, and Barthes, along with brief excursions to take up other critics, considering both divisions of the self and also examining the implications of psychoanalytic criticism for what he sees in a writer who insists on the division of writer and private person. If two such selves exist, he asks, can we not avoid both the problems of biographism and the extremes of psychobiographical criticism (see chapter 12) and at least examine that self which created the work? Concluding with a discussion of the implications of an invisible author, Simion is ready to begin his assessments that not only describe practices in four writers but also exemplify how a writer can be approached as an author, an approach embracing neither the biographism of Sainte-Beuve nor a thoroughgoing psychobiography.

It is worth noting that the spirit of Barthes informs the whole of *The Return of the Author*. The discussion of Proust in chapters 1–6 is followed by what might appear to be a curious assemblage of writers on which to meditate on the role of the author, but those who stand at the center of Simion's interest just happen to be cited by Barthes in "The Death of the Author" in support of his thesis. In taking them up, Simion shows that their banishment of the author is not so complete as current criticism would have it. Valéry, like Arthur Rimbaud, ends up hedging his pronouncements (chapter 9), and the author will then be found, as Simion notes is finally the case with Barthes, in "the anteroom of . . . reading."

Proust's specific complaint, that the person who writes is a *deeper self* distinct from the social being in the person of the writer, lays the foundation for Simion to follow how the self is seen by other writers who view it as distinct from the person of an author. Reaching back to the nineteenth century, first to Rimbaud (whose self was an *other*) and then to Mallarmé (whose self is virtually the text), Simion describes conceptions of a self-as-author antedating Proust and then examines Valéry and his conception of a *pure self* (chapters 8–10) creating and created by the work, this despite whatever else Valéry might have said regarding a work and the agency of its creation. Simion plays off their conceptions of the author who is an *other* in its variety of manifestations (the deeper self, the pure self) to show that the author is not altogether absent.

Though it is clear enough in the text, both in the opening chapter of the first part of the book and again in chapter 24, the reader should perhaps be reminded that Eugen Simion never yearns for a return to that biographism of the sort practiced by Sainte-Beuve that dominated nineteenth-century criticism. He does ask questions about the role of the author, questions which could well prove embarrassing except that he asks them with the same gentle good humor suggested by the slight irony found in the title he chose. When his quest through a number of twentieth-century writers is complete, one can still question the contemporary role of the author, but the return of that author clearly shows the alleged death was, as Mark Twain put it, greatly exaggerated. Moreover, those writers, beginning with Proust, who rang the author's death knell with such vigor provide the most telling evidence that the return of the author was not a particularly lengthy journey. In fact, as Simion demonstrates again and again, the very idea of authorship is barely out of sight among authorship's greatest detractors.

After dealing with writers on the topic of the author both conceptually and as the subject of biographies, Simion turns to examine more closely writers who, despite their sympathies with those who interdict the notion of the author, have themselves become autobiographical. Without losing sight of the paternal authority implied in the idea of the author and without being in the least derisive of the contradictions in these figures, Simion considers where the autobiographical writings of Sartre, Malraux, Ionesco, and, yes, Barthes can finally lead.

It is something of a sign of Simion's good faith that he refrains from resurrecting the story of Jean-Paul Sartre's rejection of the Nobel Prize on the grounds that it would cause people to buy his books because a Nobel laureate's name was on the title page instead of for what was said in those writings. Alluding to the rejection of the Nobel Prize would diminish Sartre, and that is not Simion's purpose, which is to examine the unquestionable presence of Sartre the person in his writings and to examine the consequences of Sartre's decision to write of the formation of the person he had become. Simion wishes to show that the pronouncements of those who would efface the author are at odds with their practice.

Taking Sartre's autobiographical work *The Words* as his exemplum, Simion dissects the poseur in the character of this work describing Sartre's childhood to find Sartre the person. Examining how Sartre, like so many other writers, grows up without a father, Simion finds that the absent patriarch presents not a case for psychoanalysis so much as a subject who in the course of becoming a writer has had to invent himself and that the impostures of his childhood, described by the middle-aged adult, indeed are the author. The poses struck by the child, as described by the adult, in fact, are what the adult is: the child who has mystified the adults is later on the adult who mystifies. Or, as Simion quotes Sartre toward the end of *The Words*, "Though they are worn out, blurred, humiliated, thrust aside, ignored, all of the child's traits are still to be found in the quinquagenarian." That is, the impossibility of knowing the person of the author becomes for the reader a knowledge of the author.

Nor is Malraux twitted for his megalomania, for choosing to live his life through a series of roles. It would seem, as with Sartre and more fully with Ionesco and Barthes, that Simion rather admires Malraux, but that he will not let his admiration blind him to flaws in the person responsible for the writings he admires. If Malraux can point to himself as a model for almost any admirable quality— humility, perhaps, excepted—his habit neither detracts from his achievements nor demonstrates the author's demise. While a nineteenth-century biographism could easily see the flaw in the author as the flaw in the work, Simion will have none of it. Establishment of the author's undeniable presence is enough.

As if to draw upon the deeper self, the pure self, the other, Simion looks to Malraux to see that there is something besides the biography that can be called the author, something that lies between the total being a nineteenth century biographer sought to capture and the author pronounced dead by modern criticism. Malraux the author is actively present in his works. In Malraux's works Simion looks both to what would ordinarily be called autobiography (accounts of his own acts) and to biography (his encounters with Charles de Gaulle) to demonstrate that for Malraux "the individual life is a point of intersection for the great roads of history." Like Sartre, Malraux is creating an existence—one might say an author—but his differs by his standing at a Parnassian distance from his subject.

The dismissal of author as idea continues in Simion's chapter where he takes up Ionesco, but here the rationale, unlike the case with Sartre or Barthes, is by no means theoretical. Ionesco's abhorrence of theory is well established. The one constant, however, is that thread going back to Proust: the absence of the father who stands as authority, the definitive arbiter who is not to be challenged. Simion's theme holds as well where, as is the case with Ionesco, theory is abhorred.

In his meditation on Ionesco, a fellow countryman though an expatriate, Simion comes to grips with the fragmentary character of what the playwright finds in his past and marvels at Ionesco's lack of concern at this state of affairs. "Here is a writer who describes the great misfortunes awaiting a human destiny, yet whose sentences convey his intense delight in retelling all these misfortunes." Ionesco, in fact, read Simion's work and endorsed what was said about him. And this endorsement undoubtedly came with an awareness that the author of a work called *Anti-Memoirs* presented an all too human author behind all the paradoxes.

After the bravura essay on Ionesco, Simion's concluding piece on Barthes may seem somewhat anticlimactic, but the thread of the absent father running through the lives of so many of the figures treated earlier extends to Barthes as well. Simion takes up *Camera Lucida*, Barthes's final work, and shows that what Barthes earlier has called the "formidable paternity" residing in the concept of the author also applies to the Barthes who in examining photographs ponders some of his own history. At the same time, in this last section Simion knows he is attempting over and over to classify a writer who will not be classified. It is as if Simion seeks in Barthes a validation of the position that the *Tel Quel* critics have parted company with the person so responsible years before for their grounding. And if Barthes cannot be tidily classified into a single category, he at least demonstrates finally that he can be present in his writings.

With these concluding sections on Roland Barthes, it would almost seem as if Simion is relieved to find a living person, an author if you will, behind the critic who erected what is perhaps the definitive epitaph for the author. When Simion was a visiting professor of Romanian language and literature at the Sorbonne from 1971 to 1973, he sat as an auditor in Roland Barthes's seminar. Despite this proximity and despite his obvious fascination with Barthes's writings, Simion could not be called a disciple of Barthes, for he was early troubled with the formalistic character of Barthean structuralism, a misgiving working itself out in his questioning here of Barthes's writings, in both the latter's structuralist and poststructuralist periods. When Barthes one day, in reply to Simion's question regarding literature, responded, "I'm not interested in what flows through the pipes but rather in the plumbing system itself," Simion knew that he himself was destined to raise some questions in a longer work. The "author" of *Camera Lucida*, Barthes's last work, is clearly the Barthes that Simion wants to see, for in this final work Barthes finally becomes human, becomes an author. The man who decreed the author dead once and for all becomes an author himself before he dies. Barthes is not rescued by Simion; he has rescued himself.

It remains to say something of the author who would call us to see authors in assessing their writings. Born in 1933 in the village of Chiojdeanca, Eugen Simion now lives with his wife in the center of Bucharest, where from their windows they watched an ancient monastery being razed a few years ago to provide a yet-to-be-realized parking lot. After receiving the Ph.D. in philological sciences from the University of Bucharest in 1969, he taught at the Sorbonne (Paris IV), where, in addition to participating in the Barthes seminar mentioned above, he attended lectures by Jean-Pierre Richard and Jacques Lacan. Simion edits *Caiete Critice*, a monthly publication of criticism, theory, and information, and is the president of GIR (Grupul Interdisciplinar de Reflecţie), a group of writers, sociologists, doctors, architects, and economists whose purpose is to serve as a bank of ideas for educating Romanian public opinion by offering support to democratic institutions in the country. In addition to these activities he is a professor at the University of Bucharest, where he teaches twentieth-century Romanian literature.

He serves as vice-president of the Romanian Academy—hence his title is now Academician Simion.

Simion is a prolific writer, having published among his ten books of criticism the four-volume *History of Contemporary Romanian Literature* between 1974 and 1990. In 1980, just before the appearance of *The Return of the Author*, he published *Dimineaţa poeţilor* [The Poets' Dawn], a book about the first Romanian poets, who, in Simion's words, "intending to speak about the art of love, discovered that they had to invent an art of writing." His Parisian diary, *A Time for Living, a Time for Confessing* (1977), received notice in European literary publications and no doubt is the impetus for his current work on the diary as literature.

Simion's character as a person—if we are to accept what he says in *The Return of the Author*—should emerge from his book. Yet a story he tells of his childhood reveals still another dimension of the man. Growing up near Ploesti, where he watched waves of Allied bombers attacking the Romanian oilfields that supplied Hitler's armies, Eugen Simion one day found a tattered pulp novel among some rubble. This romance, he tells friends, lacked not only a cover but both its initial and final sections. As a remedy, he created make-believe endings which he wrote and then read to his sisters. Though the sisters eventually tired of his attempts to frame the narrative devoid of beginning or ending, the boy continued to speculate on the possibilities inherent in the part of the text he knew. This story, Simion feels, is emblematic of the course of his subsequent career, for he is still searching, looking for the ending, still trying to imagine where the story he knows might lead, where the known can lead to the unknown. Even today, as editor and a writer, his critical works, in his own eyes, carry this stamp.[1]

Imagining the possible endings to the story can hardly bear up as a full-fledged theoretical position, and Simion does not pretend to offer one to the readers of *The Return of the Author*. All the same, what he has to say raises issues too often ignored both by the varieties of formalism that have dominated western critical thought in the twentieth century and by the more recent critical positions centered on political, historical, and cultural discourse.

In bringing this book to its present state, I must acknowledge my co-translator, Lidia Vianu, whose talents for finding a phrase or a rhythm in English so often leave me in awe. My gratitude must be extended as well to the Romanian Writers Union for both a generous grant and the unmatched hospitality that provided me with the opportunity to visit and work with Eugen Simion in Bucharest and Predeal. My guides in Bucharest, Transylvania, and Moldavia, Dan and Mihaela Constantinescu of Bucharest, deserve special mention as people whose interest in all things Romanian is as contagious as it is thorough. Financial assistance enabling me to accept the invitation of the Romanian Writers Union was provided generously and on short notice by William E. Carpenter, dean of the College of Arts and Sciences at the University of Memphis.

Professors Lynnette Black and Raymonde Niel helped to shape difficult French passages into English. Lila Saharovici proved helpful with the intractable Romanian phrases when communication between this country and Romania proved slow. Finally, I must offer special thanks to my colleague Thomas C. Carlson, who introduced me to Eugen Simion's work and to a larger body of Romanian literature.

A Note on the Text

The text of this English translation of *Întoarcerea Autorului* carries Simion's argument but omits a number of chapters present in the Romanian version. Simion himself trimmed these chapters for the English translation in the interest of focusing his work and removing what might be considered extraneous. Most of the omitted chapters refer to Romanian writers who would be unknown to an American audience. In general, English translations of French works are taken from published translations. In a few instances these translations have been silently emended to render a phrase or sentence more idiomatic in English or to achieve a greater fidelity to the original French.

I

The Life of the Author

1

Proust on Sainte-Beuve's Method

And so, by failing to see the gulf that separates the writer from the man of the world,
by failing to understand that the writer's true self is manifested in his books alone. . . .
Proust, "The Method of Sainte-Beuve" (*On Art*)

In *Contre Sainte-Beuve*, written around 1908–10 and posthumously published in 1954, Marcel Proust expressed an idea that has since become commonplace in twentieth-century criticism. Nowadays, this idea is so widely known that it seems pointless to quote it. If I repeat it here, nevertheless, it is only because in the pages that follow I shall often be talking about the relationship between the *deeper* and the *social self*, regarded by Proust and by quite a large number of *newer critics* as independent of each other. I must state from the very beginning that it is not part of my intention either to deny what is more than obvious (the *writer* and the everyday person are *not* one and the same) or to defend *biographical criticism*, which can no longer be defended, if we take into consideration the opinions of eminent literary figures such as Mallarmé, Proust, Valéry, or Barthes. I am not going to recall the biography of an idea, even though the attempt might be worthwhile. Such an attempt might reveal the evolution of a commonsensical idea that has influenced our century, modifying the critics' opinion concerning the fundamental connection between the *writer* and the *work*. My scope is narrower and, I hope, somewhat deeper. I mean to reconsider this correct distinction that managed to do away with a certain amount of confusion and intolerance in literary criticism, but which has given rise to confusion and intolerance of a different kind in its turn.

Proust formulated his idea in the following short statement: "that a book is the product of a different *self* from the self we manifest in our habits, in our social life, in our vices" (*On Art*, 99–100). This idea recurs in the essays in similar words, in "The Method of Sainte-Beuve" (from which the epigraph above was quoted), in "Sainte-Beuve and Baudelaire," in "Sainte-Beuve and Balzac," and in a number of articles published by Proust during his lifetime and reprinted in various anthologies. Its recurrence suggests that the idea was not accidental in Proust's aesthetic outlook and also that it was far from being a finite idea, frozen in one immovable phrasing. Proust constantly comes across it while meditating upon literature and defines it over and over again, making use of similar terms. As the idea is invariably associated with Sainte-Beuve's name, the writer's insistence makes us feel that, even more than the aesthetic distinction, an obsession is, in fact, at stake here. From a psychoanalytical point of view, we might say that Proust suffers from a kind of Sainte-Beuve complex that springs out of some obscure awareness of both facility and aggressiveness or, to be more specific, an awareness of aggressive facility. The matter is worth looking into since, if it is true that recurrent issues bear significance, then Sainte-Beuve is to Proust's mind more than a facile critic: he is the very symptom of intellectual violence.

"The Method of Sainte-Beuve" opens with a confession: "I have reached the moment," the author states, "or if you prefer it, I find myself in circumstances where one may fear that the things one most wanted to say . . . one may may suddenly be prevented from saying" (On Art, 94). Supported by a quotation from the Bible, the writer attempts to break his inertia, his hesitations: in short, he means to say aloud what he thinks of Sainte-Beuve and of the connection between art and criticism. The solemn, almost prophetic air of this confession arouses the reader's curiosity, even suspicion: why surround with so much earnestness some ordinary thoughts concerning a critic's method, and how can we account for this feeling of their author that he is at an important point of his intellectual life? There is only one explanation for it: the forthcoming confession bears upon some intimate aspect of the writer's deeper spiritual life.

As we well know, the confession was left unfinished. The failed project was first abandoned then later taken up again here and there in other articles. It looks as if the writer was trying to put aside a phantom that would not vanish: it turned up at every bend in the road, in the darkness of other hidden thoughts.

For the time being, the idea is foreshadowed by an unfinished confession and several quotations (from Paul Bourget, Hippolyte Taine, and Sainte-Beuve himself) meant to warn us against the reputation of a false method, the reputation of a method,[1] but also the reputation of a myth that had conquered the century that had barely come to an end: the myth of Sainte-Beuve. The judgment is pronounced only after the evidence has been collected. It is a clear-cut verdict: "Sainte-Beuve's work does not go very deep" (On Art, 99). It is not profound because it resorts to a false method. We know now why Proust indicted the critic who had been and still was regarded at the time as an incomparable master in the matter: the critic in question aimed at more than an analysis of the literary work as such (self-sufficient, that is); he always appraised the work by relating it to its author. The excerpts quoted from Sainte-Beuve's chronicles demonstrate this amply. Before deciding upon the value of a book, the critic must know of the author " 'what were his religious views? How did he react to the sight of nature? How did he conduct himself in regard to women, in regard to money? Was he rich, was he poor? What governed his actions, what was his daily way of life? What was his vice, or his weakness?'"[2] Sainte-Beuve considers that all information of this kind is useful in pronouncing judgment upon the author of a book and upon the book itself. The essence of biographical criticism is thus laid bare.

Theoretical justifications can be found in other articles by Sainte-Beuve besides those quoted by Proust. Biographical criticism lies, first and last, in the ability to find the *person* behind the creator and reach the *work* after the person has been exposed. Is the detour necessary? It is, to Sainte-Beuve, who decides that the person is the only explanation for the work. If we know the nature, the abilities, the weaknesses, if we get to know, in short, the genius of the person who writes, we can hope for a faster—and better—understanding of what the person is writing. The critic acts like a botanist in a vast spiritual world; the critic means to describe and assess the minds, to find out secret bonds between gift and character, since we must by all means know the cause if we are to appreciate the effect properly. Sainte-Beuve warns his readers that the attempt must be diligent and patient, an arduous task, since it is easier to know the writer than to know the *person*. "As a rule, it is fairly easy to value the writer, but, as far as the man is concerned, things are not easy at all." That is the reason the critic is supposed to begin the study of a biography very early, while the person in question is still alive. The work can well wait, the person cannot. The individual's life has unexpected turns; the critic must take time by the forelock and make sure that the writer's portrait is true to life, that nothing has been overlooked, not even the writer's "warts and scars."

Sainte-Beuve looks upon the biographical study as a comprehensive spiritual project, or, to use a fashionable term, a specific *approach* in the course of which the critic must make use of both talent and perspicacity. In the introduction to his 1829 article on Pierre Corneille, Sainte-Beuve offers the pattern of a biographical inquest that comes very close to the procedure of a Balzacian novelist: the biographer must *steal within the author, inhabit his world, bring him to life, make him move, make him talk; the biographer must pry into the writer's inner and domestic life, as far as his sight allows; in all possible ways the writer must be tied down to his real existence and daily routine* (1:677). If the critic here has never met the author he writes about, he makes recourse to friends, quotes anecdotes, uses documents; in short he ignores nothing of what might throw light upon the writer's existence. Sainte-Beuve even goes so far as to state that the first stage of criticism consists in "the delight of understanding whatever was real." Was Bayle or wasn't he Mme. Jurieu's lover, as Father d'Artigny thought?[3] The critic answers in an earnest, somewhat disappointed voice: "This matter of some importance has not been settled yet" (1:985). Another time Sainte-Beuve remembers Viollet-le-Duc told him that while he happened to be having supper at Edon with Bernardin de Saint-Pierre, the latter had lost his temper and . . . (2:108).[4]

What is the use of all that? Proust wonders. If one happens to have met Stendhal, can one understand his work better? Sainte-Beuve concludes that Stendhal's novels are "frankly wretched," so what is the use of his knowing the man?

Proust questions here two sides of Sainte-Beuve's criticism: his method and his taste. He uses the latter's errors of taste in order to discredit his critical method. The association is rather questionable, as questionable, anyway, as the one Proust himself questions. Can the man's errors of taste prove that the method is false? Proust pays no attention to the questionable nature of his association; he simply means to demonstrate that the famous biographical inquest fails, and we all know its disastrous results: Stendhal's novels are undervalued, Baudelaire's poetry is disparaged, Balzac's prose too, etc.

Proust's strategy is successful. He is right. The demonstration of force, the friends, the anecdotes, the biographical indiscretions are all useless if they fail to throw a clearer, fairer light upon the work. This is the point pressed by Proust: Sainte-Beuve's striving is impressively unavailing. He searches for the truth of a work precisely where it cannot be found—in its author's life. Proust notices that Sainte-Beuve treats all his contemporaries in the same way. Halfway through his essay "The Method of Sainte-Beuve," Proust as much as promises *I shall do my best to prove it*, and he is as good as his word.

The demonstration focuses on the books written about *Chateaubriand et son groupe littéraire* [Chateaubriand and His Literary Group] (1861),[5] then, somewhat more harshly, it shifts to the article on Charles Baudelaire, and, at last, it reaches the article on Honoré de Balzac, a novelist whom Marcel Proust himself does not value highly. Sainte-Beuve's most grievous fault lies in not having grasped "that there is something special about creative writing and that this makes it different in kind from what busies other men and, at other times, busies writers" (*On Art*, 103). He made constant recourse to biographical information, but the poet's true self is not manifest there. The *deeper self* lies elsewhere, in the poet's *books*. Before inhabiting these books, the poet's *self* dwells in the deep recesses of the human being.

> If we would try to understand that particular self, it is by searching our own bosoms, and trying to reconstruct it there, that we may arrive at it. Nothing can exempt us from this pilgrimage of the heart. There must be no scamping in the pursuit of this truth, and it is taking things too easily to suppose that one fine morning the truth will arrive by post in the form of an unpublished letter submitted to us by a friend's librarian, or that we shall gather it from the lips of someone who saw a great deal of the author. (*On Art*, 100)

This long quotation appears to be essential to a correct understanding of Proust's idea. Besides the deeper *self*, Proust finds there is a superficial *self* as well. The former lies in the deep recesses of the human spirit. Sainte-Beuve overlooks it, while the latter engrosses his whole attention. To support his opinion, Proust enumerates Sainte-Beuve's errors of taste and even—unexpectedly—his weaknesses as a man of the world. No exaggeration: Proust briefly outlines the life of the *Lundis* critic, his habits, his vanities.[6] His Monday morning vanity, for instance: in a little street in Montparnasse, the critic unfolds the *Constitutionnel* and (Proust notes sarcastically) he has the feeling that "in rooms all over Paris, the words he had enlisted were proclaiming the brilliant ideas he had hit on" (*On Art*, 109). Sainte-Beuve the man is conceited, even haughty. His opinions vary according to his moods, this being the only possible explanation for his contradictory articles on Victor Hugo, Alphonse de Lamartine, Félicité de Lamennais, etc. Without the least compunction, Proust places Sainte-Beuve's moral portrait under a most unfavorable light: "his thin-skinnedness, his natural inconstancy, his rapid intolerance . . . one didn't need to die, it was enough to have fallen out with him" (*On Art*, 115).

Is it an unfair accusation, is the critic's moral portrait untrue? Proust does not lie to us, only he acts precisely as Sainte-Beuve acts in his contemptible biographical criticism. He uses the weaknesses of the man of the world in order to dispute his writings. It is true that Proust quotes Sainte-Beuve's chronicles, but he gathers from them the information that, to use his own words, relates to the superficial *self*, and that alone: the worldly tastes, the exacerbated pride, the poses, the vices of the man of letters. What about the *deeper self* of the critic who, every Monday morning of the 1850s, would fill the literary world with admiration or with fear? Marcel Proust volunteers no answer and does not show the least intention of finding out.

2

Proust on Sainte-Beuve on Baudelaire

The article "Sainte-Beuve and Baudelaire" is written in the same biographical manner, the Sainte-Beuve manner. A routine introduction is accompanied by the following argument: Sainte-Beuve, to whom Baudelaire was greatly attached, "never responded to Baudelaire's reiterated entreaties that he should devote even one article to him" (On Art, 120). He continues in an obviously reproaching—and biographical—manner. "The greatest poet of the nineteenth century, and his friend to boot, has no place among the *Lundis*, where so many Comte Darus, d'Alton Shées, and the like have theirs" (On Art, 120).[1] Proust goes even further. He finds another, again biographical, detail in the story of the above-mentioned relationship, a detail that can hardly fail to impress the reader and stir hostility toward the critic. It is Baudelaire's famous trial.[2] What is Sainte-Beuve's reaction when the poet sends him a letter asking for help? Proust can hardly wait to talk about the critic's despicable behavior under the above-mentioned circumstances. "Sainte-Beuve felt his connection with the court of Napoleon III forbade it, and contented himself with drafting in anonymity a plan for the defence, authorising Baudelaire's lawyer to make use of it, provided his name was kept in the dark." The same Sainte-Beuve, Proust continues, wrote a letter about *Les fleurs du mal* that he published in the *Lundi*, but (the man's moral pettiness is underlined again) the critic made it clear at once that the aim of the letter had been to defend Baudelaire on that particular occasion. The reason for this particular information? "To qualify the strain of praise, no doubt" (On Art, 121), Proust concludes.

And that is not all, Proust warns us. As soon as Sainte-Beuve learned that Baudelaire was going to publish the letter, he asked to have it back. The reason again: he must have wanted to make sure his praise had not been too high. The previous incident in the critic's life is accompanied, between brackets, by Proust's confession that he merely assumes this to be the truth. The supposition is, however, shortly confirmed by the observation that, on publishing the letter in the *Lundi*, Sainte-Beuve explained its origin and nature in a preamble. Why a preamble? Merely to belittle and shadow the praise of the poet. Proust is positive about it: "I will speak plainly." His indignation is no less genuine when he quotes excerpts from the critic's letter, moreover those expressing, in his opinion, "concealed meanness."

The novelist is no longer in control of himself here. His anger against the critic's supposed hypocrisy ignores all intellectual good manners: "How often Sainte-Beuve tempts one to cry out, What an old ass! or, What an old blackguard" (*On Art*, 123)!

Proust's irritation gets even worse when he reaches the moment of the poet's candidature for the Academy (an incident that Proust would by no means miss). What does the critic, the old blackguard, do then? Tongue in cheek, he utters his well-known statement about *Les fleurs du mal*: "this little lodge which the poet has built himself on the tip of the Kamchatka of literature, I call it 'the Baudelaire folly.'"[3]

Baudelaire, however, looks pleased by Sainte-Beuve's attitude. When, indignant at the critic's cowardice, the poet's friends publish notices of discontent in the press, Baudelaire apologizes to Sainte-Beuve in more than one letter, voicing his esteem and regard for the critic. Aggrieved, Proust quotes the fragments in question and claims he is at a loss. He mistrusts the poet's sincerity. He feels beyond any doubt that Sainte-Beuve acted cowardly in the above-mentioned incident. His behavior was dictated by his political interests alone. Baudelaire, too, pretends to ignore the insulting air of the critic's praise, which borders on calumny. The poet swallows his pride and sends Sainte-Beuve a flattering letter in which he thanks the critic for having strongly encouraged him, and later, as if he had not humbled himself enough, Baudelaire even sends an unsigned article to *Revue anecdotique*, in praise of Sainte-Beuve's own article. Imagining that Sainte-Beuve may fail to detect the truth, Baudelaire sends yet another letter, in which he reveals the author's identity.

Bewildering incidents, all of them, Proust concludes as he did before:

> All this bears out what I have told you, that any man who shares his skin with a man of genius has very little in common with the other inmate, yet it is he who is known by the genius's friends, so it is absurd to judge the poet by the man, or by the report of his friends, as Sainte-Beuve did. As for the man himself, he is just a man and may perfectly well be unaware of the intentions of the poet who lives in him. And perhaps it is best so. (*On Art*, 126–27)

When we read the work, Proust exclaims, we see the grandeur of the poet. Seeing it, we decide, *he is a king, I see him as a king;* consequently we should like him to behave like a king. But the poet sees another image, he feels humble and is flattered by a duke's invitation or by the Academy prize awarded to him. "And if this humility is a condition to his sincerity, and to the sincerity of his work, let it be called blessed" (*On Art*, 127).

With this clever turn of the sentence, Proust exonerates Baudelaire. With Sainte-Beuve it is an altogether different matter. Proust can understand, even allow, though unwillingly, Baudelaire to humble himself in front of Sainte-Beuve for practical reasons, but he will not have Sainte-Beuve act as he did. His anger against Baudelaire is directed at Sainte-Beuve. The poet's weaknesses must not affect the image of the genius. "We [know] only the books, the man of genius, that is," Proust writes. And yet, so far, we have heard him talking about nothing else but the human being with which the genius coexists. He has commented upon the disheartening relations between individuals, to the exclusion of everything else. The work seems to have been waved aside, even Baudelaire's poetry, which Proust frankly admires.

The truth of the matter is that Proust has two standards, consequently two morals. A poet is allowed to make mistakes, a critic (Sainte-Beuve, especially), never. Baudelaire's humility may be blessed if it is required by his frankness and his work; Sainte-Beuve's wariness is unforgivable. Cowardice lies hidden behind the wariness, and Proust draws heavily upon it in order to prove that both man and method are unpardonable.

In Baudelaire Proust sees a complex personality; in Sainte-Beuve he finds only meanness and vanity. A poet may experience varous contradictory moods, since "like the heaven of Catholic theology, which is made up of several heavens one above another, . . . our spiritual man is made up of several people one above another" (*On Art*, 128). This is true for poets first of all since they "have an extra heaven, a mezzanine heaven, between the heaven of their genius and that of their intellect, their virtues, their everyday shrewdness." This intermediary heaven is not inhabited by the poet's genius. It is the heaven of prose, inhabited by the accessible individual, so much—and so inevitably—cherished by none other than Sainte-Beuve himself. "Nothing of [genius] remains in the man, the everyday man who goes out to dinner and has his ambitions; and it is from this one, who has kept none of it, that Sainte-Beuve claims to extract the essence of the other" (*On Art*, 129).

For a while, Proust leaves Sainte-Beuve aside and shifts from Baudelaire's *life* to a brief review of his poetry. His mind, however, can hardly struggle free from the obsessive Beuveian *evil*. When he stumbles upon one or another of the critic's coinages (*to love Baudelaire*), he explains it between brackets, accepts, then rejects it with distrust, viewing everything with preconceived hostility. At the time Proust was committing his thoughts to paper, Baudelaire no longer needed supporters. His poetry had won recognition, he was unanimously ranked as a genius. The reason for Proust's insistence may have lain elsewhere, in his attempt to skewer the critic who had used such an improper method in his analyses. While aiming at the method, Proust also attacked the man. Sainte-Beuve the man turns up again toward the end of the essay, where Proust is ready to conclude and state the moral, and this moral points at both an inadequate critical manner *and* an exceedingly vain individual. The novelist quotes some more of Sainte-Beuve's unfortunate coinages (*Kamchatka, nice fellow,* . . .) and comes up with unexpected biographical information: Sainte-

Beuve's letter to Baudelaire's mother, on the poet's death, a letter that charms the bewildered mother. In the long run, the conclusion must be that a critic who dwelt at such length upon so many fools, describing Baudelaire as a *nice fellow*, can hardly be looked upon as a great critic.

We may accept the novelist's harsh judgment, but can we also accept the method Proust uses in order to demonstrate the critic's limitations but even more conclusively the inadequacy of his *method*? This method is strictly and obsessively biographical, but Proust himself labors, we might say, in the spirit of the most obvious and vigorous *Beuveianism*.

3

Balzac's "Vulgar Genius"

The third fragment, "Sainte-Beuve and Balzac," defends an idea (the idea, already expressed, that the creator's genius can be found only in the books) and disputes a novelistic pattern, the one used by Balzac and by most nineteenth century realistic novels. In a strange way, the aesthetic judgment, quite credible and convincing as such, is haunted by the shadow of the same black sheep, Sainte-Beuve. Balzac, one of Sainte-Beuve's contemporaries, was wronged by the critic. These are the opening words of the essay. When we finish reading this essay, we almost feel that Balzac's major merit lies in his having been misread and misjudged by Sainte-Beuve. Proust himself is rather harsh on the author of the *Comédie humaine* ("conceiving the noblest feelings in a vulgar way," *On Art*, 161; "a vulgarian's refinement," *On Art*, 159; "half-baked realism," *On Art*, 165), but the novelist hardly remembers his own harshness when confronted with Sainte-Beuve's blatant injustices. Noticing that Sainte-Beuve disputes Balzac, Proust is all the more eager to accept the novelist in question. There is vulgarity in Balzac's feelings and style, no doubt, but once Sainte-Beuve pronounces an opinion to the same effect, the situation changes, the vulgarity of the Balzacian style becomes bearable after all.

Sainte-Beuve seems to lack the most elementary power of understanding. He makes foolish objections, such as the one concerning the traffic of characters from one novel to the next. As for his other negative remarks, well, they are "no less absurd." It was to be expected. Sainte-Beuve never leaves the "height of his false and baleful ideal of the gentleman of letters" (*On Art*, 188). He treats Balzac as he treats everybody else; instead of talking about the thirty-year-old woman in Balzac's work, he talks about the thirty-year-old woman in general. Almost always, Sainte-Beuve ends by beating around the bush. He is a dilettante, and "dilettantism has never created anything" (*On Art*, 189).

Proust is undoubtedly right as far as Sainte-Beuve's judgment of Balzac is concerned. It cannot be denied that Sainte-Beuve failed to perceive the genius in Balzac just as he failed with Stendhal and Baudelaire, but we cannot help remembering that Proust himself shared, in a way, Sainte-Beuve's harshness. He himself rather dislikes Balzac's vulgar genius, his eagerness to reveal everything. He feels that Balzac likens the *victories of real life* to those of *literature*, while Gustave

Flaubert, by contrast, realizes that "the writer's life is centred in his work, and that the remainder only exists 'to provide an illusion to describe'" (*On Art*, 159). The victories of life as important as those of literature! Loathsome confusion. We know who else is guilty of the same thing. Proust knows too, but will not tell us yet. As far as Balzac is concerned, there is an explanation. Proust can hardly wait to provide it: "the verisimilitude of some of his pictures may be due to that same vulgarity" (*On Art*, 159–60).

In this way, Balzac's *vulgarity*, like Baudelaire's *humility*, has been associated with his gift. Sainte-Beuve's limitations and prudence, however, are invariably loathsome. Forgiveness is out of the question mainly because Sainte-Beuve stands for more than a mere critic in the world of Proust's mind. Sainte-Beuve slowly turns into a *character*, a *complex* that must be taken into account.

Proust's editors and critics (among them, Bernard de Fallois, the author of the preface to the French edition of these essays) have tried to piece together the circumstances under which the fragments on Sainte-Beuve were written. Proust started talking to his friends about Sainte-Beuve as early as 1905. He had long cherished the idea of writing a book about the critic. In 1912, when *Du côté de chez Swann* [Swann's Way] had already been completed, he made the following confession to Mme. Strauss: "for quite a while now I have wanted to write about Sainte-Beuve—I have wanted, that is, to write about your family seen as Jesse's tree, whose blossom you are, and about Sainte-Beuve at the same time" (Fallois, 17). Oddly, we have here a book dealing with both Mme. Strauss's family and the critic writing for the *Globe* and the *Constitutionnel*. Proust's biographers feel sure that this book is *Remembrance of Things Past*. A great novel was born out of reading Sainte-Beuve and was structured around a critical commentary, the same one that had not been concluded in "The Method of Sainte-Beuve," "Sainte-Beuve and Baudelaire," "Sainte-Beuve and Balzac," etc. A biographer advances a thrilling idea—Sainte-Beuve is more than a mere pretext for the novel; Sainte-Beuve steals into it as one of the characters. "Swann is an invisible presence, hidden in *Sainte-Beuve*. On the other hand, Sainte-Beuve is already present in Swann's first drafts . . ." (Fallois, 26).

The Swann/Sainte-Beuve overlay is a dangerous association, a transfer that can hardly be pinpointed, if at all. I feel it might be more accurate to say that, by meditating—in *Contre Sainte-Beuve*—on major themes, such as the deeper self, the *écriture* [writing], the aim of a work, etc., Proust was training his spirit in view of a vast, frescolike novel. There certainly exists a continuity in the discontinuities of the spirit, the forsaken and fulfilled projects must all cohere. Swann, Charlus, Albertine, Gilbert de Guermantes, the narrator himself (the mysterious Marcel), like Jean Santeuil, are all of them products of this workshop, inside which a *new style*, a *new form*, a *new écriture* were born.[1] Some of the critics contend that Proust's biography is more deeply and more visibly involved in these forsaken projects than in the novel itself, since in the novel the incidents become more complicated and are modified. The resentment aroused by emasculating parents, which is essential in *Jean Santeuil*, is changed in the novel into a feeling of family obedience, as at least one has noticed. Biography seems to have been absorbed into fiction. We shall not press this idea further since it is beyond our scope. Our interest focuses on the way an *idea* is structured by a great spirit, on the connotations associated with it by the increasingly contradictory evolution of its argument, an argument that, as we have seen, ends by using the method it has disparaged.[2] It is an argument left unfinished, forsaken, then taken up again at various successive stages, strewn with insertions: Do the inconsistencies and the discontinuities of this complex narrator influence in any way the idea of the two selves? One thing is certain: the person who spots the errors of a method is unwilling to remain in the role of a mere dissatisfied essayist and so becomes a genuine *narrator*, while the critic in question turns into no less than a character.

4

Sainte-Beuve: The Critic Who Was Never Right

Sainte-Beuve's presence can be detected both before and after *Contre Sainte-Beuve*. Allowing for due variations of tone, Proust's attitude is the same, ranging from indignation to scorn. The examples he chooses demonstrate the same thing. Talking about the act of reading in 1905 (in the preface to John Ruskin's *Sesame and Lilies*, translated into French by Proust and Marie Nordlinger), Proust remarks that great writers turn to older works. He does not miss the opportunity to bring in here Sainte-Beuve and his *Lundis*, in a note, claiming that the critic's major features are his *blindness* and his hypocrisy, his ungrounded conviction that he is clear-sighted and prophetic:

> Sainte-Beuve completely failed to understand the great writers of his own day. Nor is it any answer that he was blinded by personal antipathies. After quite incredibly underrating Stendhal the novelist, he praises, by way of compensation, the modesty and delicacy of Stendhal the man, as though that were the best he could say of him! This blindness in Sainte-Beuve to all that concerned his own times is in curious contrast to his claim that he was both clear-sighted and far seeing. "The whole world," he says in his *Chateaubriand et son groupe littéraire*, "is ready enough to pass judgment on Racine and Bossuet, but it is only when dealing with new works, with works not yet stamped with the hallmark of popular approval, that a man shows whether he possesses the wisdom of a judge and the perspicacity of a critic. The gift of genuine criticism consists in being able to judge at first sight, to uncover buried talent, to be in advance of one's times. How few have it"! (*Pleasures*, 216–17)

There is more to the truth, however, than Sainte-Beuve's failure to realize who "the great writers of his day" are. Does Sainte-Beuve ignore Hugo, Chateaubriand, Madame de Staël? Of course not, even if he does not always treat them in the same way. It is not part of my intention to plead on behalf of the critic or to justify his faults. Rather I should like to grasp the complex reasons for a cultural resentment at the turn of a new century, against the critic who had carried the highest authority during the preceding age.

Proust carries too far his idea that Sainte-Beuve suffers from critical blindness. This exaggeration is, in a way, the first moral image of the character who is beginning to haunt Proust. We find here the inability to adhere to the sensibility of his age (his *blindness*), and the spiritual Bovaryism (his claim to clear-sightedness). One more feature, always present, must be added: the pretense that goes hand in hand with bad taste. Proust regards Sainte-Beuve as a judge whose verdicts are pronounced in a compensatory manner. The critic extols the refined manners of Stendhal the *man*, in order to obliterate his failure to understand the latter's *work*. His ignorance is deftly concealed; he strikes a clever balance between the two.

In a note dating from the same period (*On Art*, 314–15), Sainte-Beuve is mentioned again, and the already known objection follows close behind: Sainte-Beuve was on too intimate terms with his contemporary writers; he knew their weaknesses too well. It is, essentially, a fair objection. A critic does not have to—or at least need not—spend time either behind the scenes of literary life or, even less, in the private hell of the author. This is hardly desirable, but in Sainte-Beuve's time the critics were eager to know one another, they would meet in salons, they would exchange letters, and they knew by heart each other's loves and enmities. Sainte-Beuve shows the utmost curiosity for such relations and even becomes involved in them himself rather tactlessly. Such is, for instance, his affair with Adele Hugo. His is an age of indiscretion. George Sand "worships adultery," as it has been said; famous couples are born outside the realm of marriage; Hugo is at once the lover of Juliette Drouet and Mme. Biard; Mérimée has an affair with Mme. Delessert; Chateaubriand, Musset, Liszt—all of them experience no less than an "erotic and mystical madness" (1:25).[1] Nor is this the only characteristic of literary life. Sainte-Beuve is far from being a hermit, he is a man of the world and has his calling days, pays visits, leads a public life, has his own private life, experiences illicit love affairs. Is this way of life mirrored in his work? Proust claims that it is, thus associating the *man* and the *work*, without fully realizing what he is doing.

> Where Sainte-Beuve is concerned, I grant that he was too close, I won't say to the works of the writers he pronounced on, but to the writers themselves. He had seen too often that Alfred de Vigny had less social grace than Molé, and was somewhat of a simpleton compared to him, he had been too well aware that in the circle of Mérimée, and Jacquemont, and Ampère, Stendhal was by no means the foremost, and far from being esteemed the man of genius we have since decided—or as I think discovered—he was; as if in the sight of even his most intelligent friends, the superiority of the genius ought to clothe and transfigure the man it dwells in. (*On Art*, 315)[2]

Proust may not object to this line of judgment, but he undoubtedly hates it. Yet, whether Proust hates it or not, this is how literary life has always been. "If too much information is a dangerous thing, too little does not help matters either" (*On Art*, 315). As a rule, Proust mistrusts the *proximity of models*. He resorts, by way of explanation, to the field of painting. An artist must not draw too close to the model, the work created would be harmed by too long an intimacy betwen writer and model. I conclude from this—and other cases that I shall mention later—that Proust felt the intimacy of the model was sacred, and any attempt to reach it from the *outside* appeared downright repellent to him. This conclusion bears undeniable relation to Proust's idiosyncratic reaction to the *Sainte-Beuve method*; it is yet further evidence that a *Sainte-Beuve complex* is aroused by the experience of reading.

Consequently, Sainte-Beuve came "too close" to the writers' lives and not close enough to their works. These *lives* prevented a fair view of the *work*. In the same way, Proust's friend Jacques Blanche endeavors to explain painting "by making use of information concerning the mortal being" who "shares the same prison with the artist" (Proust, *Essais*, 578). Proust's objections to his friend Blanche are, however, fairly mild. His voice grows harsher whenever Sainte-Beuve's name turns up on a page (which, of course, is bound to happen). The proofs of Sainte-Beuve's heresy are already known from the cases of Stendhal and Baudelaire. This bulky brief consisting mostly of reiterations includes Flaubert as the only case not dealt with by Proust before. Proust is sarcastic here, he feigns acceptance, shrewdly strives to understand his opponent's point of view while meaning to discredit it in the end— all this from the very core of its image as seen, as created by Proust himself. During this act of demolition, Proust lavishly uses both his intelligence and subtlety in a style of complex derision:

Sainte-Beuve attempted to do the same, and the direct consequence is that anyone ignorant of nineteenth-century literature who tries to study it by reading his *Lundis* will learn that the important writers of that age in France were Royer-Collard, Comte Molé, de Tocqueville, Mme. Sand, Béranger, Mérimée, and more of the same kind.[3] Certainly Sainte-Beuve also knew personally some intelligent and pleasant people who happened to be fairly useful at that particular moment, but it would be sheer madness to view these people as great writers today. Such was Beyle, who had, for no clear reason, chosen the pen-name Stendhal for himself, and who had a real gift for biting paradoxes, quite meaningful on the whole. But it would hardly be proper for anyone to jump at the conclusion that Beyle is a great novelist. His short stories are not bad at all. But who can read his novel *Red and Black*, or his other works? They were written by someone totally devoid of any literary gift. Beyle himself would have been greatly astonished if anyone had really thought of any of his works as a masterpiece. Anyway, the idea would have puzzled such people as Jacquemont, Mérimée, Comte Daru, all of them endowed with infallible taste, people in whose houses Sainte-Beuve used to meet the affable Beyle, people to the truth of whose opinions in the matter Sainte-Beuve can by all means testify, as a protest against the absurd idolatry we witness nowadays. Sainte-Beuve states, "*The Charterhouse of Parma* is hardly the work of a novelist." One might as well believe him, he knows more than the rest of us, he used to share suppers with the author himself. Man of the world as he was, Beyle would have been the first to laugh at the idea that he might be a great novelist. Baudelaire, on the other hand, was quite a decent young fellow, whose manners were quite refined. Quite gifted he was, too. Yet his idea to come forward as candidate for the Academy was certainly a distasteful farce. Sainte-Beuve's misfortune was, as it seems, to have commerce with people whom he was not prepared to admire. Flaubert was another decent fellow. But his *Sentimental Education* can hardly be read, if at all. Yet there are in *Madame Bovary* certain things "stated with real subtlety." Whatever people may feel, Flaubert is definitely better than Feydeau.[4] (*Essais*, 578–79)

The fact that Proust keeps turning around such names as Mérimée, George Sand, and Béranger must not be overlooked. These errors committed by Sainte-Beuve's enthusiasm are systematically contrasted to the other kind of error caused by the critic's lack of taste and his sour nature.

The foreword out of which the previous fairly long excerpt has been quoted is interesting from more than one point of view. Proust changes there one side of the *author-work* equation, replacing *author* with *History*. Consequently, the denial of biographical criticism is somewhat modified too. Art is wronged by those who hold the point of view of *History*. So does Proust's friend Jacques Blanche, "from time to time," so does Sainte-Beuve, "pretty often," though. Then, when least expected, we are told that Jacques Blanche is right ("this is where his merit lies") to look upon art from the side of History, since in this way he throws light upon the scene and brings it to life. Sainte-Beuve, however, is allowed less than Jacques Blanche. The former is a mere prisoner of history:

Sainte-Beuve does not go any further than this particular point of view, which often makes him rank the writers of his time in very much the same order as Mme. de Boigne or the duchess de Broglie might have devised,[5] unlike Jacques Blanche, who uses the above-mentioned point of view for only a very short space, almost as if it were a game meant to multiply the contrasts, throw light upon the picture, bring the scene to life. (*Essais*, 579)

Taking for granted the afore-cited statement, we might conclude that the failure is not caused by the *method* itself, but by a stubborn use of this method. The historical (biographical) view is not mistaken unless it becomes permanent. Proust seems to me to be making a concession, albeit a small one, here for the sake of Jacques Blanche, a concession that he nearly withdraws within the space of the very same essay: "Yet, this historical point of view shocks me, since Blanche, much like Sainte-Beuve, appears to attach too much importance to ages and models" (*Essais*, 577). As a matter of fact, the shock appears to be caused by the mere name of Sainte-Beuve written on the page.

Proust's harshest denial of Sainte-Beuve's criticism is to be found in his extremely interesting 1920 essay "About Flaubert's Style," written in reply to Thibaudet's article.[6] Proust is no more fond of Flaubert than of Balzac. He even says so himself: "It is not that I am not particularly enamored of Flaubert's style, as we find it in his various books" (*Pleasures*, 223). And then again: "his images are, generally speaking, so weak" (*Pleasures*, 224). Consequently, Flaubert is not *quite* to Proust's liking, but the fact that Sainte-Beuve disliked him as well is to Flaubert's advantage. It makes all the difference in the world. When one Daniel Halévy wrote an article on Sainte-Beuve in *Les débats*, introducing him as one of the most important literary guides, Proust chose to recall what the very same Sainte-Beuve had written about Flaubert. Making a long digression, Proust deals, not for the first time, of course, with the image of this literary guide during the nineteenth century. No longer sarcastic, his style is direct, negative, uncompromising. All of a sudden, Proust forgets about the *method*. He keeps blaming here the critic's errors of taste. He rejects Sainte-Beuve's criticism on the whole, down to its marrow. Nothing is said now about the critic's dutifulness to *history*, or about his *biographical* outlook on literature (to a certain extent, these objections had been meant to justify errors of judgment). Proust focuses upon the very nature of the critical judgment, on its utter falsity.

Beyond any possible doubt, Sainte-Beuve is the critic who devised the worst, the most untrue literary hierarchy ever known. He was never right about anything, Proust claims, not even once, which means that Sainte-Beuve always failed to place contemporary writers where they really belonged.

Not even once? An unusual statement, I should say. Here is a critic who wrote about his contemporaries for as long as he lived, yet he was never right about them. Has there ever been such an intellectual fate? Certainly, Proust says, it is the fate of Sainte-Beuve, the false guide, the man who took no notice of things and people that deserved it. Sainte-Beuve's mystifying spirit is attacked:

Now I have more than once debauched myself by indulging in the delicious but shoddy music of Sainte-Beuve's florid conversational style, but surely no one ever failed so completely as did he in performing the functions of a guide? The greater part of his *Lundis* are devoted to fourth-rate writers, and whenever, by chance, he does bring himself to speak of somebody really important, of Flaubert, for instance, or Baudelaire, he immediately atones for what grudging praise he may have accorded to them by letting it be understood that he writes as he does about them simply because he wants to please men who are his personal friends. It is simply and solely in this way, as personal friends, that he mentions the Goncourts,[7] who, whatever one may think of them, are infinitely superior to the general run of authors for whom Sainte-Beuve habitually expresses admiration. Gérard de Nerval, who was, without a shadow of doubt, one of the three or four really great writers of the nineteenth century, is patronizingly dismissed as "that nice fellow Nerval" and only mentioned at all in connection with a translation of Goethe. Sainte-Beuve seems to be quite unaware that he produced work of his own.[8] As to Stendhal, the novelist, the Stendhal of *La Chartreuse*, our "guide" laughs out of court the idea that such a person ever existed. . . . It would be fun, had I not less important things to do, to "brush in" (as Monsieur Cuvillier Fleury would have said),[9] in the manner of Sainte-Beuve, a "picture of French literature in the nineteenth century," in such a way that not a single great name would appear and men would be promoted to the position of outstanding authors whose books today have been completely forgotten. . . . But the error of which Sainte-Beuve is guilty is far more serious, because he was forever maintaining that it is easy to appraise at their true worth writers like Virgil and La Bruyère,[10] long recognized and duly classified, but that the really difficult, the true function of criticism, that by virtue of which it deserves the name of criticism, consists in establishing the hierarchy of contemporaries. It is important to realize that he himself never once did this, and that fact alone is enough to justify us in refusing to think of him as a guide. (*Pleasures*, 235–37)

Never appears to me to be too drastic a word. Nobody trusts a guide who can find no road at all. Can a whole age have been mistaken about Sainte-Beuve? Why had Baudelaire been so happy to receive a few kind words from the critic? Why did important writers want to be his friends, why did Hugo himself, the barbarous genius, value so much the articles of this critic who was totally inept? Proust's final statements stir our doubts when he denies Sainte-Beuve everything. By contrast, he admires Jacques Boulanger, "by far the best critic—though he is more than that— of his generation" (*Pleasures*, 247). He also admires some other people, whom this century now drawing to an end knows much less than Sainte-Beuve, the critic who was never right about anything.

In another 1920 preface (*Essais*, 606–16), Proust goes back to Sainte-Beuve the man, the critic's character. The critic has been destroyed. The *man* follows. Maybe *follows* is not the right word, since the man had been examined before too. Proust had long before formed an opinion of the critic's character. He merely writes and publishes in 1920 what had been in his mind since 1905. His thoughts have constantly grown roots all along, building a denying kind of literature around themselves, deeply affecting Proust's imagination. To the Proustian spirit, Sainte-Beuve plays the part of the eternal obstacle. Proust's indignant, sarcastic, or despising demonstrations leave the impression that the obstacle is hardly notable. No hesitations, no fears. Yet this so easily defeated obstacle keeps turning up again and again. The repetition makes us suspect there is more to it than what we know. In the above-mentioned *Preface*, the pretext is Baudelaire again, with the same wretched letter of recommendation to the Academy; the poet is introduced, as we already know, as the *agreeable fellow* who *wins sympathy when seen in flesh and blood* . . .

Nothing new. Compared to the 1908–10 texts, Proust's tone is sharper now. The *man* is reduced to nothing (his stupidity, his pretense, his cowardice), his language (critical style) is sniffed at, "this phrase monger" (*Essais*, 610). In short, everything is denied, nothing is spared. To Proust, Sainte-Beuve symbolizes a huge moral and intellectual hoax.

Sainte-Beuve's name is present a few more times in Proust's later essays, joined to that of Baudelaire. Such is, for instance, a 1921 letter to Jacques Rivière (*On Art*, 241–46). Proust does not press there his already formulated accusation. In a footnote, he merely quotes Fernand Vandérem, an authority on the matter, who, in a remarkable pamphlet, seems to have come to the final "fearful truth" about Sainte-Beuve. The things stated with such remarkable authority by Vandérem do not satisfy Proust, though. In a postscript, Proust goes back to Sainte-Beuve's admirer, Halévy, and implicitly to Sainte-Beuve himself, who seems to have said something somewhere, we do not know what. Anyway, Proust curtly decides that the excerpt referred to is "nothing especially remarkable." This excerpt, dealing with Baudelaire, is as unremarkable as another one about Virgil's poetry: "Nor is there any particular reason why we should go into ecstasies over those very accurate observations of Virgil's, which the author of *Les Lundis* takes so much delight in trotting out" (*Pleasures*, 263).

Something is rather abstruse. Does Proust dislike all Virgil's faultless lines, or does he only dislike the lines Sainte-Beuve quotes? From what we have seen, I tend to accept the second possibility. It rounds off the critic's image. Besides his lack of authority as far as contemporary literature is concerned, Sainte-Beuve cannot be taken for granted when he deals with past authors either. No hope left. Sainte-Beuve is a total failure, a huge hoax, an obstinate, mean pretender, which Proust's genius will not tolerate.

Proust's exegetes have found some more random remarks in a notebook dating back to Proust's youth. Bernard de Fallois quotes them in his preface to the volume *Contre Sainte-Beuve* (1954). Proust's short unfinished sentences intimate that he meant to continue studying Sainte-Beuve's style as well as to enrich the critic's moral portrait with new details. Few of these remarks are really new to us. They all support the idea that Proust loathes the critic's worldly inquiries. As a matter of fact, Proust hates all those who violate the mystery of art. He says, "Poetry is something mysterious. Sainte-Beuve failed to realize this" (30). A few juxtaposed notes follow, then again, "this failure turned him into a bad writer." Further on: "Interested in the color of the age . . . Sainte-Beuve sees things from a historical point of view" (31). "Sainte-Beuve's continuous prattle" and "his errors are caused by his failure to realize that genius is original and conversation is useless" (32). A more serious accusation follows, scholarly and subtle: Sainte-Beuve, as seen by Proust, has no feeling for the *irrational*.

The critic's moral faults are stated more sharply than in Proust's articles: "mean and small . . . obscure when he praises . . . honest when he blames" (33), "recurrent justifications, cowardice following death" (the death of the author analyzed), "the hypocrisy of this delight," "his mediocre self prevents him from experiencing the author's mood; it also bars his understanding" (33–34), "his wisdom has absolutely nothing to do with literary insight."

The errors of judgment we already know are not overlooked; Flaubert is placed between Barrière and Dumas fils, Balzac made equal to Eugène Sue and Soulié, Baudelaire to Monselet, Nerval is described as a salesman going from Paris to Munich and back again, Vernet is declared to be splendid, while Flaubert, Stendhal. . . .[11] Then there is his tendency to see literary groups and nationalities, instead of individuals. Sainte-Beuve talks about too many nationalities, Proust notices with irritation and sarcasm. Having drawn a list of faults of the critical style (the automatisms of the "artistic" style, its false elegance, its false subtlety, the pedantic order of the adjectives in a sentence), Proust concludes with a memorable definition: "a second-rate Chateaubriand."

Is there anything remarkable in this ambitious grocer's work, has anything been preserved out of his lengthy writings? Toward the end of "The Method of Sainte-Beuve," Proust seems to approve of Sainte-Beuve as a poet. The recognition is rather slippery. The novelist writes, "At times I wonder if after all Sainte-Beuve's best work is not his poetry" (*On Art*, 118). A hesitating praise, an approval focused in fact upon a speculation, *At times I wonder. . . .* As the demonstration proceeds, this approval appears less and less justified. Why, then, does Sainte-Beuve's poetry appear good? Because in the poems Sainte-Beuve is more open than in his other writings. "When he leaves off writing prose, he leaves off telling lies" (*On Art*, 118). Sainte-Beuve the poet does not handle borrowed words, his language exhales honesty, he experiences things on his own, the games of his spirit, their innumerable hints and references, come to an end. Trying to express approval for Sainte-Beuve's poetry, Proust devises a fierce comparison: "As a student obliged to put his thoughts into Latin," Sainte-Beuve faces reality for the first time in his life. Having left behind his shallow words, has the poet reached his goal at last? Not really. The comparison which follows is even harsher. "Like some habitual drinker put on a milk diet, along with his artificial vigour, he loses all his strength." Proust's praise is drowned in pity. "Nothing could be more touching than this technical destitution in the great spell-binding critic, practised in all the elegancies, fine shadings, drolleries, all the emotional effects, all the paces and graces of style."

Two or three more praising statements like these could make even hell look more agreeable than Proust's text. Proust refuses to withdraw his generosity. How does Sainte-Beuve write his poems? Well, it is obvious that he must try to emulate his favorite lines in Theocritus, James Fenimore Cooper, and Racine. The poet's true, "subconscious, deep, personal" self (the *deeper self*, so to say) will only be present in his "awkwardness." It is not much, but at least it is honest, personal, deep. The famous polygraph has got no more to show than "this charming handful of his poems—charming, and also sincere" (*On Art*, 118–19). His poetry, his striving to put into words the purity of love, the sadness of waning afternoons, the excitement of reading, are seen by Proust as the mere reflection of a heinous truth, the weakness of a work of art, a whole wonderful, immense, yet meaningless work. Consequently, *Les lundis* reveal only a semblance of Sainte-Beuve's personality, the huge hoax. "A little poetry" reveals his real, true depth. The text ends with a last stab: "In the scales of eternity, a critic's verses outweigh all the rest of his works" (*On Art*, 119).

The opening statement seemed to hold something in store for Sainte-Beuve. The closing sentence denies him everything. It is indescribably sad if, out of a large *wonderful work*, only "a charming little thing" is preserved. Proust's praise is more dangerous than the bitterest of accusations, because it springs out of an immense scorn, which I feel Sainte-Beuve does not deserve. This is a widely used strategy. One praises a critic's poetry or fiction in order to belittle the criticism. Sometimes literary critics themselves use this weapon against their fellow critics. Proust's calculated imprecision aims at more than merely annoying or belittling a well-known critic. Shall we now make it plain, at last, why a profound creator like Proust resented Sainte-Beuve so intensely, what the real meaning of his resentment is? What demons is Proust trying to exorcise by means of this long polemical practice?

5

Proust against the Deeper Self

Sainte-Beuve's critical method is the main object of Proust's discontent. His dislike of *biographism* is sincere and justified. The *work* can hardly be explained in terms of its author's *life;* knowledge of a *character* will not lead to an understanding of *talent;* virtues and vices are not transferred to the work such as they are, they can by no means justify the qualities or defects of the work in question. Proust shatters the foundations of biographical criticism, although he is neither the first nor the last to attempt a separation of the *work* from its author's civil status. It is his particular merit to have pointed out that a work does not originate in external circumstances, that its roots draw upon the creator's *deeper self,* that this *deeper self* is present in any *work.* The work must, therefore, hold the most important part in criticism. This work is independent, far apart from the author and the person seen in various salons by contemporaries. Such theoretical statements have been preserved and continued by the aesthetics of the present century. The prestige of the biography-oriented method, a positivist method ignoring the very essence of creation, crumbles. Creation is absolutely free, mysterious, peculiar, and complex.

Still, Proust's examination of Sainte-Beuve's method reveals more than that: Proust's determination is somehow suspicious. At some point in the demonstration it suddenly becomes obvious that behind Proust's profound aesthetics something lies hidden, concealed from a first hasty glance, something that may have passed unnoticed by Proust himself: an opposition of the *deeper self,* as the writer himself would have put it. I think it is much more than a mere opposition to an outlook on art and its connections with real existence. Proust objects, in fact, to a more general way of acting, of understanding, of living, of writing. In Proust's aesthetics, Sainte-Beuve symbolizes a major evil, and this evil arises from deeper down than a shallow method.

At a close examination, we find that Proust's arguments touch constantly upon *intimacy, discretion, the creator's secret, the unconscious, the deep self,* etc. This particular layer of the work created, implicitly through the creator's being, is threatened by the biographical critic, who cannot help being indiscreet. This critic hopes to reach the work by delving into its author's character. The road leads nowhere, as Proust amply demonstrates, and, of course, he must be taken at his word. This research acquires a certain efficiency only outside the work (the *superficial*, the *social self*, the *self* with a particular social status). But even more, it implies an aggressive indiscretion, a violent strategy, a striving to penetrate within an intimacy that must not be soiled by alien eyes. Inside the world of Proust's imagination, Sainte-Beuve plays the part of the vile aggressor. Due to accumulation and reiteration, the latter's superficiality turns into a threat. Proust's repeated portrayals endow the critic with the attributes of a traditional monster. The substance mainly consists of fierce cowardice, meanness, vanity, hypocrisy. Here is a critic who *insists* although he never understands anything, a spirit who *persists* although he can hardly discriminate, a coward who, however, makes a point of *being present* everywhere and *having a finger in every pie*, a person who must *have his say, commend*, or *reject, praise*, or *slander, belittle* by means of sour praise and worship, promote with the help of slimy utterances.

As has been seen so far, Proust soon turns from the aggressive method to the aggressive man who uses it—his proverbial indiscretion, his restless presence in the literary life, his curiosity, that unbearable curiosity concerning biographical details. All these come together in an extensive attempt to burst upon the intimacy, the secret of a life. The *Sainte-Beuve complex*—since a complex it is, clearly suggested by Proust's intolerance—has its strange, though understandable, origin in a double movement of the spirit for self-protection. First, Proust rejects a shallow method, which does not lead where it should (i.e., to the work and further, to the deeper self), an approach that looks toward an insubstantial *biography* of the person who lives, instead of examining the author who writes. Suppose the approach went further and reached the *self* hidden inside the work, the one who writes? Proust's second, implicit, reaction comes into play here. Though merely superficial, indiscreet, and talkative, the biographical method is a threat, nevertheless. It prowls about a secret space, an area of safety that must by no means be infringed upon. The area of the deeper self must not be transgressed. The restless, biographical ogre waiting at its gates is a constant danger. Sainte-Beuve's superficiality is thoroughly disquieting. His endless hypocrisy, his utter lack of taste, his proud illusion of being the *guide* of public opinion, his conviction that his verdicts never fail—all these are clear, disturbing signs of a coming onslaught.

This conclusion relies on Proust's whole demonstration, or, rather on his understatements, but there is one particular scene in which, more than anywhere else, we can easily read between the lines. It describes the very moment when the narrator announces his decision to write an article on Sainte-Beuve. The episode almost willingly lends itself to psychoanalysis. It is part of the fragment "Talking with Mamma." It opens with a confession of filial tenderness that, I am sure, can amply be psychoanalyzed, if researchers have not already done so. The confession follows a symbolic sentence: "To escape from the memory of that *brazen minute* I should not always, as now, have Mamma at hand to turn to" (*On Art*, 88; italics added). This sentence is preceded by an episode in Venice, a disagreement between mother and son. The stage is set in Proust's memory. Trying to flee from the remembrance of a brazen minute, then, the narrator asks the protecting memory of his Mamma (the guardian god, invariably capitalized) to join him in intimate surroundings.

> The unbearable recollection of the distress I had caused her brought back an agony that only her presence and her kiss could heal. . . . I felt how impossible it would be to set out for Venice, for any place on earth, where I should be without her. . . . I am no longer a happy creature, dallying with a wish; I am only a vulnerable creature in torments of mind. I look at Mamma. I clasp her in my arms.
>
> "What is my silly-billy thinking of, what nonsense is this?"
>
> "I should be so happy if I never saw anyone again."
>
> "Don't say that, my lamb. I am very fond of these people who are nice to you, in fact, I would like to see you with more friends who would come in and talk, without being too much for you."
>
> "All I want is my Mamma."
>
> "But your Mamma would rather think of you seeing other people, who could tell you things she doesn't know, things you could explain to her about after they had gone. . . . It's a bad plan to live quite alone. . . ." (*On Art*, 88–89)

Then Proust's memory goes back in time, choosing another moment of intimacy. The child is ill, a doctor sees him while Mamma witnesses, nods politely at every piece of advice ("you were only listening for politeness' sake"), which he is certain she will not take ("you put no trust whatsoever in the doctor"). Soon memory retraces its steps toward the time when the narrative is being written, and the dialogue between mother and son is continued, after it had been interrupted by the childhood memory. Mamma must go out, but she first sees her son to his bedroom.

> "Mamma, my pet, you know it's late. I don't need to remind you about noises."
>
> "No, goose! While you're about it, why not ask me not to show anyone in, not to play the piano?" . . .
>
> "Will you be going out?"
>
> "Yes."
>
> "But you won't forget to say that no one is to come into my room?"
>
> "No, I've got Félicie on guard outside already."

"Perhaps it might be as well if you would leave a little note for Robert, to make sure he knows, and doesn't walk straight into my room."
"Walk straight into your room?
'Can he be unaware how strict a law
Fences our Monarch here from men in awe,
And that for mortal rash enough to come
Unbidden to his sight, death is the doom?'" (*On Art,* 90–91)

These lines are quoted from Racine's *Esther* and are relevant for the strict law which Marcel has imposed upon himself and which he will not have anyone disobey. The narrative continues:

She leaves me; but my thoughts return to my article, and suddenly I have an idea for another one. *Contre Sainte-Beuve.* I re-read him not long ago, I made, contrary to my usual habit, a great many rough notes and put them away in a drawer, and I have some interesting things to say about him. I begin to think out the article. More and more ideas occur to me. Before half an hour has gone by the whole article has taken shape in my head. I want to ask Mamma what she thinks of it. I call, there is no sound, no answer. I call again, I hear stealthy footsteps, they pause outside my door, and the door creaks.
"Mamma." . . .
" *'Whose footsteps trespass here?*
What imperious mortal bent on death draws near?
You, Esther? And unlooked for?'" . . .
"Listen! I want to ask your advice. Sit down."
"Wait till I've found the armchair. It's not very easy to see in here, I may say. Should I tell Félicie to bring the electric lamp?"
"No, don't. I might not be able to go to sleep again."
"Still Molière," she said laughing. " *'Forbid the torches to approach, sweet lady.'"*
"I've had an idea for an article, and I want your opinion on it . . . . The subject is to be: Objections to the method of Sainte-Beuve."
"Goodness! I thought it was everything it should be. In that article by Bourget you made me read, he said that it is such a marvellous method that there has been no one in the nineteenth century who could make use of it."
"Oh yes, that's what he said, but it was stupid. You know the principles of that method?"
"Assume that I don't." (*On Art,* 92–93)

I have quoted these long excerpts out of a text made up of layers of memories (the technique of the palimpsest, Gérard Genette would call it), because the ideas in the text, either obvious or understated, point to what we have already found out: to Proust, Sainte-Beuve is more than the creator of a critical method. Proust's imagination attaches some deeper significance to this man of letters, whom the marquise de Villeparisis contrasts to Balzac (in "Monsieur de Guermantes's Balzac"):[1]

> a charming man, so witty, such a gentleman, he never put himself forward, and one never had to meet him unless one wanted to. Not like Balzac. And then, he had been to Champlâtreux;[2] so he, at least, would have been able to write about society. But he took care not to because he was a gentleman. (*On Art*, 205)

There are several stages in the dialogue between Mamma and the son. The confession of total, perpetual affection for the mother, preceded by the need to flee from the memory of a *brazen minute*; an episode of intense tenderness, culminating in a decision of isolation from the rest of the world; Mamma objects, she wants her son to see people who can tell him about incidents she ignores; a doctor is then remembered, having come for the sick child, an intruder whose advice the mother did not take; then the narrator's repeated wish that "no one is to come into my room," not even his brother Robert, who might burst into the room while Marcel is asleep, not knowing he is sleeping; the mother is amazed, she recites a stanza from Racine, something about a strict law protecting the king from the mortals' indiscretion, and a few more lines from Racine intimating that those who dare enter without being called will be killed; suddenly, it occurs to the narrator (Marcel) to write an article about Sainte-Beuve, and half an hour later the article is completed in his mind; he needs his mother's opinion, and, called back into the room, the mother quotes another line, from Molière's *Amphitryon* this time, in the same foreboding tone: "Forbid the torches to approach, sweet lady"; rather surprised, since she before regarded Sainte-Beuve in a favorable light, the mother accepts her son's idea with eager complicity.

Several conclusions can be drawn from this succession of significant moments. It seems better to leave psychoanalysis aside, since it is perhaps too easy. The son will not travel with anybody else but his mother, and when he is ill will not have anyone share the intimacy of his room except the same affectionate, protective mother. Everything points to Marcel's experiencing a *parricidal crisis*; during it, Sainte-Beuve's name springs forth, the writer decides to kill him in an article. Sainte-Beuve could be replaced by the *Father*. After all, it is he who promulgates laws in literature, selects, rejects, recommends for the Academy, shares people's private lives, questions them, draws their portraits. This conclusion might be correct. Young Proust's inner life is haunted by a phantasm, and this phantasm borrows the dark, grotesque appearance of a man of letters whose name is Sainte-Beuve. I would not know whether his subconscious really hides a parricide; the quoted excerpts show me that Proust's imagination sees in Sainte-Beuve the man who must be kept out, the intruder from whom his mother and Félicie must protect him.

The idea of writing *Contre Sainte-Beuve* is born in a highly suggestive atmosphere —the perfect intimacy created by a deep affection between mother and son, the repeated request that nobody should be allowed into the space of this intimacy. "I should be so happy if I never saw anyone again," Marcel confesses. Then the fear that his brother Robert might come in followed by the lines from Racine and Molière about the strict law that conceals the secret of the king's life. Under the pressure of all these details, Sainte-Beuve is easily identified with the *imperious mortal* who disobeys royal orders or with the one who fetches torches so that he may see what nobody is supposed to look at. He is the aggressor who strives to trespass upon a space of happy intimacy, the inopportune, insistent, cunning guest who defies an agreement of peace and solitude.

In the dialogue quoted above, there is also another meaningful sentence. Mamma says, "It's not very easy to see in here . . ." and asks for permission to have the maid *bring the electric lamp.* Marcel withholds it with the trivial explanation *I might not be able to go to sleep again.* Marcel's desire to protect the darkness of the room, his refusal of the lamp Félicie might bring, could mean something more than what has been found so far. The light might rend an intimacy that the solitary son holds dear. At the same time Félicie's lamp is the *outside* contrivance rejected by the narrator. It is the contrivance of indiscretion.

The things stated plainly in "The Method of Sainte-Beuve" and in "Sainte-Beuve and Baudelaire" are here merely suggested by Proust, only half revealed, with great subtlety, in an episode where we detect a hidden thought, a wished for, obscure interdiction. The biography written by Sainte-Beuve infringes upon the agreement that protects the secret of the creator's life. It disobeys the *strict law,* it bursts into the house and spies on the great man's solitude in a bedroom guarded by the loyal Félicie and watched over by the charming Mamma.

There are a few more details worth examination in the anticipatory scene. First of all, the idea to write against Sainte-Beuve occurs to Marcel as soon as *Le Figaro* publishes his first article. A previous chapter of the book amply narrates the incident.[3] Several details there (the expectation, the surprise, the joy to see his name in print, his hesitation to read the article, the wish to learn his mother's opinion) anticipate a similar image described further on: Sainte-Beuve the columnist, awaiting the Monday morning issue of the paper he contributes to. Such coincidences may or may not be accidental. So, as soon as Marcel has become an author, the first thing he can think of is to write another article for the purpose of destroying the method of Sainte-Beuve, the critic who . . . This looks to me like a metaphor for an attack against the creator's realm of safety, a secret realm, seriously endangered by too intense a light. Félicie's guilty lamp plainly suggests the other, figurative lamp of the biographical critic who violates the solitude of the *deeper self*, both the solitude and the secrecy.

In short, biographism presupposes compulsion—compulsion of the writer's intimacy—and Sainte-Beuve is the very image of this reprehensible striving to infringe upon the creator's essential secrecy.

Having reached this far, I wonder whether psychoanalysis was here before me. The books I have consulted all seem to have overlooked the above-mentioned scene. As was to be expected, *Contre Sainte-Beuve* attracted attention, and researchers have detected in part of Proust's assertions a "certain special evil intention," as Dominique Fernandez, one of Proust's psychobiographers, calls it (304). The analyst sees in Proust's rejection of Sainte-Beuve an intimate impulse, a kind of transfer that can be explained away, if necessary: "the vehemence of Proust's words intimates that the noisy pride taken in the creator's independence is not exactly an aesthetic creed or a literary manifesto; it is, rather, a subterfuge meant to avert too inquisitive eyes from the sight of an unavowed truth" (Fernandez, 304).

Whatever view of these facts we may take, whatever method we may adopt, one thing is certain. Proust's aversion to the method of Sainte-Beuve is far from harmless. He reacts to the biographer's offensive curiosity with an intolerance which operates at several levels of his imagination, as we have seen. Here is an unexpected side of Proust's criticism.

6

Proust's Biographism

The rest of the essays contain repeated references to temperament, life, and historical circumstances. In a dissertation on Corneille preserved as a manuscript, Proust uses the idea of temperament as a help to discrimination in poetry. "The creations of poetry and of literature are not works of pure thought; they express, besides that, each poet's particular temperament, which alone gives a work its distinct identity" (*Essais*, 59). This is as much as to say that the poetic temperament differentiates one creation from another. But *temperament* is a term used by Sainte-Beuve as well. This point of an inner biography is the exact destination of our indiscreet critic. In some notes ("La création poétique"), possibly written about 1900, the novelist briefly theorizes upon the *prolongation* of reality (not upon its *imitation*) in the work of art, in order to evince the major advantage of a poet, the advantage of seeing what is invisible to everyone else. This unsophisticated aesthetics is common coin. Its interest lies in the fact that, talking about the poet's *life* (*existence*, in general), it seems to ignore the distinction made between the two *selves*, postulating quite the reverse.

> The poet's life has its small events like the lives of other men. He goes to the country. He travels. But the name of the town where he spent a summer, written at the foot of the last page of a book, with the date, tells us that the life he shares with other men serves him for quite another purpose, and if, as sometimes happens, this name of a town, establishing at the *Finis* where and when the book was written, should be the very town where the novel is set, the whole novel affects us like a sort of immense extension fitting into real life; and we understand that for the poet real life was something totally unlike the real life of others, something holding the precious vein he was in search of, and not yielding it up for the asking. (*Essais*, 412–13)

Proust himself writes brief biographies when he feels the artist in question is worth it. Such is the 1900 biography of John Ruskin, published in *La chronique des arts et de la curiosité*. I wonder, does it really matter that the "spiritual guide" Ruskin was the son of a wine merchant or that his mother was a chemist? Or that his father used to travel in a hired coach, stopping here and there in order to admire nature or art monuments together with his family? Not from the point of view of the *deeper self*. Such irrelevant details belong to *biographical criticism*, the method of the superficial Sainte-Beuve. But this time it is Proust himself who handles them, making up a short biography. He feels sure that Ruskin's childhood deeply influenced his later books. He states it plainly: "As it often comes to pass, in his last books he amply describes his early life. He was haunted by the charm of his childhood, and he voiced it in his book *Praeterita*, which is a kind of biography . . ." (*Essais*, 439).

If that is true (we may as well believe it is, since Proust himself does the same in his great novel), why should it be considered stupid of a critic to try to find out, from documents or elsewhere, what actually happened during those beautiful childhood years?

There is also the use of *anecdotes* in literary criticism. Sainte-Beuve is never tired of spicing his agreeable, shallow texts with funny incidents from the writers' lives. We already know Proust's aversion to such intrusions. Yet here is Proust himself, eagerly telling us an anecdote from the life of Dante Gabriel Rossetti (*Essais*, 472–74). The novelist records the words he has heard from a gracious lady who once told him that another lady, Mme. Michelet (Mlle. Mialaret, at the time),[1]

> experienced what may have been the greatest joy of her life on the day when, during the most beautiful lecture Michelet delivered at Collège de France, she identified—although now it referred to the nations of Europe, not a single word had been altered—the first sentence of the first love letter she had written to him.

Well, now. Proust learned from someone—a lady—how another lady reacted when, during an academic lecture, she identified a sentence from a love letter. This is decidedly a perfect instance of Sainte-Beuve's style inserted in Proust's critical text.

In another essay, I find another statement that stands in strange relation to the strict theory of the two *selves*. While discussing the books of Montesquiou,[2] whom Proust knows intimately, Proust stresses their *human value*. "The reason why these books will last in time is that they spring out of real life, they are fired by a love that constantly kindles them, they are tirelessly faced with reality" (*Essais*, 187). Does it really matter that M. de Montesquiou's works *spring from real life*? Doesn't this sound like the grievous, meanly biographical, inquisitive fault of the light-minded Sainte-Beuve? Of course it does, though this time it belongs to Proust himself, the opponent of biographism, the ever tireless disparager of the *Lundis*.

These are not the only remarks in Proust's essays that point to his involuntary Beuveism. Exhausting them would prove irrelevant. It must be obvious now that I am not going to deny the merit of these subtle intellectual distinctions. I mean only to demonstrate that Proust himself found it rather hard to banish *life* altogether from the literary text. *Life* in the form of biography, anecdotes, and circumstances can hardly be avoided in an examination of the world of art. It steals even into a text directed against biography. I will only provide one more instance, an excerpt from the essay "Gustave Moreau":

> Do circumstances count for nothing? There are times when it would appear so. Rodenbach,[3] however, said that Baudelaire was Baudelaire because he had been to America. *I myself think circumstances count for something*. But any circumstance is one-tenth chance and nine-tenths being disposed to fall in with it. That Gustave Moreau [painting] seen on a day when I was feeling out of my element, and disposed to hearken to inner voices, enriched me more than all that tour of Holland, hurried through, my heart dutiful, but untouched. (*Essais*, 674; italics added)

The answer is more intricate than before. Circumstances *do count for something*, Proust says. Not much though, merely ten percent. The question is, need we know this ten percent that comes from outside the work (and from outside the *reader*, of course)? It seems so, since Proust himself decides to let us know disgraceful incidents in Sainte-Beuve's life and since in his portraits he mentions the stories of so many literary salons: *The Countess Aimery de la Rochefoucauld's Salon, A Historical Salon: The Salon of Her Highness, the Princess Mathilde, The Courtyard with Lilac and the Studio with Roses—Mme. Madeleine Lemaise's Salon, Princess Edmond de Polignac's Salon—Music Today, Echoes from of Old, A Grandmother*, etc.

What are all these, if not scenes from literary life? Do they bear any relation whatever to the major works of art of the age? The "grandmother of our dear friend and collaborator Robert de Flers," who has just passed away, does not bring us any closer to what the dear friend Robert de Flers writes.[4] The grandmother, whom Proust once saw "crying like a little girl," has no such power. We shall, however, be more tolerant than Proust. Such portraits fail to explain the life of a work, but they are far from being useless to literature. Anyway, we enjoy reading them without involving them in our judgment of the works, whose creation is governed by other forces and laws. These portraits will not explain a literary work, but they provide interesting information about the conditions under which a literary work was born and about the public for whom it was created.

7

The I Is an Other

Car je est un autre.
[But I is an other.]

Rimbaud

The contradictions in Proust's essays—injustices, I should call them without any compunction—do not dismiss the essential idea which Proust examined with so much wit and understanding: the distinction between the *work* and the *social self*, between a *book* and its *author*. Proust is not the first to think of this, but he is the first who has the revelation of an *abyss* separating two elements which were considered by nineteenth-century criticism to determine and explain each other, one being the cause, the other the effect. Separating the two, this idea contradicts the aesthetics of romanticism, which was grounded on the image of the genius. As early as 1871 in a well-known letter to Paul Demeny, Rimbaud wrote the famous sentence *Car je est un autre.* And he couched this thought:

> Romanticism has never been carefully judged. Who would have judged it? The critics! The Romantics? who prove so obviously that a song is so seldom a work, that is to say, a thought sung and understood by the singer. *Car* **Je** *est un autre.* . . .
>
> If old imbeciles had not discovered only the false meaning of the Ego, we would not have to sweep away those millions of skeletons which, from time immemorial, have accumulated the results of their one-eyed intellects by claiming to be the authors! (Rimbaud, 305, 307)

The meaning of this *I* who is an *other* cannot be grasped unless we retrace Rimbaud's steps along his argument. Posthumously published in 1912, the letter turns around a limited number of ideas, *inventions of the unknown, new forms, the disarrangement of all senses*, the *mystery* of poetry once again. Acting as the spokesman of younger generations, who are "captivated by visions," Rimbaud rejects almost all previous poetry. His sarcasm does not spare Musset's followers into romanticism. All those poets refused to look at the unknown, they failed to "inspect the invisible and listen to the unheard." Rimbaud agrees that Baudelaire is the first prophetic poet. Consequently, Baudelaire may be considered the "king of poets, a real God." Unfortunately, he loved literary circles too much, and his form, so much admired, is in fact rather mean since "inventions of the unknown call for new forms" (Rimbaud, 311).

If we follow the train of Rimbaud's thoughts, we realize that in the above-quoted sentence the word *other* has several meanings at once. The "I" whose voice is heard in poetry is *other*, not the one we meet in everyday life; this *other* must also have something to do with the hidden meanings of a poem. It is related to the *unknown*, the *invisible* which must be inspected, the *unheard* which the *voyant* poet is listening to. This second meaning appears to me to be more important than the first. Rimbaud dreams of a poetry able to create its own new language, to bury (he says elsewhere) the tree of good and evil, to anticipate a deed, instead of merely following in its traces.

Car je est un autre! The initial question has been left unanswered. Who is this *other?* Most of the aestheticians and poets who have tried to find out from 1880 to our own day have thought that the answer can hardly be the *author.* The romantics had a cult of the creator; the postromantics replace it with a cult of the work. Beginning with Mallarmé and ending with the *Tel Quel* theoreticians,[1] the aspects of the relationship between the author and the work have been carefully examined, almost exhausted in fact. The major tendency has been to ignore the annoying character known as the author. At a first stage (Rimbaud, Mallarmé, Proust, Valéry to some extent), the name on the title page (the "man of the world," to use Proust's words) is replaced by a mysterious force, residing in the depths of the being which can only be identified in and by means of its work. The *I* who speaks inside the book is not the I whose name is written on the cover. The former is an *other*, an *impersonal* voice. Mallarmé says, "I am impersonal now, not the Stéphane you once knew, but one of the ways the Spiritual Universe has found to see Itself, unfold Itself through what used to be me" (Mallarmé, *Selected*, 87).

A voice which speaks for the whole universe! The conceited romantic *I* is not so very far behind, neither is the romantic love for perfection and fulfillment, but we have definitely changed sides. The *voice*, which has meanwhile become the spokesperson for the whole universe, belongs to nobody in particular. It is an impersonal voice. It has preserved its force, but its identity has been lost. This voice does not have a social existence, its only life is within the *book*. A peculiar pride informs Mallarmé's words: "the whole world exists so that a *book* may be born [*tout au monde existe pour aboutir à un livre*]."[2] The change in the order of the universe is terrifying. The existence of the work justifies the existence of the world. This new order leads to the *creator's* disappearance. The demiurge is devoured by its own creation. Galatea consumes the artist who brought her to life.

Our century was anticipated by these prophetic poets and is fascinated by the myth of the work which has lost its author. In *The Crisis of Verse* Mallarmé writes, "The pure work implies the disappearance of the poet as speaker, yielding his initiative to words" (*Selected*, 75). The same Mallarmé, in an 1896 inquiry, while commending the Poet (capitalized), mentions the "eternally impersonal nature of all those who write beautiful poems" (*Oeuvres*, 873). This impersonal existence, which is turned by the work into a messenger of the universe, cannot be explained by means of *cheap anecdotes*, of course. Discussing Rimbaud in 1896, Mallarmé declares it is superficial to talk about "the main directions of a significant destiny" (*Oeuvres*, 514–15). A destiny can only be expressed by means of a *work*; no current biography can capture it.

The excerpt is well known, it need not be quoted. Its meaning is quite obvious, too. The poet has no biography, and, if we are keen on making one up, we can hardly fail to realize that it will explain nothing. When talking about Villiers de l'Isle-Adam,[3] Mallarmé refuses to start by expressing his curiosity as to the man's identity. He begins with something that is essential, *the truth about the act of writing* ("the madness of writing presumes, by virtue of doubt—the taste of ink is connected to the night sublime," *Oeuvres*, 481). Consequently, if we really mean to find the creator's *impersonal voice*, we must look for it in that "drop of ink," not in the incidents of his life. Did Villiers de l'Isle-Adam ever actually exist? Mallarmé can only say that he once lived in Paris, inhabiting a *nonextant, lofty ruin*, that his eyes were riveted upon the *heraldic sunset*. He is not interested in the real address. Because Verlaine insists, Mallarmé reveals a few facts of his own biography, but, devoid of anecdotes, his *life* has a smooth surface. "I examine my life, I can see only daily worries, joys, inner griefs" (*Oeuvres*, 664). Just that. He was born in Paris, spent his childhood there, his mother died when he was barely seven, a kind, loving grandmother raised him. He learned English so that he might read Edgar Allan Poe, which was one of his major experiences. In short, the poet's life is like a flight of stairs leading to a *book* which must provide (the words are memorable) "an orphic explanation for the Earth." Unwillingly *summing up his life*, Mallarmé concludes that the poet's only duty is to find this explanation. It is also the poet's only identity, I should say. By virtue of this explanation alone can we understand the destiny of a poet, since in everyday life the poet looks totally different?

Proust is not so drastic as Mallarmé or Valéry, as we shall soon see. Talking about a *deeper self* ["au fond de nous mêmes"], he implicitly feels that there must be some point where the creator can be identified, somewhere in the depths of the being, and only filtered by the work, of course. Forgetting about the "man of the world," the analysis should focus upon the depths of the creative spirit. If that is possible (Proust thinks it is, though on certain conditions), then the idea of a creator's *life* is not totally banished. The sentence "I is an other" bars the way of *biographical criticism* and opens it for a *criticism of the depths*. The work is written by someone (by an other, an impersonal voice, a deeper self); the work is not born out of itself, or not yet. But even this will come to pass soon enough.

8

Valéry as Precursor

Who is the author of the beautiful work?
"He is not positively anyone."

Paul Valéry

The idea of an *impersonal voice* is taken up again, enlarged upon, even complicated by Valéry, who seems to be the most respected aesthetician of our century. His influence has grown mostly after his death, and he now has quite a number of followers. He is at the origins of the formalist *nouvelle critique*. In order to understand Barthes, the *Tel Quel* theoreticians, and the semioticians properly, one must first read *Variété, Dialogues, Tel Quel, Rhumbs, Mauvaises pensées et autres*.[1] "Monsieur Teste" outlined everything in advance. And more often than not he was right about everything. Others have complicated things after him. Paul Valéry's skeptical genius thought everything over and over again. His flawless rationalism infused rigor and passion into what seemed to have been understood, evaluated, ranked once and for all.

As far as the issue of this essay is concerned, Valéry is the fundamental point of reference. First of all, he concludes what Mallarmé started. He explains, goes deeper into what had merely been stated. Valéry's spirit is in search of the *whole*, but eagerly deals with nuances, too. His ideas aim at a rhetoric of the text rather than at the depths of the *self*. From the very beginning, Valéry discredits the idea of the author (existentially speaking) and focuses his attention upon the *work*, which is, he paradoxically states, the daughter of forms. His rejection of biographical criticism is the natural consequence of such a statement: "All criticism has been dominated by the outworn principle that the man is the *cause* of the work—as in the eyes of the law a criminal is the *cause* of his crime. Much rather, they are the effects of it in each case" (Valéry, *Works*, 8:105)! Fortunately, the author and the person are not one and the same, Valéry further remarks. Their lives differ. We may know everything about Racine's life and yet understand nothing of his art. "A man's true life, which is always ill-defined even for his neighbors, even for himself, cannot be utilized in an explanation of his works" (*Works*, 8:106).

What about that *deeper life* Proust was talking about? Valéry ignores the distinction. There is no room for uncertainty with him. His interest focuses upon the work alone; what is outside the work does not exist. The *author* is a useless source of confusion. Who is the true creator of the beautiful work? "Not anyone," Valéry replies (*Works*, 7:20) And again, "it's my *error* that plays the author" (*Works*, 14:562). This means that the work conveys something else, something more, infinitely more than the author meant to say.

In *Dialogue de l'arbre*, Valéry pushes the statement even further. Using Lucretius's voice, he lets us know that "the author is but a detail, useless more or less" (*Works*, 4:164). All works are the "daughters of their form," a form which preceded them. If, therefore, we try to reach the author by means of the work, we shall, at best, reach an imaginary hero. The creator of the work has nothing in common with Proust's *deeper self;* the creator is only a hero born in the reader's fantasy. Therefore, the *work* does not lead the way toward the depth of the being as imagined by Proust. The work points to a *mask*, the mask to a *machine* (*Works*, 14:138), the same machine for producing works which Chateaubriand once mentioned.

Consequently, biographies are futile, even harmful, Valéry decides in an essay that has already been mentioned several times in this volume, "Villon and Verlaine" (*Works*, 9:232–52). We know next to nothing about Homer or Shakespeare, and, if you mean to find out anything about me, says Faust in *The Only One*, "all you know about me is nothing but a fable" (*Works*, 3:205). While writing a work, the creator is made, is altered; the work, once finished, changes the creator again (*Works*, 14:230). The creator is thus badly humiliated and cannot help becoming the child of his or her own work. That is why the real person who created the work must not be mistaken for the person latent in the work (*Works*, 9:95). The latter is fashioned, comes to self-knowledge and to accept each new image in turn. The creator becomes a new person; the creator is, at last, the person who is doing what he or she alone of all people can do.

Valéry speaks of the artist, or the free artist, and states that an artist's major work is the artist. The artist writes in order to develop his or her own being into shape. This idea is very popular among the critics who have come after Valéry (Jean Rousset is among them). For somebody who accepts this idea, the *creator* might easily forget about being the humiliated child of the work and become more important than the *work* itself. At this point, Valéry hesitates. Usually he is not on the side of the author (i.e., the artist), but now and then he seems to feel sorry for the author and holds out a helping hand. Such is Valéry's idea that by writing his work the artist becomes *somebody else*. Such returns of the author to the front are, however, very rare. At the turning point of each demonstration, Valéry takes back everything the author possesses. The author ceases to exist altogether. Valéry's logic leaves no hope. The creator is molded by the work, but it is no use trying to find the creator inside the work, because the attempt will lead our curiosity to the discovery of a mask. Created by the work, the creator loses identity. The author becomes pure rhetoric, a "paper being," as Barthes later puts it. Proust's theory is expanded.

Let us now go back to biography for a while. In the above-mentioned essay, Proust declares it to be futile, even harmful. We already know his arguments, they are correct. We are interested in *Phèdre*, rather than in Racine's love affairs. Do we know anything at all about the poets who wrote the Bible, about the author of Ecclesiastes or the author of the Song of Songs? Certainly not. Valéry is right to use this question in order to discredit those who like biographies and cheap anecdotes, as Mallarmé used to say. Unfortunately, the illustrations offered by him—by Proust, too, as by all those who deny the creator civil status—are not so very convincing. The Bible and Homer's poems are extremely old creations, works of a very remote collective imagination. We do ignore who Shakespeare was, but, at the same times, we all wish we could know more. For several centuries now, critics have been busy making up numerous imaginary biographies, incited by the absence of the real one. These imaginary biographies have nothing to do with Shakespeare's great theater plays, but they feed the cult of this mysterious creator, the most important writer of the Renaissance. It is true that we can enjoy his plays even if we know nothing about his life. We are offered no choice, but we often experience sadness that we know nothing definite about the man who created Hamlet. His shortcomings, his moments of superficiality or betrayal, are unimportant, but we should like to learn about the great directions of his destiny.

The situation of a modern work is different, and so is the situation of the modern author. We keep bumping into this author, whether viewed as a *social self*, a *deeper self*, or an *impersonal voice*. The author is alive, very much like the dwarf imagined by Sainte-Beuve strolling about the gardens of literature, with a stick in hand, eager to strike at our legs. The author's life will not explain the work, but the main thing is that we should like to understand how much of real life goes into a work of art. It seems to me that the existentialist critics have made a notable contribution to this great debate of our century. Valéry lingers in the realm of rhetoric, so—as one of our philosophers (Noica) would have put it—we must pause a minute longer amidst his words, whose peace reminds us of a setting sun.[2]

9

Valéry as Biographer

*Yet, there is nothing
outside myself.*

"A Few of Monsieur Teste's Thoughts"

In our century, literary theoreticians could be divided into two groups according to their attitude toward the creator's existence. There are those who consider this existence and those who try to ignore it. Valéry belongs to the second group, although, as has already been seen, he is from time to time overwhelmed by nostalgia and casts a glance beyond the fence of the work at the artist waiting outside. The words unexpectedly uttered by Monsieur Teste—"Yet, there is nothing outside myself" (Valéry, *Works*, 6:77)—point to an alert subjectivity, the revolt of the creator who feels the work is going to suck him in.

Monsieur Teste, who is so good at distinctions, is less intolerant than Valéry. He does not deny the author authority; the weakness of the author, who *allows the molding of the self*, is accompanied by the same author's ability to *create*.

> I shall even make beings who are somewhat like me, and I shall give them eyes and a mind. I shall also give them a very vague hint of my existence, so they may be brought to deny it to me by the very mind I have conferred on them; and their eyes will be made in such a way that they see an infinite number of things, but not me. . . . And I shall be the prize of this riddle. (*Works*, 6:77)

The creator brings to life, then, beings who are going to see further than their maker. The creator endows them with eyes and reason and makes them suspect that he or she exists. The creations will know just enough to be able to deny their creator and pursue their denial up to the point beyond which this authoritarian, haughty creator can only be perceived as an enigma by the beings created. Valéry is a perfect dialectician of ideas, so he can easily join these two requirements. On the one hand, the work requires utter independence and supremacy; on the other, the creator requires preservation of identity in spite of this urgent liberation movement. Presuming to draw a comparison between this and geopolitics, I should say that Monsieur Teste acts very much like the English politicians who, while permitting the British colonial empire to be abolished, still keep an eye on the liberated countries by means of the Commonwealth. A faint idea of its existence is thus still preserved. The creator looks satisfied, pride has been humored. The creator has not been banished but still has a finger in the pie.

Although Valéry strongly denies the use of biography, he himself resorts to it several times. Discussing Paul Verlaine and François Villon, he admits that the two poets are a particular case requiring the help of biography. Valéry says:

> A very important part of their respective works is concerned with their biography, and the works of both are no doubt autobiographical at more than one point. They both make definite confessions. We are not certain that these admissions are always accurate. If they tell the truth, they do not tell the whole truth, and they do not tell nothing but the truth. An artist selects even when he makes a confession. Perhaps most of all when he makes a confession. Here or there he lightens or darkens the colors. . . . (*Works*, 9:235)

This text must be carefully perused. We learn here that there may be particular cases in which the poet's biography must be discussed. This is necessary, for instance, when a work is largely related to its author's life. Some writers openly confess what they are doing, though, very often, their confessions are incomplete. Since particular cases may always turn up, Valéry admits that biography may be of some use, that it must not be rejected. He no longer feels that knowledge of a poet's life is inevitably harmful. On certain occasions, the honest researcher cannot afford to ignore the creator's outward existence. As Valéry puts it, "This means that we are bound to concern ourselves with the life and adventures of François Villon, and try to reconstruct them in the light of the details that he gives, or to unravel the allusions he is continually making" (*Works*, 9:235–36). Consequently, Valéry actually brings to light Villon's mysterious life; he traces and explains the hints in his poems and deplores the absence of documents. "The life of François Villon," he sadly admits, "like his work is somewhat murky in every sense of that term. There are great obscurities in both, and in the character of the man himself" (*Works*, 9:237).

Are these the words of Sainte-Beuve, Taine, or Lanson?[1] Actually, none of them. They belong to Valéry himself, the enemy of literary biography, the theoretician of the self-made work. He even praises the biographers and bibliographers who have dug up information about Villon's life, holding in high esteem the splendid work of those three or four first-rate scholars. Valéry knows some of them personally, and he describes his useful, agreeable conversations with these learned people. Due to his peculiar spiritual honesty, Valéry never stops until a thought has been carried to its furthest consequences. He thus comes to conclusions one could hardly have expected of him. Such is the statement that Villon's "infamy" increases our interest in his work and that the poet's scandalous life lends brilliance to his poetry. These statements are followed by a short observation that could very well belong to the school of Lanson: "and extracting from the horrible and pitiful mixture the masterpieces we all know . . ." (*Works*, 9:247). Another statement, about Verlaine this time, seems to have been written by a fanatic adept at biographism: "every possible vice had spared in him, had perhaps planted or developed in him, that power of graceful invention, of expressing gentleness, fervor, pensive tenderness . . ." (*Works*, 9:248). Does Valéry go too far? I wonder. Anyway, he makes an important concession to biographical criticism when he states that the man's infamy can justify the force of his poems or that the poet's vices play any part in the tenderness of his lyricism.

Like Proust, Valéry fortunately contradicts himself. His nimble mind accepts what is obvious, it complies with any subject. Can Villon's poetry be separated from his life? It cannot, since his poetry and his existence are intricately mingled into a unique, fascinating myth. It is the myth of the demoniac artist, the sublime rebel. Theories are of no avail in such cases.

There are other occasions, too, on which Valéry resorts to biography. He uses it again when he discusses Johann Wolfgang von Goethe, an author at peace with the world, not a poet damned like Villon:

> To these must be added an infinite number of incidents and private circum-
> stances, meetings, opportunities, friendship with his king, women, literary
> rivalries; and we must try to decide how this man, a very handsome man, a
> human being terribly alive, a wild voluptuary, but at the same time a mind
> continually discovering its own increasing vastness, came to terms with
> the complexities of life, discovered his own destiny, and ultimately won
> to immortality. (*Works*, 9:155)

Valéry presented this speech at the Sorbonne, on April 10, 1932. He sounds very much like Sainte-Beuve, the critic passionately interested in the artist's ideas about religion, women, fashions, in the way the artist dresses and lives. A hundred years later, Valéry corroborates the usefulness of biographical inquiries which Proust so vehemently indicted. This shows that there is some meaning attached to the author's existence as such, that the author should not be doomed to knock forever at the closed gates of the work. This great exile must from time to time be allowed into the imaginary country he or she created. Even if the author fails to produce a satisfactory explanation concerning this creation, even if this country turns out to be something totally different from what the artist may have planned. We must not pretend to ignore the essential truth that, though the life of this imaginary country may run contrary to its creator's wishes, it certainly is not placed outside the frontiers of the creator's power.

10

Valéry's Pure Self

*Every work is
the work of lots of other things
besides an "author."*

"Rhumbs"

Valéry holds that the work is more important than everything else. The work is the pattern for everything else, in the same way that God is seen by theology. Valéry is certainly right. The author's life may be of some interest only if the work has a certain degree of excellence. As a great lover of nuances, Valéry hurries to add that no work can ever be finished. The excellence of a work has nothing to do with perfection, because perfection can never be attained. The so-called end of a work is a mere accident, caused, for instance, by the fact that the writer felt tired or was compelled to deliver the book to the editor by some appointed day. Sometimes a work is finished only because its author has ceased to be. Why this powerlessness? Because the work is no more than a stage in a succession of inner changes. The creator of the work (*the free artist*) is unable to attain an end, a state of fulfillment, a peaceful mood. Better than anybody else, Valéry knows how to suggest this vague, tormenting mood of the modern creator at work. "I work with full knowledge of what I am doing . . . , my choices are never final; I work over my work, I traverse deserts, lands of plenty, Mount Sinai, Canaan, Capua, I know the time for excess and the time for elimination . . ." (*Works*, 14:227).

One work is one section made in its author's inner evolution, a fragment set free in the *act* of writing. The critic must judge this act more than the work, Valéry explains, just as a judge passes sentence on the circumstances of a murder, not upon the murder as such. All these nuances are significant because they seem to announce that Valéry is now ready to send his probing thoughts beyond the work. The supremacy, the power, and the independence of this work are gradually pushed aside. This is the second step taken by this great distinguisher of ideas in the direction of a *Poetics*, whose foundation he lays. Valéry warns us that our attention must concentrate upon the *act* of bringing a work to light, rather than upon the *work* itself. The arduous process of creating a work, the effort required by a definite obstacle, must be considered before everything else. The obstacle is meant to check the writer's facility. A greater number of obstacles lend depth to the work (seen as effort or act), since perfection can be achieved only by means of hard work. Valéry does not think much of inspiration or talent. He does not deny that they exist, but they are much less important than the matchless effort of creation, which is the only proof of a creator's calling. Valéry carries this opinion so far that he brings himself to prefer a work which, though unsuccessful, is the fruit of hard work and unimpaired lucidity to a masterpiece issued out of a drunken elation of inspiration. This paradox stresses that a book must be, first and last, consciously worked out. The *new novelists* and the *newer critics* take up the idea and derive their particular aesthetics out of it.

Soon the opinion appears stated a little differently, and the small change it undergoes is significant. *"It is not the finished work or the impression it makes on the world that can develop or complete us, but only the manner in which the work was performed."* Then we find: "I withdrew some degree of importance from the *work* and transferred it to the will and purposes of the *agent*" (*Works*, 8:249). Jean Ricardou decides that Valéry's *agent* introduces the *scripteur*, and his creative act leads to what is later termed "the productive effort" (Ricardou, *Théorie*, 70). Ricardou may be right about Valéry's *agent* being the forerunner of the semiologists' *scripteur*, yet Valéry certainly had no intention of separating the creative *agent* from the *work*. It is true that Valéry feels the agent to be more important than the work, yet he hastens to add, "It does not follow that I was willing to see the work neglected, but rather the contrary" (*Works*, 8:249). This essential statement was overlooked by Jean Ricardou, who quotes only the ideas that prove his point. Valéry is a lover of nuance. His spirit makes room for exceptions and is ready to consider contraries. He dislikes intellectual terror as well as the fanatic use of any method, even when he praises the *agent's* forethought and will. Still, he cannot do without the *meaning* of a work; he never forgets about the idea of value. The resourcefulness he uses in judging of a work lies in the standards he imposes upon the *act of writing* (*écriture*).

Valéry thinks that there is more than one meaning to a work, however hard its author may have tried to impose one final meaning alone upon it. A work creates its own meanings, which are then multiplied in the minds of ever so many unpredictable readers. Valéry broaches here the idea of a pluralistic reading, so much cherished by recent critics, and he also starts an aesthetics of the act of reading. The author awaits necessity, looks forward to receiving an unambiguous answer to this "question that is *essentially incomplete*" (*Works*, 13:59). The author anxiously expects the work to create the self in hopes of seeing understanding gain in depth and precision.

The case is paradoxical. Valéry sees the author as a victim in love with the hangman, expecting this hangman to bring truth to light. This truth is uncertain. Amidst all these approximations, we find the place allotted by Valéry to the romantic *genius*. The latter is a result of interaction, rather than a creator of the universe. It only happens once to Valéry to write author with a capital *A*, thus restoring the authority denied by modern literature. The authority is temporary, the power is conditioned. "A work is executed by a multitude of minds and circumstances (ancestors, climates of opinion, chance events, previous writers, etc.) under the Author's supervision" (*Works*, 14:120). This is the image of a splendid conductor, the old image of the creator, dating back to a time previous to that which separated the *work* from the *person* who created it. And yet, we shall not be fooled. Valéry, or somebody else, reminds us to contemplate this director of the orchestra from behind. Over the author's shoulder—we must peek at what is written—the orchestra makes the music. The conductor can just as well be absent, after all.

But is this true? Valéry does not make up his mind to banish the conductor from the stage. In the complex dialectic process of creation, the author is an almost useless detail, of course. Almost, yet not entirely useless. The author becomes useless when the work has been created but is needed until then. We must also remember that a work is not created by its author alone: "every work is the work of lots of other things besides an 'author'" (*Works*, 14:201).

While reading such subtle remarks, we can hardly fail to wonder whether the skeptical, penetrating Valéry is or is not the prey of an undeniable sophism, like Proust and all those who acknowledge the author's absence from the work. Whose is the voice that will have us believe that there is no author and that the real maker of the work is *"not exactly a person"*? It belongs to an author who makes subtle distinctions concerning this absence: an intellectual with a traceable biography, academician, professor at the Collège de France, Mallarmé's friend and admirer, the administrator of the Mediterranean center, the father of two boys and a girl, if I am not mistaken, an admired and respected poet, who, while still alive, became a true myth (as true as a myth can be) to part of the new generation of writers. Doctoral dissertations, studies, monographs have been and are still written about him; an important direction of postwar criticism claims to have originated in him. Valéry himself can hardly be said to have been banished from his work; he is actively present in what he writes. His *self* is not impersonalized and, as a matter of fact, assumes great responsibilities, just the same as Proust's, even the responsibility of judging itself, of *thinking its own thought*, as Mallarmé admirably put it. All meditations on the author's absence from the work end in a paradox since the author who talks to us about this absence does not forget to write his name on the title page.

The subject is not devoid of importance but makes clearer the nature of a literary *object* and its connections with whatever goes into its making. It is useful, too, because, by defining the essence of a work, it corrects the excesses, the errors of a criticism seeking the truth of a work outside the work as such. Mallarmé and Proust brought into literary criticism the idea that the artist's superficial social existence must not be mistaken for the artist. A creator is a *person of the depth*, the work is the true biography. Valéry sees the artist as exclusively the fruit of the *work*. Once the work is finished, the artist and the person who began writing it are no longer one and the same. An artist is, by far, more complex than the creation. The work goes beyond the author's rational intention, the work *comes into being* somewhere beyond its author's expectations though not outside the author. As a matter of fact, what Valéry called "positivement personne" is a lucid creator, determined to grasp everything, to go beyond lucidity itself. Unlike Proust, Valéry offers the image of a *person of abstractions*, who thinks out the work and the tools that create it.

Marcel Raymond quotes Valéry (Raymond, 35; cf. also Valéry, *Oeuvres*, 2:1505) with a text not very well known which attempts a definition of the *self* as a spirit of spirits, the absolute stage of consciousness. I find it worth quoting in full (it is one of Valéry's last texts) because it makes us see that the author of *Monsieur Teste* means to define both the nature of the object (the *work*) and the status of the agent that creates it. The origin of a work is said here to lie in a *pure self* that absorbs and transforms everything, even the author's biography. Valéry writes:

> My remarks are all centered around my *Pure Self*, by which I mean the absolute of my consciousness: the steady, unique operation of automatically struggling free from *everything*, our very person included, with its history, peculiarities, various abilities, and private complaisance. I eagerly compare this *Moi Pur* [pure self] to the valuable *Zéro de l'écriture* [italics added] in mathematics (*Oeuvres*, 2:1505).

Valéry's *pure self* comes after—and, in a way, against—Proust's *deeper self*; the former brings all contingencies (history, biography) to the level of the supreme stage of consciousness. That stage is the origin of the *work*. This *moi pur*, which includes the creator's social and moral life, is the cause that generates the work. Where can this *pure self* be found unless in its faithless creation?

Just as God left the world after making it, the artist is seen by Valéry as withdrawing, or being banished, from the work. The artist withdraws from the work in order to enable the work to invent the author—a fruitful absence, a strategic withdrawal. Gérard Genette says that Valéry, like Jorge Luis Borges, decides that the true creator does not invent, but discovers: *invents what expects to be invented*. (Genette, 263) The statement is ambiguous. It might mean that no creator invents at random; the creator is guided by the will to understand, which is amplified and turned from its initial meaning by the process of creation. Who hides behind this will, who, without the least grain of innocence, accepts being overtaken or invented by the work? The great absent, of course, the Author, symbolized by the *Pure Self*, which brings everything up to the *zero stage of the écriture*.

11

Tel Quel *and the Author*

*Whenever the artist is preferred
to his work, this choice, which
exalts the genius, suggests a
degradation of his art.*

Maurice Blanchot, *Le livre à venir*

In *Logiques* by Philippe Sollers we read, "Nowadays, the interest in the *writer* and his *work . . .* has been replaced by an interest in the *act of writing* and of *reading*" (237–38). In *Théorie d'ensemble*, Sollers adds:

> by bringing the *text* to the front, with its existence in history and its mode of production; by systematically opposing the metaphysical valuation of the concepts of "work" and "author," by questioning the ideas of subjective or so-called objective expressiveness, we have reached the nerve centers of the contemporary social unconscious; in short, we have modified distribution of our symbolical property. Our contribution to literature is meant to be as subversive as Marx's criticism of classical economy. (68)

Julia Kristeva goes even further: "For semiology, literature does not exist" (92). For the *Tel Quel* group, the work is a suspicious concept. The author is even more so. The author was dismissed a long time ago. The only reality is the text, which, as Julia Kristeva concludes, "is written with other texts, not only with sentences and words." Raymond Jean impatiently urges us to stop "wondering about the meaning of a book, its author, or its readers" (Jean, 101–2).

Section G in Jean Ricardou's study "L'Impossible Monsieur Texte" is meaningfully entitled "The Abolition of the 'Author': Anonymity." "First of all, isn't the concept of the author the fruit of some retrospective illusion?" the author (sorry, the text producer) wonders (*Théorie*, 68). He goes on: what we call author may easily be a mythical hero, an invention, a phantasm preventing us from actually seeing the text. The words "may easily" are mine since Jean Ricardou never hesitates. Commenting upon Valéry, he firmly concludes that the author must be abolished.

Not only the *author* is at risk. The following section of the above-mentioned study is entitled "The Abolition of the 'Work'" (Ricardou, *Théorie*, 68, 70). With the author gone, the work might soon become a fetish, a cult object. Someone is on the lookout to prevent such a thing. Someone who is, perish the thought, the *author* of these uncompromising remarks on the existence of the author and the work.

"The root cause of the idea of the author" is a vast critical undertaking. The *new novel* and *la nouvelle critique* prefer not to talk about this concept at all. The author should stop signing books, Ricardou explains (*Nouveau roman*, 389–90). An anonymous book could spare its interpreter (i.e., the reader) the additional effort of destroying its author's image. Readers would thus be enabled to use the text in order to form a suitable image of the text *producer*. Jean Ricardou confesses that he, for one, has tried to replace "that symbolic name by a productive word." Productive of texts, certainly. Has his attempt been successful?

The language used by *la nouvelle critique* replaces the author by *scripteur, écrivant, écrivain, donateur de récit, producteur*, etc. The idea that a work of art does not need an author is accepted even by those who look upon the work as an aesthetic entity. I quote from a study by a review for poetic research:

> We ignore Homer's life because we are fully satisfied with his poems. They were written by no one in particular, they are the creation of an *impersonal spirit* [italics added]. Together with the realistic element, individual psychology is also thrown overboard. Neither referent nor author can create the work. (Todorov, 29)

This *impersonal spirit* has, of course, everything in common with Mallarmé's impersonal voice; the denial of *individual psychology* is suggestive of the denial of the concept of *creative personality*, which dates rather far back in time. The novelty lies in the radicalism of this opinion.

Even the writers who are not very much involved in this new rhetoric seem determined to banish the author from the work. I have already mentioned Blanchot, who feels that the function of language is to destroy the author who uses it. He talks about an old confusion the romantics exacerbated. Glorifying the myths of Prometheus and Muhammad, the romantics imagined they were glorifying art. Instead, Blanchot remarks, they extolled the creative artist, strong individuality. Further, when the genius is extolled, the work is degraded, and one finds oneself "withdrawing from one's own force, in search of compensatory dreams" (266). Neither Mallarmé nor Paul Cézanne appears to Blanchot to have deemed himself an uncommon individual. They never concentrate upon their existence as individuals; they are involved in an essential "obscure search" (268). The essay out of which these statements have been quoted is significantly entitled "The Disappearance of Literature." What is literature heading for? Blanchot answers, "Literature advances toward itself, toward its essence, which lies in its disappearance" (265). The disappearance of traditional literature, of course. Blanchot follows Valéry closely as far as the relationship between author and work is concerned. Glory appears to him to be a word without glory ("that ardent, bright void, a halo cherished by artists from the Renaissance to our days," 267). The work is all important, yet its main function is to "facilitate the search of the work" (269) in the end. *Book* and author must live far apart, the book must escape literary genres, it must exist isolated in its "concentrated singularity" (276), in its uninterrupted flow. Like Valéry, Blanchot prefers the projects to the finite work or masterpiece, because these projects contain a more intense search, a more significant restlessness.

Still, we must not forget that Maurice Blanchot, who is more anxiously skeptical than Valéry, believes in the existence of the *work*. In order to reach its aim, this work must by all means struggle free from its author, the haughty, impetuous *genius* who, since ancient times, has been positive of being the messenger of a god. Both the god and the oracle must get lost. The book can do without them.

> The book has no author because he wrote beginning with the spoken dis-appearance [*la disparition parlante*] of the author. It needs the writer, inasmuch as the latter is absence and the place of the absence [*absence et lieu de l'absence*]. The book is a book when it does not refer back to someone who would have written it—as pure as his name and free of his own existence as it is the literal meaning of one who reads it. If the lucky man, the individual, does not have a place in the book as an author, how, reader, could he be considered to have an important place in it at all? (Blanchot, 310)

Several cryptic formulas are present in the excerpt above. What can *l'absence* and *lieu d'absence* possibly mean? What about *la disparition parlante*? I cannot help noticing that in critical texts the author's exile, disappearance, or removal is hardly more that just metaphorical. At least Proust's opinion is clearer. His Manichaeism denotes a discipline of mind. Most contemporary essayists are satisfied with mere hints. They are in no hurry to explain why the author must leave the work and its vicinity. Blanchot is a first-rate discriminator of ideas, and yet, while reading him, I cannot help feeling that, by denying the author's existence, the essayist renders the author all the more present, as a matter of fact. The *absence* and the *place of absence* suggest the opposite—plenitude, presence, an organizing force. Even seen as an exile, the author resembles those *blanks* in modern sculpture, unspeakably more meaningful than *shapes*. The author's absence is suspicious, an interrogative absence, an exile arousing thoughts and inciting us. It incites us to think of the author's absence, exile. Here is, then, one more form of presence, after all. Concealed, murdered like the *father* of psychoanalytic literature, the author is still there. Oedipus's guilty conscience feels the dead Laius to be more intensely alive than the living Laius.

The newer rhetoric dispenses with the author, and we must admit there are enough grounds for it to do so. A mechanism can very well be examined in the absence of its maker. The existence of this maker's projects (the work) is sufficient. A new, flourishing discipline (the *poïetics*) has come into being; some become fanatic about it, others, on the contrary, utterly deny its use. It has been and still is spectacularly battling against the conservatory spirit in criticism. It has most often come out victorious because the truths defended by *poïetics* are, to a great extent, truths for *literary criticism* as well. Contemporary criticism has renounced—for good, I hope—a certain manner of examination felt to be unsuitable. *Biographical criticism* is dead beyond doubt because we no longer accept the idea that the relationship of the work to the person who wrote it is as uncomplicated and direct as one's relationship to one's clothes. A person's clothes hardly ever reveal anything essential about their owner anyway. A fashion is merely a *system of signs*, as Barthes put it; it is the language of an age, and only by small changes, nonconformities, combinations (of the common signs) can it become an individual's private language as well. Art is another language, by far more intricate. Consequently, it is not easy at all to define the relationship between this language and the person who gives it a body in the *act of writing*. Literary criticism—having a different function from *poetics*—is called upon to examine both the structure of this specific *language* (who was it that said poetry was a specific language within language?) and its value. A critic can only detect a structure in the presence of a certain degree of aesthetic value. At that point, the critic steps away from the "poetician," even if the same train still carries them both. The critic moves to another car and gets off at another station than the poetician.

But where can the author be found meanwhile? Well, the new rhetoricians make a point of depositing the author at the luggage office beforehand. The author is a useless burden. Yet a day will come—Tzvetan Todorov foretells—when the relationships between writer and work will be examined from the structural point of view, and value will be determined only in relation to the joint existence of reader and work. Well, the relationship between work and reader has already been examined (by Barthes, as far back as 1973, in *The Pleasure of the Text*; by Hans Robert Jauss—from the sociological point of view—in his studies on the aesthetics of reading; by Gérard Genette, and many more). The other relationship (author-work) seems to be taking its time. The author has not reached the end of the desert yet. Rhetoric does not look ready to welcome the author. Its attention is still engrossed by the *paper being*, the *text producer*, the *grammatical person*, in short, by the Great Absent.

12

Probing the Unconscious

Before the problem of the creative
artist analysis must, alas, lay down its arms.

Freud, "Dostoevsky and Parricide"

In the meantime, the laboratories of psychoanalysis offer a different view of the person, consequently of the *author*. The author comes to the front, the work is seen as a way of access to the person who, while writing, expressed there the traumas, the complexes, the phantasms of the unconscious. The beginning of any work is an intense childhood trauma. An *écriture* is not started by another *écriture*, but by something preexisting ["tout—l'arrière-monde inconscient sous-jacent à l'oeuvre"] (Fernandez, 21), that is, something previous to the work, yet not outside the person who writes. Psychoanalysis redeems the *author* and the *biography*, subordinating the work to its creator once more, which does not mean that the author (creator) really has a choice. Quite the reverse, the author's acts are dictated by a well-timed mechanism. The author is tyrannically guided by the unconscious, present in the phantasms, obsessions, projects, *themes* of the individual, therefore of the work as well. From Freud to Lacan (and later), quite a number of such interpretations of the *work* have been published. Marie Bonaparte, Charles Baudouin, Jean Delay, Marthe Robert, Dominique Fernandez—all use psychoanalysis in hopes of laying the foundation for a new critical method meant to restore the broken engagement of the *author* with the work.

I am not going to attempt here a *criticism of methods* or a definition for a *method of criticism*. I should merely like to examine the evolution of the position of criticism in our country as opposed to something that dominated all literary debates for centuries on end. All types of psychoanalysis call back the one who had been exiled from the radiant city of rhetoric. Psychoanalysis offers a definition for the individual, and, in literature, it surrounds the creator with a complex web of problems. Biography is redeemed and, if I am not mistaken, Proust is reconciled to Sainte-Beuve more or less. The procedure opens with Proust. *The deeper self* is interpreted in the light of Freudian theories. This interpretation is in fact an appropriation of the term, which is then inevitably thwarted. Proust accused Sainte-Beuve of making his social inquiries in order to learn what he could (superficial information, of course) about the "man of the world," and the psychoanalyst, adept at psychobiography, eagerly agrees to the proposition that the *deeper self*, indeed, can hardly be found in the author's behavior to women, religious views, etc. When the same Proust states that a book is the fruit of a *self* that ignores everybody else, even the *self* that knows others, the genetic critic is overjoyed:

> The author of *Remembrance of Things Past* endorses a method that identifies the "deeper self" with the self born in the depths of childhood and perceives in his work the solitary, faithful melody of this self that lies hidden behind the social deposits. The "sacrifice" of life to an inner "god" might even support the law of involution that psychobiography finds in every great book: we write only because we mean to retrace, beyond daily life and common incidents, the life before life, the only life that is ours alone, waiting intact and violent in the furthest recesses of our being, for the moment we can plunge back into it and begin worshipping it exclusively. (Fernandez, 40)

Things are quite clear: by means of a clever speculation, Proust's *self*, the self that writes, is lured into the deep unconscious. As a matter of fact, Proust is the favorite topic of psychoanalytic criticism. He makes it very easy for us to see how the child's traumas, complexes, and phantasms are transferred to the work. His attempt to protect the mystery of creation is of no avail to him these days.

However, Proust's theories are not all accepted. Psychoanalysis refuses to separate the self that writes from the self that lives. On the contrary, they appear connected like a cause to its effect. Consequently, the distinction of the two selves is strongly opposed by psychobiography, psychocriticism, and, as we shall soon see, even by existential psychoanalysis. As far as our subject is concerned, we shall examine the psychobiographers' objections to the arguments expressed in *Contre Sainte-Beuve*. The same critics who eagerly approve of the "deeper self" and the hidden "god" now change their mood and reprimand this opponent of biography. There is no real chasm between the person who writes and the person who lives; there is no causal relationship of determination between a work and its author's life. Therefore, we must not accept the provocation of this great, complex writer who is obsessed with guilt and phantasms, both in his life and in his works. Creation is not pure fiction or free invention; creation descends (or climbs, it is the same thing, after all) toward the deeper self of childhood frustrations. Part of Proust's theory is deep enough, but the other part of it is vulnerable, downright repulsive, since

> talking, in *Contre Sainte-Beuve*, about the incompatibility, the total lack of com-munication between the self that lives and the self that writes, Proust makes room for . . . the worst confusion known in this field, which is confused

enough as it is, anyway. It is obvious that he provokes, incites us to reply that his paradox does not hold water, that his very life and work are a perfect demonstration of how close the work is to its author's life. (Fernandez, 301)

The work is close to the author's life. Its author's exclusively. As a consequence, genetic criticism examines the work and the author's biography at the same time. In the psychobiographic approach, the work and the biography are simultaneous. They exist and merge together, they explain each other. Here psychoanalysis parts with Beuveism. The former makes room for the person's faults and vices, but not all biographies are acceptable. The biography of the "man of the world" can be considered only insofar as it hides another essential biography, waiting in the furthest recesses of the being, in the remote childhood, a biography of repressed impulses, or parricidal fits, of sexual interdictions and thwartings, well, a biography that keeps an eye on *parents*, whether they are tyrannical or weak, present or absent. The work constantly hints at some relation between father and son, son and mother. Creation, the same as life, centers round several complexes (the Oedipus complex, the narcissistic complex, the Cain complex, the Jocasta complex . . .). They can explain the biography of a genius as well as the birth of a work because to create means to murder the father and thus become the father of the work (Freud).

Sainte-Beuve is only partly rehabilitated by genetic criticism.[1] The "man of the world" still is quarantined. Psychobiography, psychocriticism, archetypal criticism, monothematism are all interested in the individual as a *web of complexes*, as a product of the unconscious, of childhood traumas; the author of a work is merely the result of these agents. Criticism must simply delve to the roots of the tree. "The function of psychobiography is to make known the unconscious mechanisms that caused both life and work. Consequently, psychobiography could be defined as the study of the interaction between man and the work, the study of the unconscious roots of their unity . . ." (Fernandez, 38–39).

But Freud stopped short when the Poet was in sight. His method came to a standstill. "Analysis must cease when the Poet is in sight," which means that the psychoanalytic approach leaves out two aspects of creation, first, the mysterious power of the genius, then the form of the work, that is, the world of forms, the paradise of neo-rhetoric. Must we see here caution, a certain strategy for the benefit of the reader, or merely the powerlessness of this father of psychoanalysis? The new psychoanalysts refuse to give in. They will not admit that there are limits to their method. Psychobiography like other approaches is determined to find a way out. The secret "gift" of a genius may be examined, the forms of a work are not inviolable. The ironic motif, the theme of frivolity in Gustav Mahler's tragic symphonies, can be explained by a traumatic experience in his childhood. The child witnesses an atrocious incident. One day his father ill-used his mother and the child ran out into the street, where he heard a Viennese folk aria. This remote tune, behind which a trauma is hidden, is the origin of the frivolous motif in Mahler's work. Mahler himself confesses it, and psychoanalysts take him at his word. This is how one must make use of an author's life. Psychobiography is not satisfied with fragments but aims at a global image of both author and work. Structuralism, which merely analyzes the inner connections within a text and rejects any association with what is outside the text, is discarded, psychoanalyzed, made to feel guilty. It is described as the *Son* trying to get even with his *Father*. The father is the author, of course, the son is the analyst (rhetorician).

Traditional biography is not spared either. Saying that psychoanalysis tries to reconcile Proust to Sainte-Beuve, I told only half the truth. Psychoanalysis would like to reconcile a thwarted Proust, who has been made to feel guilty and has been pushed toward the mechanisms of the unconscious, to a Sainte-Beuve out of whom only the meaning of the biographical inquiry, without its substance, has been preserved. Sainte-Beuve's biography is a chronology of surface incidents, a *curriculum vitae* that psychoanalysis openly hates. When, talking about André Gide, Jean Delay says that "whether tale, journals, or fiction, each work is a portrait of the author" (3), the critic does not have in mind the author as viewed by Sainte-Beuve. Delay is interested in Gide's *secret life*: he seeks the author who hated his father, who was brought up by a tyrannical, bigoted mother or by a mother who was affectionate and watchful. Somehow, unwillingly but irreversibly, the child found himself bound by a chain of causality that could not be broken. His freedom is temporary. The creator is an eternal prisoner, released on bail. His grown-up life is no more than a prolongation and expiation of his childhood.

It would be absurd to deny the scope of psychoanalytical criticism. But its limits must also be considered. Psychoanalysis offers one way of *reading* the work. It is not the only way, nor is it even an all-inclusive one, as psychoanalysts claim, just a partial way of reading. Psychocriticism (Charles Mauron) accepts Proust's dichotomy (*the creative self* and *the social self*),[2] as it accepts, of course, the effects of the unconscious, but inserts there, as modeling agent, the *myth*, which becomes apparent in a succession of obsessions. The critic must trace these obsessions in the work, must detect their coherence and meaning. Mauron is trying to avoid here two positions he disapproves of: the attempt to justify a work by means of a biographical accident and the wish to separate a writer's imaginative life from its true roots. Or, we might say, the error, for instance, of explaining a work in terms of conscious thinking or of a metaphysical choice. The second specification separates psychocriticism from the rationalistic, spiritualistic tradition in aesthetics; the first specification separates it from part of psychoanalysis. An "unfair attack," the psychobiographer says. *Monothematism* [identification in a work of a unique theme, born in early childhood, the result of some initial trauma] also leaves the road of traditional psychoanalysis. In this way, the writer is reduced to only one obsession, however vast that may be, a unique theme—the clock, the statue, a tree, etc.

Such narrow analyses look suspicious. The critic uses a template in reading the work, and the work usually supports and reinforces the template. With a little patience and hard work, everything on earth can be confirmed—Hamlet's unwillingness to kill his father's usurper, Blaise Pascal's anxieties, the structure of a symphony, Friedrich Nietzsche's vitalism . . .

It is fairly obvious that the psychoanalytical way of reading only sees a scheme in both work and biography and an implacable mechanism instead of the relationship between the individual and the work. They overlook something essential, something that might very well be the specific of creation as an art: its irreducible nature, the work seen as a stage for ideas, for a personality. Psychoanalysis does not encompass the whole universe of a work, nor can it account for all sides of the author's existence. Psychoanalysis provides literary criticism with fruitful suggestions, but it will never replace literary criticism as such, since critical examinations are based on such concepts as value and existence. It is not in the power of psychobiography to make us drop the vice of reading the biography of the social, moral, or intellectual person, who lives on the surface and whose life continues even after the age of three or seven, the biography of one who is changed in the act of writing, and whose writings depend upon the life led. By its *procedure of conscious probing*, psychoanalysis makes us acknowledge the dark depth in a creator's being, but it rejects any conscious contributions to the creation of a work. This is, in fact, the paradox of psychoanalysis: a method that uses the devices of conscious intelligence in order to prove the power of the unconscious. Was it not Proust who said, after all, that intelligence alone is able to decide that the instinct comes first?

Psychoanalysis examines the artist aggressively. Jean Starobinski, to whom the method is not unknown, psychoanalyzes this aggressivity. He sees in it a kind of complex (the "literary complex"), caused by the very origins of psychoanalysis. It is a method that uses only elements provided by literature. This aggression has a specific rhetoric (a *rhetoric of the unconscious*, as Starobinski calls it), expressed by means of a text that aspires to sound scientific, although its style is hard to grasp: a *style of obscurities*. I must also add that this style deals with something outside the work, even outside the mind examining this work. In psychoanalysis we find an aggression against the author, since the work is on the point of vanishing as an independent world, complete in itself, as an act integrated in a preexisting reality. In its attempt, successful to a certain extent, to redeem the link between *life* and *work*, psychoanalysis ends by dismissing the *work*, by humiliating the work, as someone put it. Instead of listening to the work itself, we learn the complexes of its author, and these complexes are, in turn, replaced by the talkative almost suspiciously coherent voice of the analyst, who avidly holds the work as a precious prey in both hands and feeds upon it gluttonously. The analyst knows everything about the remote past, knows all its hidden recesses, and the analyst's explanation is meant to prove that the work is no more than the consequence of some accidents that happened long ago. A hidden hand guides the hand that is writing, the hand of a frustrated, unconsciously perverse child, prey to some trauma or another. The child's hand is guided, in its turn, by the analyst's firm hand. This double tyranny is, of course, resented. I shall quote Jean Starobinski again; he can hardly be suspected of programmatic hostility against Freud and his adepts. The Geneva critic is a worshiper of lucidity and never fails to see the limits of a critical method.[3]

> The meaning of any work contains the past life and private history of its author, but the work transcends this private history. We must never forget that this history looks out upon the work; the work consumes it. The author's past life is intimately blended with its implicit or explicit image of itself as seen in the present life of the work, which work is busy inventing a future for it, too. Seen in this light, every work contains a true life in the past, and an imaginary life in the future. If we base our examination exclusively upon the side of the past (childhood, etc.), the work will appear as a mere consequence, but we all know that, more often than not, the writer uses a work in order to anticipate his own fate. The work is much more than the result of an initial experience, of some previous passion; the work itself is an initial act, a moment of discontinuity when its author, no longer prisoner of his past, endeavours to use the past of the work to the purpose of inventing some fabulous future, a timeless pattern. (Starobinski, 282–83)

Well said, indeed. We shall only add that in the act of writing the creator's life undergoes a change too. The act of writing opens in front of the writer's biography the prospect of a fabulous, mysterious future. A biography redeems the past life, enriches the present, and definitely modifies an individual's existence. It is undoubtedly true that the *self that writes* alters—we can hardly learn how or how much—the *self that lives*.

13

Sartre, the Writer, and the Reader

*Each painting, each book is a
recovery of the totality of being.*

Sartre, *What Is Literature?*

In his preface to *The Family Idiot*, Sartre begins by asserting that he took to writing this book in order to answer the question, "What can we know about a man?" In order to find the answer, he examined the case of Flaubert. What can we know about Flaubert? An incredible number of things; perusing the existing information, anyone can easily learn the truth. Yet, putting the data together, the analyst notices they are often irreducible, ambiguous, that Gustave Flaubert's sincerity is far from flawless, that the meanings of his work and the meanings of his life are heterogeneous. What is the analyst going to do about it? Will he renounce the hope of redeeming the writer's whole being? Here is Sartre's answer:

> This book attempts to prove that irreducibility is only apparent, and that each piece of data set in its place becomes a portion of the whole, which is constantly being created, and by the same token reveals its profound homogeneity with all the other parts that make up the whole.
>
> For a man is never an individual; it would be more fitting to call him a *universal singular*. Summed up and for this reason universalized by his epoch, he in turn resumes it by reproducing himself in it as singularity. Universal by the singular universality of human history, singular by the universalizing singularity of his projects, he requires simultaneous examination from both ends. (Sartre, *Family Idiot*, ix)

The method had been defined and used before (in the books *Baudelaire* and *Saint Genet*); it consists in a kind of back and forth or a to and fro, from work to individual, from individual to history. A "progressive-regressive" method that attempts to link all abstractions to the meanings of the concrete, a method devised "in the labor itself to comply with the exigencies of its object," this object is born while it is being analyzed. Flaubert turns gradually into an *author* while writing

Madame Bovary. Does the quality of *author* imply that Flaubert is any different now from the man he was when he began writing the book? Sartre does not say. He feels that the relation between the author and the work is fairly intricate. In *The Family Idiot*, Sartre uses psychoanalysis and Marxism in order to build a new anthropology that, besides the *deeper self* and the *social self*, aims at portraying the *complex self* as a whole.

Does existential psychoanalysis, Sartre in particular, manage to relate in any way the person who lives to the person who writes? Does it finally reconcile Proust to Sainte-Beuve? Anyway, Sartre and his followers replace this dichotomy with a superior synthesis. New concepts are added to the old relationship (work-creator): *history, action, freedom, alienation, involvement,* etc. Sartre tells us that an individual is a *singular universe.* An individual is a singularity with a calling for totality. A *self* who, by reflection, wishes to partake of wholeness as a being. The immense desire of the self for introspection cannot be completely gratified: "In reflection in fact if I do not succeed in apprehending myself as an object but only as a quasi-object, this is because I am the object that I wish to grasp . . . ; I can escape my selfness [not] by taking a point of view on myself (for thus I do not succeed in realizing myself as being)" (Sartre, *Being,* 300). Although people know that their understanding has certain limits, they will not give up trying to go beyond them, since they strongly feel that their power of understanding is their fulfillment as beings, their force to dominate themselves as *objects.* Sartre's distinctions upset traditional categories. He attaches a totally new meaning to biography, since he places the individual not only in relation to the *écriture,* the *imaginary universe,* "a deep pleasure always hidden" (which is mentioned by Flaubert in a letter, and which hints at Flaubert's neurotic nature) but also in relation to a whole universe, to which the individual willfully belongs and strives to understand. We can conclude from all this that Jean-Paul Sartre brings the individual back to the surface of existence. Not the "man of the world," though. Sartre sees the individual burdened with biological fate and the laws of history. Faced with both, Sartre's individual will not give in. The individual has two formidable weapons: awareness and action.

Sartre closely associates the issue of the creator with the issue of people in general. In order to explain the condition of the artist, one must first know the artist's position as a being in this universe. The author is, in fact, a being who has taken to writing. The act of writing is a way of life. Consequently, the nature of the aesthetic act can only be examined after the nature of the existence that generates—and determines—the aesthetic act has been defined. In this way, Sartre aims at redeeming a lost sense of unity, together with the major meaning of a relationship. He brings the great exile back into the city and joins again the two faces of the symbol: the creator *within* the work (the rhetoricians' grammatical person) and the creator without—the deeper self (probed by psychology and by psychoanalysis), who assumes existence. Sartre's existentialism may redeem the whole, but it does not remove the contradictions. The redeeming act is part of the method, not of the object. Sartre's creator (Sartre's person in general) is a swarm of contradictions. Stability in the world is ensured by a dialectics of opposites. The striving for freedom, which is fundamental, and the feeling of alienation encompass a large area of chaos that consciousness tries to set in order. Is the effort of this consciousness successful?

The modern creator's existence is essentially an interrogative one. Camus, Sartre, and Malraux repeatedly say so. "The interrogation has become a thing as the anguish of Tintoretto became a yellow sky" (*Literature*, 12), Sartre writes. The important subjects of meditation lie under the sign of a major, profound question: *What is the meaning of the act of writing? Why do we write? Whom do we write for?* These are chapters out of an essentially interrogative book, *What Is Literature?* The answers are only temporary because truth itself keeps changing. A dialectic "to and fro" is felt everywhere, from the work to its author, from author to history, from history to the work, from the work to the reader and back to the author, work, etc. Malraux decides that the modern person's dignity resides in the ability to keep asking questions. There is hope because of the person's fundamental interrogative morals. Sartre renders this dialectics even more complex. An interrogation is the beginning of an answer, even if the answer is provisional and debatable. The *act of writing* (a recurrent concept with Sartre) is the result of human awareness of *interrogative existence*.

The relationship *author-work* is extended to a third character, usually over-looked by traditional criticism. Modern criticism (part of it, at any rate) brings him to the front again (Valéry, the *nouvelle critique*, the Constance school),[1] but readers can only seldom find at once *all* the elements of the play that is being acted under their very eyes and in which they take part themselves. Rhetoric leaves out the main actor (the author), psychoanalysis generally ignores the spectator (the reader), biographical criticism considers the spectator with indecision—the reader seems to be either tolerated or absent. Before the theoreticians of the new novel and before Jauss, Sartre carefully considers the act of reading. In *What Is Literature?* (1948), the creator and the work are examined in relation to the reader, the third element of the relationship. The classical binomial is replaced by the triad author-work-reader. None of the three can be understood in the absence of the other two; each character bears upon the whole. The *act of writing* acquires a new significance, unknown both to the new rhetoric and to psychoanalysis. The person who writes strives, in the act of writing, to find the best possible position to face the universe, or, to use Sartre's words, to feel "essential in relation to the world." This ought to mean set the land of disorder in order, assert "the unity of mind on the diversity of things" (*Literature*, 33).

To feel we are essential in relation to the universe! Something in this splendid sentence reminds us of the haughty romantic genius. Anyway, it conveys the dignity of the modern creator, who cannot help questioning the universe. Instead of creating beings (Sartre tells us), the creator "detects beings," and the better the creator detects, the more numerous the detected beings are. The work is a "recovery of the totality of being" (*Literature*, 51). But the attempt is only half successful unless the third actor, the *reader*, takes part in it as well. The reader turns the inner *écriture* into a work, infuses a meaning into the aesthetic object, which reacts like a "strange whirligig." The work comes into existence only if the author and the reader agree to trust and help each other. Otherwise, the act of creation cannot be complete. It is incomplete and abstract:

> If the author existed alone he would be able to write as much as he liked; the work as *object* would never see the light of day and he would either have to put down his pen or despair. But the operation of writing implies that of reading as its dialectic correlative and these two connected acts necessitate two distinct agents. It is the conjoint effort of author and reader that brings upon the scene that concrete and imaginary object that is the work of the mind. There is no art except for and by others. (*Literature*, 36–37)

Consequently, the work encloses in it both creation and the way creation is received (i.e., read). The act of creation is only finished when the reader, who is created in the act of reading, takes it up and carries it to its end. The act of reading lends substance to the work and helps the reader find an identity. And yet, the act of reading is not free. It may stimulate a sense of freedom, it is a creation, an invention, but the creation is *guided*, the freedom conditioned, the invention preordained. It is guided, conditioned, preordained by the *author* and the *work*, since both author and work (or part of it) exist before the reader's arrival. At this turn of the debate, Sartre makes a meaningful statement: "Thus, for the reader all is to do and all is already done" (*Literature*, 40). What can this double assertion signify?

14

Sartre: All Is to Be Done

Reading is a pact of generosity between author and reader. Each one trusts the other; demands of the other as much as he demands of himself.

What Is Literature?

The *nouvelle critique* quite frequently finds there is a distinction to be made between *truth* and *verisimilitude* in a literary work. Older criticism was obsessed with truth; new criticism is rather interested in the *validity*, the *possibility* of any point of view. The former means to reach the absolute, unique, total meaning; the latter makes do with a possible, acceptable significance. Barthes is uncompromising in this respect. Criticism deals with what is valid rather than *true*, as no language (that of the work included) can be true or false in itself; it is merely valid or not when seen in relation to a coherent system of signs. The nature of the work is not objective, and positivists are wrong in describing it to use qualifications meant for objects. A critic is not supposed to tell us the *truth* about Balzac, Proust, etc., but must produce a coherent text that should include in it as many elements present in the language (text) of the work as possible. The critical text concentrates both upon the work and upon itself. Criticism is *connaissance de l'autre* [knowledge of the other] and *co-naissance de soi-même* [literally, co-birth of oneself] (Barthes uses Paul Claudel's pun here). Sartre had made a similar statement before Barthes, only Sartre felt that a work (criticism included) was grasping of consciousness, a way of recapturing the wholeness of existence. An individual can choose a manner of understanding this totality. The freedom of choice is, to Sartre's mind, essential in criticism as well. The act of reading is a choice in itself, a direction selected by the spirit implying both giving and receiving. When we read, we integrate all the elements of a work into what the existentialists call a *projected existence*. Because of this, the act of reading turns out to be subjective and creative. All words are steps toward transcendence. It is up to the reader either to revive them or to make them look like lifeless signs. The work begins its life only when its works become meaningful, when a creative reader lends them significance. "The work exists only at the exact level of his capacities; while he reads and creates he knows that he can always go further in his reading, can always create more profoundly, and thus the work seems to him as inexhaustible and opaque as things" (*Literature*, 40).

This statement is essential to an understanding of contemporary criticism, and it has become famous. A partisan of *la nouvelle critique* (André Allemand, *Nouvelle critique, nouvelle perspective*, 1967) asserts that the work does not reside within the work, but in the various ways of understanding the work. Consequently, a work cannot be called good or bad, false or true, the work is what we, its readers, are or what we make out of it. A work does not exist before it has been read. The "objectivity" and "independence" of a work are sinful words used by positivists who imagine that a word, once written on the page, means anything in itself.

These ideas are of course debatable, but we must go back to the question of truth in criticism. Can it be found in the *work* or in the *interpretation* of the work? Some reply that it cannot be found anywhere at all, since literature does not deal with what is actually true: it only deals with what might be true, what might be *valid*, and even these only appear in an analysis of the work, not in the work as such. As far as literature is concerned, nothing is objective, everything is debatable, the space of literature is, first and foremost, a space of subjectivity. Criticism in its turn, acknowledges, so to say, the *objectivity of subjectivity* (Barthes).

This way of thinking ignores a fact foretold by Sartre's extraordinary intuition. Let us have a look at the sentence already quoted. *For the reader all is to do and all is already done.* So something has been done before we start reading the book, a *spiritual project* has been carried out, an attempt to redeem the totality of a world has been made before our reading this book. *Everything is yet to be done*, of course, *but only after the work has already been created.* Maybe positivists exaggerate when they decide that a work exists in itself, independent of its interpretation. It is fairer to admit that a work has a *virtual existence.* The project of the book lends itself to interpretation; it is concealed within a text that can only be brought to life by the light of the reader's understanding.

Therefore, we can confidently conclude that literature only lives when it is confronted with a reader's sensibility, enriched by the attributes this reader attaches to it. Yet, to be fair to the very end, we must also admit that this *subjective* (personal, fluctuating) *existence* is made possible by the previous existence of a language invariable and individualized. As a matter of fact, there are two levels in the life of a work: a *historical* one (a finite project, enclosed within language) and a *virtual*, subjective variable one (born out of an interference with other projects). In order to struggle free from its historical inertness and silence, a book requires the ability of a critic, of a reader of any kind, to discover signs (symbols, myths). In short, the *historical existence* and the *subjective, virtual* one condition each other. In the absence of an intelligent reader, the book is a mere heap of scribbled sheets. Interpretation can only proceed when the author's truth has been enclosed within a system of conventional signs (the text). Critical interpretation is partly dependent on this truth. In Balzac's novels, a miser will always be a miser, no matter what critical method we may use.

What I mean is that the opinions concerning a book may be diverse but not arbitrary. The same book may be looked upon both as a masterpiece and as an imposture, which has often happened, but at least one of these assertions must be false, if not both. The value of a critical argument has been said to have nothing to do with its truth. I doubt it. Or, rather, I will no longer put up with the idea that a critic is allowed to lie, if gifted enough to do so. I take *verisimilitude* to be one side of truth; criticism is not arbitrary at all. In criticism, *validity* requires aesthetic justification, and there can be no such justification in the absence of the respect for the truth of the work. Consequently, Barthes's statement requires one qualification: in criticism there are no final, absolute *truths*, indeed there are only *validities*, but unless these validities have an eye for the truth and testify to its presence, they are doomed to die of imprecision and arbitrariness. The freedom of our interpretation is limited by the fact that *everything has already been done*, by the meaningful architecture of the work.

15

Sartre and Author(ity)

The world is my task.

What Is Literature?

The agreement of generosity relies upon reciprocal trust. The author must not fool the reader; the reader must not disregard the author's intention or willfully misread. This double requirement is stipulated by the creator in the work. As early as 1948, Sartre stated that any good work contained in its pages directions as to how it should be read, a pattern of reading implicit in the work, which, of course, could be extended, enriched, but by no means ignored. There is an *appeal* (message) in the work, which is essentially one of freedom. The "aesthetic joy" cannot be grasped in the absence of the sense of freedom. We are not writing for slaves, Sartre remarks. And further on, "the work can be defined as an imaginary presentation of the world, insofar as it demands human freedom" (*Literature*, 57). Writers have only one major topic, freedom. The act of writing is the expression of a basic desire for liberty. This conclusion relies upon the writer's *involvement*, upon the author's intense desire to *change* the object (the work) and also to use this work as an instrument of change. Sartre even accepts the older idea that moral requirements must be the result of an *imaginary involvement in action*. Is it an involvement of the work or of the author? Of the act of writing, first of all:

> To write is thus both to disclose the world and to offer it as a task to the generosity of the reader. It is to have recourse to the consciousness of others in order to make one's self be recognized as *essential* to the totality of being; it is to wish to live this essentiality by means of interposed persons; but, on the other hand, as the real world is revealed only by action, as one can feel himself in it only by exceeding it in order to change it, the novelist's universe would lack thickness if it were not discovered in a moment to transcend it. (*Literature*, 54–55)

The *world* as action; the act of writing reveals a world; to be essential in relation to life and the universe; to write is to alter; the writer is a mediator; the work as a production (reproduction) of the human being; the act of writing is a kind of freedom that generates another kind of freedom (the act of reading); the human being is marked by *existence*, and this existence has its place in *history*; a work is a proof of its author's belief in human freedom . . . These are recurrent ideas in Sartre's writings. They are the ideas of Sartre's youth, when he had just come out of a war that had been won, together with the other intellectuals who had fought in the resistance movement. Young Sartre is politically involved, he creates an ethic of action and defends a literature determined to *fight*. "The world is *my task*" (54), he writes with superb, immeasurable pride. Such a proud sentence had not been recorded in literature for quite a long time. "Each book is a recovery of the totality of being" (51). This sentence is perfect ground for hope.

Sartre does not advance a method of analysis. He is interested in an examination of both method and its object. A method is influenced by a number of factors. First, the person who uses the method. The Sartre who, in 1947, wrote *Baudelaire* is different from the Sartre who started—and could not finish—*The Family Idiot*. What makes the two differ is not their quality, but the age of their spirit. The essays in *What Is Literature?*—determined, sharp, very much like an ultimatum—fascinated by the human place in the universe, as they all are, sound rather unlike than like the essays in *Situations VIII* and *IX*. Sartre is still there, but his faith in literature has dwindled. I wonder whether the later Sartre was still willing to endorse his earlier statements: *the world is my charge, a work redeems the sense of wholeness of human existence, while writing one becomes essential in relation to the universe* . . .

The method Sartre uses in *Saint Genet* and *The Family Idiot* is far more complicated. The main theme of his criticism is the same question of the work's relation to the person, but the critic goes further, the voices intermingle. Who speaks, we wonder, and who is talked about? Is it Sartre or Jean Genet, can it be Sartre or is it Flaubert? Genet is the hero of his own work, yet he seems to be Sartre's hero too. Flaubert, who used to say that the really great works have no author at all, becomes, when interpreted by Sartre, a true epic hero. It is the image of a Flaubert who weaves, then unravels, his own being, who experiences a permanent neurosis, and who explains his existence as a writer, as a man, by this very neurosis that never leaves him. Numberless details, the works read over and over again, the whole looking like an ever-growing snowball.

The work *adheres* to the person who wrote it, and the analyst, with a diabolic dialectic, adheres closely to the object of analysis. Sartre's book on Flaubert is also a book on himself. Confronted with Flaubert's work, Sartre always finds something to say. He calls Baudelaire *the man who never forgets himself*; this definition suits Sartre too. When confronted with a work, Sartre brushes humility aside. As a matter of fact, his mood and his words are the very opposite of humility. There appears between analyst and work (author) a double and mutual *authority*. The writer's subject is the world, the role of the work is to change this world. A critic is supposed to bring to life an object that lies engulfed in inert darkness. This critic neither sacralizes nor desacralizes; the critic finds the pattern, the meanings, the hidden associations and is in search of a self all along. The use of a *method* lies in the humility with which it reaches what is essential to the creator, to existence in general.

So the analyst's intention is identified with the author's intention in an *authoritarian* way. Fully, even dramatically, Sartre takes it upon himself to fulfill the *mission* of both writer and work. *The mission of the world*, so to say. It would be incorrect to state that Sartre takes the place of the object he writes about, that he wants to master it. In fact, he takes possession of a theme, a book, a *life*, in order to detect the human being in there, which, again, is just another way of dealing with himself. There is more to it than that, though. His *authority is double*. The writer (work) and the analyst mirror each other with proud lucidity and utter fidelity. Handled by the analyst, the work reveals its numberless meanings. The analyst whose questionings are all involved in this work acquires multiple meanings. A work must provide answers to questions reaching it from outside, as well as to those questions it contains within itself. Under such circumstances, one may wonder whether the act of reading can still be looked upon as an agreement of generosity. It seems to me that the act of reading turns into an attempt at identification, a transfer of meanings, a true re-creation. Genet is no longer an author who shamelessly deals with a foul world, as we have been told. He is *Saint Genet*, a martyr of abject life. The act of reading has modified his identity, has turned him into a character who will henceforward carry in his work the cross of burdensome sainthood. To put it in a nutshell, Sartre has created an author (a life, a biography) commensurate with the potential values of Genet's work.

16

Critical Methods and Literature

Who comes first, the author or the work? Creation or its creator? The work comes first, since the work survives the disappearance of its author. Creation, because it conveys, it stirs, it yields to meanings, and acquires a body (a spiritual body) in the act of reading. The work comes first since it changes particular existence into one that can stand for and comprise everything. In *Search for a Method*, Sartre explains that existential criticism begins with the study of the work in order to reach its author, then it returns to the work, since, by objectifying the individual, this work is *more complete, more comprehensive than life*.

From a work to its author and back to the work again, this investigation reveals the *work* and substantiates the *life*. In what way, one may ask? It seems to me that, during the last few decades, methodology has abused the words *Work* and *Author* (both capitalized). They seem oddly raised to power, to the state of an inoperative abstraction. What is the meaning of such words as *Work* and *Author*? We have all known for quite a while now that *the Work* does not exist; there are only individual works, which can be read in a number of ways. Similarly, *the Author* in general does not exist; there are authors, who are related to their works in a number of ways. Criticism is not supposed to deal with such things as the *Standard Work* or the paradigmatic *Author*. Flaubert tells us that every work has an aesthetics of its own (created by it), and the statement is perfectly credible. Consequently, all generalizations are risky in that respect. When dealing with generalities, all dialogue is unprofitable. In fact, dialogue only becomes possible when the critic approaches the work in accessible language. The author's *life* becomes meaningful when it relies upon a book that is alone of its kind. On second thought, we realize that no work allows itself to be perfectly mirrored by another work. No biography can ever fully grasp the condition of the creator. Discussing the connection between a work and its author's biography, we run the risk of reducing reality to something nonexistent. Fortunately, art is made up of particular instances, special cases, norms that usually contradict the *Norm*. Every work has its models, but it does not always treat them respectfully. We accept them only in order to step aside from them the sooner.

What is, then, the nature of the relationship between author and work, how must we deal with what existential criticism calls "significant conduct"? I, for one, see only one way out. We must concentrate upon the material life of a work (its language), we must reveal and explain in what obscure way a life acquires the colors of a destiny, as Camus used to say. When a theoretician of art asserts that "all aesthetic objects are the fruit of a *human project*" (Doubrovsky, *Corneille*, 20), I require to know at once what particular aesthetic objects he has in mind, what human project is revealed in the work. Above all, I must know which work has prompted the critic to use this language of essentialities. And I should also like to know how far this language can go before it can no longer be understood. Generalizations are only provisional in art (G. Calinescu and so many others repeatedly tell us so),[1] because the theories that support such generalizations rely upon a limited number of situations. This does not mean that theories ("anticipatory hypotheses," Jean Starobinski calls them) are inevitably false. I merely suggest that, in criticism, a theory dealing with ideational *verisimilitude* must constantly be confronted with the truth of some particular work. Promoted by the contentious spirit of Serge Doubrovsky, the psychoanalytical direction of existential criticism voices a significant opinion concerning the matter under discussion. This direction claims to have started from Maurice Merleau-Ponty and Sartre, but, as its promoter put it, existential psychoanalysis peeps at Marx, as well as at Hegel. Sartre's position is rendered more supple, sometimes it is even corrected, especially Sartre's peremptory attitude in *What Is Literature?* Among other things, Doubrovsky has the merit of simplification, he produces statements that are readily understood. He starts from the assumption that "the inner cohesion of a work is supported by the cohesion of an individual, concrete existence—the only one there is—that uses the work in order to find its own identity . . ." (Doubrovsky, *Pourquoi*, 209). This means that, at a certain point, biography does meet the work, the question being, however, when and where?

Existential psychoanalysis diverges from both Proust and Sainte-Beuve, but, at a later date, it attempts to reconcile the two within a new synthesis. Serge Doubrovsky tells us that, failing to *explain* literature, traditional biography (the biography of acts and external facts) murders it. Murder is a strong word. Dissociating oneself from Sainte-Beuve is absolutely necessary, even if, sooner or later, one . is to go back to him. Consequently, an additional stress can do no harm. Criticism *murders* literature. Showing no mercy, I, for one, should say, by making the author's existence known to us traditional biography (biographical criticism) announces the advent of the work. Just that. Or, maybe, biographical criticism prepares us to respond favorably to the work. It creates a holiday atmosphere around a work. To make this holiday even more appealing, biographical criticism also invents a suitable hero, *the author of the work*. It watches the author closely, constantly, at home, in literary salons, taking walks, in the alcove, at church, wherever the way of life and the outlook of the social self can be seen. Traces and signs are found leading to a work that the detective critic fails to reach. What is true is true, so at least we must admit that no such indiscretion has ever murdered a literary work. The works that Sainte-Beuve praised or disparaged, out of ignorance or of spite, still exist today as a living proof, and they obediently submit now to psychoanalytical analysis, existential psychoanalysis, the intolerant new rhetoric . . .

I agree with Serge Doubrovsky that traditional biography is unable to explain the birth of the inner structure of a work, that all its attempts in this direction are bound to fail. The cause of this failure is the inexcusably narrow image of the creator's life as seen in biographical criticism. The creator's *life* is not a mere sum of details, it is a *significant conduct*, a collection of *discontinuous, partly obscure facts and gestures*, a line of *open, ambiguous meanings* (Doubrovsky, *Pourquoi*, 211) that, as we know from Sartre, tend to melt into a whole. Existential criticism replaces the *deeper* and the *superficial self* by a *Total Self*. This all-embracing *self* can explain the *life* and can hope to find its true connection with the *work*. In this way, literature appears as "the most complex revelation of an existence." From within the text, "a man talks to other people about man" (Doubrovsky, *Corneille*, 20). Doubrovsky coins memorable phrases for the simplest of truths. All art is essentially a "human presence"; psychology, politics, and aesthetics are governed by the same subject; meeting and communicating within the same *human existence*.

Under these circumstances, criticism is intelligent enough to admit that biography (letters, abandoned manuscripts, details of daily life) will never explain a literary work, that the work is undoubtedly above all possible biographies, that in criticism there is no "beyond" in the work that is not, by means of perception, on "this side" of the thing. The author does not vanish from sight as soon as a book has been completed. The death of the author will not "help the truth of the work," as Barthes used to say. A very significant ontological relationship is contained within the language. Serge Doubrovsky is right to say that, deprived of its origins and destination, prevented from communicating with reality (existence), the literary work is fatally diminished, that the writer's *deeper self*, as seen by *la nouvelle critique*, is a self deprived of its substance (Doubrovsky, *Chemins*, 153), that abusing rhetoric is no less dangerous than the abusive use of history in traditional criticism. It inevitably brings about the "utter abolition of existence."

It stands to reason that the *existence* must be brought back into criticism, not into the work (which the existence has never left). What is the exact meaning of the word *existence* one may wonder. In the texts I have quoted, the concept has innumerable connotations and is highly ambiguous. Serge Doubrovsky mentions a *project of an existence*, a *significant conduct*, without bothering to explain what he means. Three different meanings at least are attached to the idea of existence in literature. There is, first, an existence previous to both author and work, an existence that can ultimately be identified with the *universe* containing the creator and the work.

Second, there is a project of existence that can be traced in a work and is so often mentioned by psychoexistentialists. Last, the meaning of existence is, in Barthes's words, a *structure of existence*, in Malraux's words, an *experience transmuted into awareness*, in Camus's words (already quoted before), *life acquiring the colors of a destiny*. In other words, the term *existence* points to a particular position vis-à-vis the world, an exemplary life that is able to cope with both consciousness and the unconscious. This is the meaning we always try to find, either within or without a work—in documents, in Sartre's *action*, in Malraux's *adventure*, in the psychoanalytical web of complexes and obsessions.

What is the place of the work within this complex *existence*? What are the connections between *life* (the creator's existence) and the remaining aspect of existence? And again, finally, where does criticism stand when we consider all these directions of existence? We are left in the dark. Serge Doubrovsky and together with him all those who seek the work and the author through the eyes of the *total self* dispatch this matter without bothering to answer such questions. They make use of a concept that denotes too many things, and, as we all know, in literary criticism too many determinations pave the sure way to indetermination.

Interestingly, today all criticism begins by formulating its own theory of criticism. Every method questions all others. Few are the critics interested in their neighbors' affairs. This latter half of our century is an age of intolerance in the field of criticism. I take it to be an inaugural, founding intolerance. I *exist* insofar as I can differentiate myself from the rest. I *exist* in the solitude of my method alone. The methods seem to have replaced the critics. Tickets, please. Have you got a method? If so, pass, get on the train of criticism. No method, no methodological brotherhood owns you? Farewell, then. You are stranded on the platform of traditional criticism, that dull and determined biographical, positivist, psychological, impressionistic criticism.

Consequently, present day criticism produces methodologies as fervently, peremptorily, scholarly, and presumptuously as it can. Analyses, whenever they manage to squeeze in, can do no more than support the method upon which the critic has laid eyes from the very beginning. Unfortunately, more often than not, we know from the start what it is all about. From the first sentences of a psychoanalytical study I feel I am going to come across frustrated children and guilty parents. They are there all right, both children and parents, each with biographical incidents and confused thwartings, transfers, and phantasms. I will not make a secret of the fact that such a view may very well please quite a number of people. A psychoanalytical text may be good literature. Yet I cannot help objecting to the literary work being used as a mere pretext, and I sadly realize that the *all-embracing universe* of this work is lost. The hero of the critical text is not the hero of the work, or its creator; the true hero of this critical text is the unconscious, dwelling in the depths of being.

One thing is certain in connection with the criticism of these last few decades: the literary work is beginning to lose priority. Instead of the method justifying the work, things go the other way. Even those methods that claim to be faithful to the *text* alone use this text as a pretext for their own existence. The act of reading proves that the analysis is correct. Here is a significant reversal. The method is prior to the work. The work is unable to decide upon or at least to modify the critic's apparel. The more transparent and obedient a book, the greater the value of the critical text. A new quality, a new standard in the judgment of literature, has appeared, the penetrability of a work, its advantage of spurring analysis into fruitful action. Mallarmé's famous statement could now be pronounced again. The aim of literature is to lead to a *Method*. At the end of everything there is the almighty Method.

17

Starobinski and Method

Critics and analysts, keep Psyché's lamp
aflame, but remember Acteon's fate.

Jean Starobinski, *La relation critique*

T oward the end of his "Psychoanalysis and Literary Knowledge" (1964) in the volume *La relation critique* (1970), Jean Starobinski briefly mentions a little fable that is suggestive of the modern critic's connection with methods. The fable brings together two well-known myths, that of beautiful Psyche, who, disobeying the gods, lit her lamp and glanced at the face of Cupid, her intended husband, whose face she was not supposed to see. Then the myth of Acteon, the hunter who was bold enough to glance at the goddess Artemis bathing in a river. The goddess turned him into a stag, and he was rent by his own dogs. Psyche was afflicted by an unending line of misfortunes because she had the boldness to glance at the face of the man intended for her. A double interdiction, twice disobeyed and expiated in two ways: Psyche is saved by her own love and devotion, while Acteon, his identity changed by the wrathful goddess, is devoured by his dogs. In both cases, the interdiction refers to *sight*. A guilty glance that must not reach some secret; the glance is equivalent to knowledge, and knowledge to aggression. Starobinski intimates that the modern critic is in the beautiful and indiscreet Psyche's position. The critic can hardly wait to glance at the creator's hidden face and so, disregarding the agreement, lifts the lamp and takes a look. The critic sees something extraordinary, the head of a charming adolescent. But a drop of oil wakes the sleeping adolescent and turns loose the anger of all gods. Psyche (the analyst) must pay for her indiscretion, but this is worth doing, for knowledge turns into revelation even if the way toward it must cross hell.

The modern critic may equally be doomed to Acteon's fate. An indiscreet glance may bring about death. It is a symbolic death: Acteon (the critic) is devoured by the dogs of method. Before actually dying, the critic also experiences the torment of being deprived of identity. Being turned into a stag implies no longer being able to dispose of words; the critic is denied the ability to convey what he or she has witnessed. Artemis's cruelty is, to a certain extent, perverse. She does not kill the thoughtless, peeping hunter with her own hand or at once. She first degrades him biologically, depriving him of the essential human gift, his power to communicate. Actual death comes later, accompanied by a wealth of symbols. We know from mythology that, having devoured Acteon, incited by the goddess, the dogs scoured the forest in search of the master whom they were carrying in their bellies. In this search, the dogs reached the cave of the centaur Chiron, who had taught Acteon the art of hunting. The legend adds that Chiron put up a statue in the likeness of Acteon, in order to comfort the inconsolable dogs.

Acteon (the critic) does stand a chance, after all, the chance of turning into a work of art himself. His glance at divine beauty is paid for by his shameful death, but his martyrdom is followed by the birth of a statue. I have no idea what the psychoanalytical interpretation of this myth may be (Charles Baudouin does not include it among the founding myths), but one thing is clear—Chiron is Acteon's spiritual father. He initiates Acteon into the art of hunting and later erects the statue of his martyred pupil. Chiron is therefore the *father* who perpetuates the image of the *son* killed by the dogs the son had trained. I will leave the subject open to the meditation of those interested and merely remark that if we equate Acteon's fate to the fate of modern criticism we have serious ground for worry. Jean Starobinski's warning is perfectly justified, for when possessed by the drunken elation of methodology, one must always remember Acteon's myth. Criticism must not be turned into a repeated *approach to the method*, an *approach to approaches*. Chiron himself may turn out to be a vain illusion, and what statue will then appease the dogs that have devoured the critic?

Starobinski's fable applies to the connection between literary criticism and the theory of criticism. The opinion he voices in the preliminary essay of *La relation critique* is an example of lucidity. The learned Geneva critic pleads in favor of a cause that is ours as well. He supports a criticism of interpretation, guided, though not overwhelmed, by the theory of criticism. He is in search of a method that will not sacrifice the literary work, a method that, while helping critical analysis, may function to the advantage of the work. He supports that criticism that is able to consider every essential detail of a work, as well as the connection between a work and its author. After all, criticism is a free play of the mind. As Starobinski puts it, criticism has "its strokes of luck," its moments of fulfillment and of grace. Why should we deny it all that, why should we do without those things that lend nobility to this form of creation? Undoubtedly, criticism does need "firm normative principles, guiding though not tyrannical, meant to confront it with its object now and again" (Starobinski, *Relation*, 12), but, to my mind, one has to avoid by all means turning these *normative principles* into the essential theme of criticism. Otherwise, one may easily end like Acteon.

As a matter of fact, Starobinski voices a commonsense opinion. He urges us to go beyond the *spontaneous sympathy* we may experience for a literary work (the primary, impressionistic stage) and thoroughly study the "web of simultaneous connections" or, in other words, attempt an immanent examination of the work, making use of a "scientific" method (*technique*). We are not supposed to stop at this analytical stage; we must then turn criticism into a *free play of the mind*. This free play of the mind involves several things. As Starobinski informs us, at this stage criticism becomes a "knowing" that is aware of both itself and the global, all-embracing image of its object, or, in the critic's own words, "an open accumulation of things partly pointed out," an operation that emphasizes the "structural unity that informs all inner relationships" (Starobinski, *Relation*, 18–19).

This *traject* of criticism (one of Starobinski's favorite terms) is good stuff for thought. It leads from sympathy to an "immanent" study and, further, to the free play of the mind. It is an open, circular traject (elsewhere Starobinski mentions the hermeneutic circle), a trip from the interpreter to the work, then beyond the work, and back to the work and its interpreter, over and over again. These three stages do not always follow one another in the same order. The critical mind can hardly be prevented from escaping into the *free play of the mind* before it has experienced the stage of objective examination. The chronology of the critical mind is independent of the chronology demanded by the method. Those "strokes of luck" and "states of grace" hinder the cold strategy of the geometrical spirit in criticism.

Aside all that, the free meditation redeems the unity of the work (which is endangered by the fragmentary, immanent examination) and expresses the critic's personality (intention, voice, particular traject, or whatever term one is apt to use). The critic does not linger idly about the outskirts of the text. Respect for the work does not discourage the critic from creating. In describing this intricate relationship of both dependence and independence between the work and its interpreter, Starobinski finds a felicitous phrase, "the passage from an endearing dependence to a watchful independence." Then, further on, "our autonomy (in whose absence all explanation is impossible) must rely on our freely varying response to the invariable substance of the work" (Starobinski, *Relation*, 28).

Here is a spirit who takes a healthy view of the concepts operating in criticism, of the connections established between these concepts, which are as important as the concepts themselves. Starobinski's curiosity helps him glance at the world outside the walls of his method. Like all true critics, he takes a moderate view of his own importance, yet he is hardly prepared to follow humbly in the footsteps of the literary work. A work may just as well exist without my help, whether I am an analyst or a reader, but a work truly becomes itself (a spiritual force, an aesthetic object) only when it comes across a critical mind that responds to it, a critical mind that is well aware that this work exists as a universe within a universe of relationships. There is a certain something *beyond* the work, there is a "structuring subject" within all structures, and the two compel us to consider the sociocultural universe into which the subject merges and out of which it emerges as separate. In this way, immanent criticism is left behind. The work contains an original world of relationships and is itself contained within another world of relationships.

The world outside the work adjusts to the world *inside* the work. The voice *outside* as well as the voice *inside* must both be heeded. I shall quote a telling excerpt out of Starobinski's subtle essay:

> I may give up trying to find the *law* of a work outside that work (in its psychological "springs," its cultural antecedents, etc.), yet I am unable to ignore that something within the work that is bound to the world outside, in the implicit or explicit, a positive or a negative way. What are the meaning and nature of that relationship? (Starobinski, *Relation*, 19)

The question touches upon a large area of interest. We have already crossed it several times. We are bound to scour it over and over again, since nothing is ever finally settled in criticism. We keep experiencing new things, and this makes all the difference to our next crossing. When a new venture is made, we know a little more than before.

Starobinski brings sociological and psychoanalytical standards back to criticism in a comprehensive and coherent concept, which is exactly what a critic's concepts ought to be like, open enough to welcome all literature in its diversity, yet coherent, accurate enough to prompt an orderly analysis, an orderly judgment. The critic's interpretations (of Rousseau, Corneille, Racine, Stendhal) confirm the validity of the method. It must be repeated that this is a method that will not reject talent. These concepts do not despise the critic's imaginative power or, implicitly, ability to create:

> In order to fulfill its all-embracing mission, to deal with the works comprehensively, criticism must be more than a verifiable "knowing," it must turn into a work itself, and take upon itself all the risks of a work; it starts as the trace of an act . . . and finally becomes an act in its turn. (*Relation*, 33)

Consequently, the critical text ponders over its own existence insofar as it is able to find the way leading to the work and its author. It is a meditation that assumes and redeems the unity of the work. Here is a highly essential detail.

In an interview that I included in my book *Timpul trăirii, timpul mărturisirii, Jurnal parizian* [A Time for Living, a Time for Memories, Parisian Diary], Jean-Pierre Richard was complaining that the unity of a work was lost in its thematic analysis. He disliked the fragmentation of a work and likened the modern critic's position to the condition of Penelope, the woman who would unweave by night what she had woven during the day in her suitors' presence. Richard's anxiety is singular in postwar criticism. Critics do not usually doubt their methods; neither do they feel uneasy about the status of the work. Let the work come to what it may, as long as the method has the upper hand. In Starobinski's criticism, indebted to several methods at once (from psychoanalysis to Spitzerian stylistics),[1] I find Richard's and Georges Poulet's endeavor to rescue the unity, the cohesion, the very brilliance of the literary work. They are extremely careful, and loyal—I should say—not to reduce the work to a heap of dead fragments in their critical analyses. No matter in what way, all criticism must piece up again the original unitary universe of the work. The critic must imitate Hermes (this being the myth advanced by Starobinski), the patron of hermeneutics, the hero who steps over the boundary between two worlds, coming and going from absence into presence and back again, from nothing toward everything, crossing all realms of the work and those of the universe. Here is a wonderful statement: "I must first bring the work back to life if I am to fall in love with it, I must make it talk and then answer its questions" (*Relation*, 28).

But whose is the voice heard in the work, the voice that, all along, the critic catches, loses then hears again, the voice whose place the critic finally takes (since this is what the critic actually does) in criticism? Let us examine again a sentence that has already been quoted several times: "The *structuralist* structure of the work makes us consider the existence of a structuring subject" (*Relation*, 23). This *structuring subject* is not far from Proust's *deeper self*. On the other hand, I feel that it contains both the author who writes and the person who lives, in spite of Starobinski's assertion that the image of the author before the birth of the work will forever remain unknown. My opinion is that maybe, indeed, we ignore what the author was like before creating the work, but, starting from this work, we can discover the author who made it and was altered by it in turn. Starobinski himself is willing to examine this being whom the work has changed, whom the critic sees not as the original author, but as *somebody else*. *Who speaks*, then? And *whom does the speaker address?* What ("real, imaginary, collective, unique, absent") addressee is to receive the speaker's message? Unlike Mallarmé's *impersonal voice*, unlike the *linguistic being* of structuralism, or Barthes's *paper author*, Starobinski's *voice* can be traced and identified. In any book we hear the voice of its author (who has experienced the act of writing), and it is a bad mistake for a critic to stop up the ears with wax like Ulysses's men and then assure us that there is nothing to be heard at all. In *Jean-Jacques Rousseau: Transparency and Obstruction*, Starobinski states that in literature Jean-Jacques Rousseau was the first to subscribe in an exemplary way to "the dangerous compact between the ego and language, the 'new alliance,' in which man makes himself the word" (200). A question quickly arises, how much of the human voice is transferred to these words? Are these words (in language) faithful to the voice that clothed them in sounds, and to the hand which outlined their letters? Each critic handles such questions individually. I have a feeling no method is of help here.

18

Barthes and the Author

*The pleasure of the Text also includes
the amicable return of the author.*

Barthes, *Sade, Fourier, Loyola*

Paraphrasing Sartre, I could exclaim, *somebody ought to be here, and that person is Roland Barthes.* Barthes, who always thinks of everything one can possibly think of, must have his say in this matter as well. He expresses no doubt as to the existence of a *voice* in the text, as well as of a certain connection between the person who *speaks* in the text and the person who *writes* it. In *Critical Essays* (1972), there is an article entitled "Authors and Writers," (1960) that opens by formulating the very questions listed above. As usual, Barthes's answer contains both a truth and a countertruth. He is haunted (as I shall try to demonstrate in another chapter in this book) by a feeling of uncertainty that gravely endangers his stated certainties. Barthes's mind begets nuances that keep devouring one another. If one accepts the idea that *one models oneself* in the act of writing, then one might say that Barthes starts shaping his spirit only when language has grown ambiguous enough.

For the time being, we are not concerned with Barthes as *logothète* (to use one of his words); we are examining the way in which this genius, characterized by remarkable Byzantine subtlety, deals with a topic that has mastered modern criticism and now separates it from traditional criticism. First of all, Barthes uses words as mere vehicles of thought. Words are the instrument of communication. The *écrivant* [the one writing] uses the verb *to write* in its transitive meaning alone. Its object is the only thing that matters, while the idea of style is irrelevant. *L'écrivain* [the writer] has a different credo. The word is more than a vehicle, it becomes a structure, and the verb *to write* is invariably intransitive. *L'écrivain* polishes the words and, unlike *l'écrivant*, is willing to lose, as Barthes puts it, "his own structure and that of the world in the structure of language" (*Essays*, 145).

Here is an important point: the *writer* loses the structure, encloses it within the structure of the word. It appears to me to be a transfer, rather than a loss. As a matter of fact, the dispossession, or loss, is synonymous with the acquisition of a new body. Going along Barthes's line of thought, we might say that the writer loses a physical body and, in the act of writing, produces a *linguistical body* to replace the former. But the writer is not alone in the world and always springs from something. Before and after the writer there is always a *world*, which the writer bears inside and which bears the writer in its turn.

What connection can there be between the person who writes (who writes industriously, both assuming the words and yielding to them) and the world *outside?* Barthes offers a convincing explanation:

> the author is a man who radically absorbs the world's *why* in a *how to write*. And the miracle, so to speak, is that this narcissistic activity has always provoked an interrogation of the world: by enclosing himself in the *how to write*, the author ultimately discovers the open question par excellence: why the world? What is the meaning of things? In short, it is precisely when the author's work becomes its own end that it regains a mediating character: the author conceives of literature as an end, the world restores it to him as a means: and it is in this perpetual inconclusiveness that the author rediscovers the world, an alien world moreover, since literature represents it as a question—never, finally as an answer. (*Essays*, 144–45)

We must overlook the speculations that follow (all of them splendid, highly effective intellectually) if we mean to keep track of Barthes's main idea: the writer is a person who turns amazement as to the existence of the world into an amazement as to—and a justification of—the act of writing. Barthes's position in this respect comes close to Sartre's existentialism, as well to Bertolt Brecht's Marxist position, Brecht being Barthes's major model at the time. Yet soon enough Barthes starts talking about *who speaks* and *who writes* in totally different terms. To be more specific, he feels that the question belongs to another level and consequently views and ponders it from a different point of view. In his essay "The Two Criticisms" (dated 1963), Barthes dissociates himself from Sainte-Beuve's biographism and Lanson's positivism. His is a dialectical dissociation that takes the historical element into account. The paradox lies in Barthes's discontented feeling that historical criticism is unable to cope with history. He does not deny the use of erudition in criticism, he merely accuses positivist criticism of making recourse to what he calls the "analogical correspondence." By that he means that a work of art must not be viewed in the light of *somebody else* or *somewhere else* in literature (in Barthes's own words), because every work is its own model.

Taken as points of reference, the *somebody else* and *somewhere else* hint at Freudian criticism (Charles Mauron) and at Marxist-oriented criticism (Lucien Goldmann).[1] Barthes replaces the *paradox of analogy*, which supports the criticism of determinations, by the idea of "ontological correspondence," favorable to a *criticism of significances*. Out of its comprehensive sphere, Barthes singles out *immanent criticism*, that, in Ferdinand de Saussure's terms, examines the *signifiant*, rather than the *signifié* (the center of interest in deterministic criticism). At this level, the relationship between author and work, eagerly contemplated by Roland Barthes's lucidity, is looked upon as a "merging of relationships," rather than a causal connection between an author's *life* and *work*. It is a useful distinction:

> If there is a relation between the author and his work (who would deny it? The work does not descend from Heaven; only positivist criticism still believes in the Muses), it is not a pointillist relation which accumulates partial, discontinuous, and "profound" resemblances, but on the contrary a relation between the *entire* author and the *entire* work, a relation of relations, [*un rapport des rapports*] a homological, not an analogical correspondence. (*Essays*, 252–53)

A *rapport des rapports* is a remarkable coinage. *La nouvelle critique* has eagerly appropriated it. Each critic attributes an individual meaning to these words. Barthes regards the formula as the sign of fundamental modifications in the practice of examining criticism, which has switched from explaining a work to examining the functions of a text, the sign of some deep conversion of what he calls all "standards of knowing." The formula is also meant to imply that biographical criticism must be abandoned because it revolves around a *genetics of literary details*. Critical positivism must be abandoned in its turn, because it finds points of reference for a work in circumstances outside the work as such. Yet Barthes warns us that the usefulness of these hardworking, honest, learned positivist critics' activity must by no means be belittled. When he looks benevolently upon these critics, Barthes does not do so out of complaisance; he is certain that their findings can be of some use to the criticism of interpretation (in his study on Michelet, Barthes himself uses them). Elsewhere he expresses his regret that Lanson's project has never been carried out: no complete corpus of careful examinations concerning literary facts has been built.

As seen by Barthes, the relationship between author and work goes both ways. There is more to it than the connection between cause and effect, for it is, above all, a relationship mediated by language. The author and the work are not inevitably alike. A work can be—and preeminently is—*unfaithful*; it does not contain all its author's ideas and feelings however hard the author may have tried to *state* those in the text. The text changes their meanings. Barthes utters a paradox: "the writer is someone to whom 'authenticity' is denied" (*Essays*, 278). He means to say that the writer's sincerity is thwarted by the work, by a language that has its own exigencies, norms, and authenticity. The work alters its author's "good faith," it calms down regrets, naiveties, fears, and scruples. Maybe it does, yet are we to believe Barthes when he says that "a work can keep nothing" of all that? It seems more accurate to say that by changing their destination, the text changes their quality as well. The work encloses them and gives them another identity.

To put it briefly, Barthes feels that the act of writing changes the whole world into a text. It is a text that takes over the questions of this world (its fundamental *why*), in order to formulate its own. The impersonal concept of *world* also encloses the creator's existence. Barthes never denies it, he never banishes it outside criticism, he merely leaves it out of his examination for a while. As will be seen, the author's existence enters the critic's analysis from an unexpected area: it looms out of the *pleasure of the text*, veiled by the joy of reading.

Until we learn the pleasure of reading a literary text in some other way, however, we must without delay leave behind the way of reading of traditional criticism. In his famous study *Criticism and Truth* (1966), Barthes beheads the university hydra, represented by R. Picard.[2] For about a decade, a famous war was waged between *paleo-criticism* and *la nouvelle critique*. Besides Barthes and Picard, forces from various methodological directions took part in it. The Sorbonne defended a certain way of conceiving literature and a way of writing about literature that were attacked by some young barbarians who wanted to take the university by storm. Barthes starts by questioning the legitimacy of the prevailing point of view. His starting point is Racine, the eternal subject of all critics, whether they belong to the university or not. Before that, Barthes had written three essays on Racine, grouped in a book, *On Racine*, that had created some notice in 1960. He had managed to snatch Racine out of the clutches of the Sorbonne critics and had created a new Racine in whose works Andromaque was no longer du Parc.[3] Racine was not a 26-year-old Orestes; he had nothing to do with Nero, nor had Burrhus anything to do with Vitart. In "History or Literature," the last essay of the book, Barthes openly attacks the positivist method, stating that the author (creator) has no right to dominate either the work or the history outside the work. He disputes the central place accorded the author. This privilege of the author prevents the critic from looking at real history, such as the history of the institutions of an age, for instance. The *author* makes perspective impossible. Consequently, the author must be deprived of power. One may easily imagine the response elicited by a statement like "to amputate literature from the individual" (*Racine*, 162). Barthes decides that without this sacrifice there can be no history of literature. This sacrifice alone enables a work to recapture its transcendence, and the history of literature to meet real history.

This is the provocation. The reaction follows. Denouncing the *new imposture* of *la nouvelle critique*, Picard defends the authority of the author over the work, as well as the author's priority in connection with it. Barthes switches the debate to the realm of *significance* and denies the writer the right to explain the *legal meaning* of the work. As a matter of fact, Barthes is in a hurry to dispose of this troublesome character:

We are generally inclined, at least today, to believe that the author can lay claim to the meaning of his work and can himself make that its legal meaning; from this notion flows the unreasonable interrogation directed by the critic at the dead writer, at his life, at the traces of his intentions, so that he himself can guarantee the meaning of his work: people want at all costs to make the dead person, or a substitute for him, speak. Such substitutes may be his historical period, the genre, the vocabulary, in a word everything that is *contemporary* with the author; these contemporary phenomena acquire metonymically the author's right over his creation. Even more: we are asked to wait until the author is dead so that we can treat him with "objectivity"; a strange reversal indeed: it is at the very moment when the work becomes mythical that we are supposed to regard it as a precise phenomenon. (*Criticism*, 75–76)

Thus formulated, the questioned is settled. It stands to reason that Barthes is right. We need neither the writer, whether alive or dead, nor *substitutes* in order to reach the meaning of the work. As a matter of fact, the writer's meaning, if he or she happens to have communicated one, may just as well be a superficial one. It is absurd to look for the *legal meaning* of a poem or drama, when it is well known that no work suggests one meaning alone. Barthes's arguments look unquestionable. Together with the structuralist *nouvelle critique*, Barthes is certain that all meanings are inherent in the work and they need no outside justification. "Independently of any *situation*." Except for this situation, Barthes concludes, the work lies asleep, enveloped in its pure ambiguity, until some intelligent reader attributes one or several meanings to it. "Its ambiguity is absolutely pure . . . it always has something of Pythian concision." Pure ambiguity? Barthes treats his words lightly here, but we must not blame him, since his plays upon words lead to such astonishing meanings. His idea takes an unexpected turn, and we learn that, emerging out of pure ambiguity, the work acquires the *status of a prophet*. The work is always in a *prophetic situation*, because it hides a Pythias who will not go beyond suggesting, who will not digress. The work goes hand in hand with its reader, the person who elicits the words of this taciturn Pythias.

Of changeable nature, the reader's status joins the ambiguous and prophetic status of the work. In this way, the work *shapes itself*, reveals its meanings. In this way, the science of literature (Barthes did not question the possibility of such a science at the time but did later) obliterates the author's name. The work is unable to share the author's predicament, and Barthes's realization exhales a slight regret, as honest as can be expected ("the sacrifices which such a science would impose . . ." [*Criticism*, 75]). The science of literature can hardly descry anything beyond the work. It deals with a work "made independently of any *situation*"; "no practical life is there to tell us the meaning that should be given to it."

All these remarks are perfectly justified. One can hardly deny that when a reader meets a work there is no witness present. Some readers may happen to be acquainted with the antecedents of the work (who wrote it, when it was written, under what circumstances, what the author's intentions were), but usually they are not. Even if they do know a few things, the work itself is their main concern. Everything is settled between the two of them (reader and work). The act of reading as such requires solitude and absolute silence. This fruitful silence is the best witness there can be.

19

Barthes's Paper Author

*As institution, the author is
dead, . . . but.*

The Pleasure of the Text

It is at this point that the author's friendly return, mentioned by Barthes in his preface to *Sade, Fourier, Loyola*, takes place. A paradox becomes apparent and one must begin by explaining it. As we have seen, the act of reading separates the work from the outside world. Both reader and work take refuge in a space and a time unknown to real existence. Common laws and connections are disregarded. Yet, no sooner has the work shown its face to a reader who kindles its life with meanings, in the utter silence of the act of reading, than the great exile, the author, comes back. It is a *special* image of the author. In his preface Barthes deals admirably with the arrival of this unexpected guest. In the beginning there is the pleasure of the Text (capitalized, pronounced as sacred in an analysis that—another paradox—ends by desacralizing literature). Therefore, in the beginning there is the pleasure, and the name of this pleasure is Author:

> The pleasure of the Text also includes the amicable return of the author. Of course, the author who returns is not the one identified by our instititutions (history and courses in literature, philosophy, church discourse); he is not even the biographical hero. The author who leaves his text and comes into our life has no unity; he is a mere plural of "charmes," the site of a few tenuous details, yet the source of vivid novelistic glimmerings, a discontinuous chant of amiabilities, in which we nevertheless read death more certainly than in the epic of a fate; he is not a (civil moral) person, he is a body. (*Sade*, 8)

The statement cannot be understood properly unless one knows that Barthes attaches quite a number of connotations to the *body*. The term may denote a linguistic, that is, grammatical body, or it may point to a wealth of details, microstructures, as it seems to be doing in the statement above. Here Barthes talks about fragments belonging to the pattern of a life. The essayist explains that, while reading Sade, he fails to remember Sade as the grandiose victim oppressed by society because of his obsessive passion (his *fire*, Barthes calls it), he fails to remember Sade's particular fate and conjures up something else instead, Sade's use of *milli* instead of *madamoiselle*, the white muff he wears when he accosts Rose Keller, or his last games with the little Charenton washerwoman. Out of Fourier's life, he recollects that the utopist liked eating some special Parisian pies and that later in life he felt attracted to lesbians. When reading Loyola, instead of the saint's vision and pilgrimages, Barthes merely sees his subject's beautiful eyes full of tears. And so on.

In this context, Barthes also uses the concept *biographème*. He talks about a biography made up of small significant units, meant to build the image of an author (a *body*) to accompany the act of reading. Half jokingly, half in earnest, Barthes tells us that, were he a dead writer, he would give anything in the world to have a cordial, unembarrassed biographer outline his life using such details, modulations, likes, and other *biographèmes* (*reduce* his life to them, Barthes says sternly). As a matter of fact, Roland Barthes did not really wait for his death; neither did he wait for the advent of the unembarrassed, friendly biographer who was to trace the "biographemic" pattern of his life. He traced it himself in *Roland Barthes by Roland Barthes* (1977).

Let us go back now to the pleasure of the Text and the return of the author. In his explanation of this idea, the essayist uses a dismal image. The Text destroys its subject ("a subject to love"), the subject is blown into the text just as ashes from a dead body are blown into the wind after cremation, which means that, during the act of reading, the author must rise out of self-created ashes. This weird character pieces up its own body out of small disconnected fragments. It is, of course, an imaginary body, a *life* blown to the four winds and then recomposed at the will and whim of some unpredictable reader.

In *The Pleasure of the Text* (1975), Barthes uses a psychoanalytical name for this character, *le Père* [the Father]. A prodigious ambiguity envelops the word, and Barthes is in no particular hurry to clear things up. This Father is not hidden behind the text; he is "lost in the midst of a text." An encouraging sentence follows: "He is always another, the author." It's a vain hope, though, since on the same page we learn about the death of the author. As will soon be seen, this death is followed by a resurrection resembling Barthes's conclusions in *Sade, Fourier, Loyola*. The death comes first: "As an institution, the author is dead, his civil status, his biographical person have disappeared; dispossessed, they no longer exercise over his work the formidable paternity" (*Pleasure*, 27).

And yet, "in the text, in a way, *I desire* the author: I need his figure (which is neither his represention nor his projection), as he needs mine (except to 'prattle')." As a *linguistic being*, the writer is caught in the web of fiction, but is a mere toy, a jolly joker, a *zero degree*, the *dummy* in a game of bridge: "always on the blind spot of systems, adrift" (35), "always outside of place (atopic)" (34). But "death of the Father would deprive literature of many of its pleasures. If there is no longer a Father, why tell stories?" (*Pleasure*, 47). Barthes produces here a final conclusion that all stories remind us of Oedipus. When one tells a story, one contemplates Oedipus constantly breaking the Law. Barthes's dialectics is amazingly undulating. His subtle intelligence is so very whimsical. In his own critical texts, the *author* dies and is resurrected more than once.

We must go back now to the line of his thought. As an *institution* the author has vanished from the text yet, during the act of reading, puts in a friendly appearance. The author is needed, created by the joy of reading; the author needs a reader, the reader needs the author. It is not as a civil or moral being that the author returns but as a *body*, details, impulses, images blown in the text like ashes in the wind. Approaching psychoanalysis, Barthes tells us that the Text is consumed by the Text, but when the reader calls, the Father returns because his absence impairs the reader's pleasure. It is a temporary return, though, because the author (Father) can never be otherwise than *out of place*. This is, in a few words, Roland Barthes's fluctuating theory concerning the connections between the person who writes the Text, the person who reads it, and its Author, hidden within the text and brought back into sight by the true joy of reading.

The creator's external biography does not affect the act of reading. The author's civil existence stays as it is—the reader is no Orpheus to rescue it from oblivion. Only a biography consisting of *biographèmes* can be of some use to criticism. Barthes waves aside as futile a person's social biography, which registers all the acts of the one who writes, although when writing about Balzac (*S/Z*), Barthes confesses to having encoded all references to the latter's life and work. He was never interested, though, in the author seen as "the locus of property, heritage, filiation, Law" (Barthes, *Grain*, 80). Barthes only talks about the return of the author as a *paper being*. He even has several plans in this respect.

Barthes opens the door to a room we have never yet seen.

> If one day this authorial determination can be put into proper perspective within a multitext, a fabric of connections, then the author could be reinstated—as a paper being present in his text by virtue of inscription. . . .
> I would even say that I look forward to this development; I should like to one day write a bio-graphy. (*Grain*, 80)

In another interview, printed in 1971, the essayist speaks of the biography of the paper being and produces the new concept of *ergography*. It denotes the *écriture of the composition of the text* (an ergograph is an apparatus that examines and measures muscular effort). Up to a point, the essayist's remarks are rather cryptic. His disapproval of traditional biography is as clear as ever: "what we ought to do is retrace not the biography of a writer but what could be called the writing of his work [*l'écriture de son travail*], a kind of ergography" (*Grain*, 145). He does not press his point, but, from his few remarks, we understand that he has in mind a being born out of language, a writer who inhabits the Text as a grammatical character.

On the publication of *The Pleasure of the Text*, a journalist confronted Barthes about the previous statement concerning the author's return. Barthes offered an interesting justification.

> To me, that sentence seems rather avant-garde! It really would be a wonderful liberation to be able to take up the authors of the past again as agreeable, charming bodies, traces that still remain seductive. There are writers who point the way for us: Proust, Jean Genet (I'm thinking of his novels)—he is in his books. He says *I, Jean.* It would never occur to anyone, however, to say that his books express a subjective experience: Genet is in his books as a *paper character.* That is the success of his work: he is there as a completely disinherited character unencumbered by any heredity in relation to himself as *referent.* (*Grain*, 166)

Let us put aside Barthes's explanation for a while. We have learned so far that in the text the writer *is* a paper hero. The voice heard in a narrative is and is not Jean Genet or Marcel Proust. We accept his presence, but his absence bewilders us— whose is that *other* voice we hear? Barthes's repeated use of the formula *paper character* is an unsuccessful attempt at explaining what a true biography, an *ergography*, is supposed to look like. The critic says he has considered writing a biography but that his Chateaubriand "is first of all in his oeuvre, his books: a Chateaubriand of paper" (*Grain*, 350). For instance, he envisages the biography of a *Chateaubriand de papier*, a Chateaubriand unlike all images ever produced by his biographers, a Chateaubriand in his old age, a writer who had become a machine for writing books.

As far as the question under discussion is concerned, Barthes's *position* is one of *transition*, we might say, using his own definition of himself, from some other essay. He disapproves of biographers, yet he cannot make up his mind to deprive the text of its author. He announces the death of the person who writes, then he praises the resurrection of the grammatical person. He ascertains the death of the Father (the father of the text), but his tenderness at once sets about bringing back together the latter's image (a particular image, though) that had been scattered all over the work. He extols the pleasure of the text and complains that the author's absence diminishes this pleasure. His imagination sets about inventing the author with its own means, then uses the first opportunity to drop this invented being, until the act of reading is repeated and the critic's nostalgia paves the way for a new *friendly return* of the same old author.

Confronted with this rotary motion of the critical dialectics, one is at a loss. Is it ritualistic death or ritualistic resurrection that the author has been doomed to? The one thing we can be certain of is that Barthes allows this author a highly uncertain status. The author is kept waiting in the anteroom of the act of reading. Barthes's image of this act of reading resembles a room with two exits (entrances, maybe). The author uses one to go in, at the call of an intense reading, and uses the other to leave, when the reader forgets the yearning for the person who wrote the work, and consequently the author is dispatched. This endless *passage* to and fro informs the language, *constitutes* the language, the *work*, and the *text*. These will not be abandoned by the critic, no matter how eager to change places (to change ideas, I should say, as far as Barthes is concerned). The author comes and goes, dies and is resurrected, these successive deaths and resurrections resulting in the image of a *paper being*. Here is a Jacob of modern criticism, forever fighting a grammatical angel. When analyzing a work, Barthes hardly ever thinks of the person who wrote it, but, when at ease, he contemplates the possibility of a strange biography, one that could trace the *écriture of the composition of the text*, an ergography that is supposed to ignore the author's moods and concentrate on the structure of these moods and tensions, on the mechanisms of the act of writing.

In spite of all that, Barthes cannot be said to show programmatic hostility to all kinds of biographies. In the above-mentioned 1979 interview, he praises Proust's biographer, George D. Painter, for having rehabilitated "marcellism," by which he means "a real interest in the private life of Proust himself and no longer simply in the characters of his novel." Does Barthes really mean an "interest in the private life of Proust himself"? This, more than anything else, has been the true ambition of biographical criticism for more than a century now. Indeed it is the very biography that Proust and his many followers despise so fiercely.

Barthes's excursions, returns, and metamorphoses fail to unsettle me. I take them to be proofs of his critical sensibility and understanding. Barthes is far too intelligent to ignore that there is no Text without an author, that the person who writes must leave visible traces in what is written, that the *linguistic body* will never be separated from the *body* (I use Barthes's meaning of the word) of the *scripteur*. The writer may turn into a machine for writing books, but that does not necessarily mean that this machine operates on its own. At least once, in the beginning, somebody must switch it on, must start it working. In literature, this *beginning* is reiterated with every new sentence. The rest comes of itself.

Barthes's *position of transition* among radical standpoints is very much in his favor. When we read Barthes, we have the feeling that his spirit is eager to converse with any opponent. His strategy is quite intelligent. The essayist does not discard *de plano* the issues of his opponents, like so many despotic spirits in culture. As a matter of fact, Barthes does more than that, but in a very subtle way. He draws close to those issues and appropriates them, makes them his own themes, thus changing their destination. His enveloping approach is very fruitful. Methodological terrorism has lately grown increasingly irritating—much like the political terrorism that stains with blood the end of our century—but Barthes's work does not have the same fate. Its freshness is unimpaired by the new synthesis under way, by the new integrative stage of criticism so far dominated by what we have seen. "Local imperialisms" never counted with Roland Barthes during his lifetime; they can do so even less now that he is dead.

20

Barthes as Biographer

*The only biography is of an
unproductive life. Once I produce,
once I write, it is the Text itself
that (fortunately) dispossesses me
of my narrative continuity.*

Roland Barthes by Roland Barthes

Barthes declares, "I do not have a biography" (*Grain*, 259). Then he continues that since he began writing, "I no longer see myself, I'm no longer an image for myself. I can't imagine myself, can't crystallize myself in images anymore." The strange thing is that Barthes is never absent from his brilliant texts. He is always there, even in his more specialized essays (*S/Z, The Fashion System*) or in his book on Michelet. Maybe he cannot look at himself (we might as well take his word for it), but he certainly makes his readers take a good look at him. This uncommonly intelligent, unpredictable, resourceful author, engaged in an endless search, will never step aside. Readers are lost unless they can keep pace with Barthes. Sartre is less demanding, at least lingering longer in the precincts of a concept. Barthes is restless and doing precisely what he claims he will not do. He loves (while writing, because of writing) what he hates; he affectionately clasps some notion in his arms, only to let go of it when least expected. He plays havoc with the concepts and displays more vitality than a *paper being*, a grammatical hero, could possibly possess.

The pleasure of Barthes's texts relies upon a constant *friendly companionship*, rather than a return. Were I to step into the boots of the friendly biographer Barthes used to dream of, I wonder what aspects of Barthes's life—which, by the way, I hardly know at all—I should choose to describe him. First, an infinite tenderness, then his image surrounded by his younger friends—a Barthes in his late fifties playing the part of a magister, a *guru*, somehow ashamed of doing so. A photograph of this group, printed in *Roland Barthes by Roland Barthes*, is subtitled by the critic " . . . *among friends.*" I find in it Barthes in the position of a master thinker, who hides discreetly behind some pupil and hangs his head with sham bashfulness. But he carries a bundle of papers or books under his arm, and these are the unmistakable sign of his authority, his paternalism . . . There is, finally, the image of the author surrounded by the same circle of friends, boycotting himself, refusing to officiate in his seminar at the university, in which I myself took part for a semester. Barthes teaches here the language of cordiality and strives hard to dislocate traditional teaching. This affectionate, friendly professor, who drowns literary objects in *pure ambiguity*, keeps popping up in front of his words, even now, when I read (again) his remarks upon the death of the author as an institution, the Father consumed by the Text, the friendly return of the author in the guise of a lifeless character . . .

Barthes's biography (a monograph, rather), *Michelet par lui-meme* [Michelet by Himself] (1954) is totally different from traditional biographies, yet it does not ignore *Michelet's real existence*. The critic is engrossed by the work, rather than by the story of the man who wrote it. In spite of this, the story of the man steals into the text, disregarding the critic's introductory warning: "The reader will not find in this little book of mine the story of Michelet's thinking, the story of his life, or the attempt to connect the two in view of some explanation." Barthes's intention is "to trace the structure of an existence (not a life), seen as a group of themes, a systematic network of obsessions . . . ; I have tried to outline the whole, leaving aside possible historical or biographical roots" (*Michelet*, 5). The illustrations that accompany the text seem to belong to the museum of Michelet's imagination rather than to his true life or his contemporary age. That is all very well, but if we come to think of it, the photographs are, after all, images of Michelet's family: we see there Michelet's wives, Michelet as a young man, Michelet at his writing desk, Michelet at the Academy, Michelet and Edgar Quinet lecturing again at the Collège de France, surrounded by a crowd of enthusiasts in 1848. Are all these, I wonder, outside Michelet's time and life? "Gently mortals, be discreet" (*Words*, 255).

The new biographical view rests upon terms such as the *structure of an existence, the coherence of the individual*. This view has nothing to do with the biography of the "man of the world" or with *ergography*, the story of the paper hero. *Michelet par lui-meme* is a charming book, written by two hands that share the same words within the text. One of them belongs to Barthes (the narrator, the stage manager), the other to Jules Michelet, the "history eater." Barthes draws up record cards and selects fragments; Michelet has no choice except to corroborate the thoughts of this biographer besieged by numberless ideas. The man's social story covers no more than two or three pages and is taken out of one dictionary or another. The critic enlarges upon the other biography (of the man *suffering from history*) and deals extensively with the flow of the historian's work (in sixty volumes). Michelet's portrait is a masterpiece. Michelet's headaches are no less than the headaches of history. Writing about history, Michelet turns into a "history eater, priest, and owner." He is a *traveler*, a *swimmer*, a *robber* of the past. His writings are unspeakably voracious.

Barthes applies all concepts to Michelet (*Michelet as Oedipal, Michelet as voyeur,*) and he even talks about *Michelet's lesbianism* ("*Michelet lui-meme n'est plus ni homme, ne femme, il n'est que Regard* [Michelet himself is neither man nor woman; he is only the look]"). Without questioning these associations, I should like to see whether the man who, in all probability, wrote more than all his contemporaries put together is preserved alive within such unexpected biographical ciphers. He is there, indeed, and this analysis of his historical texts makes him appear truly gigantic. What can be more impressive than the image of a spirit who gulps history down, swims oceans, flies high, plunders history, gobbles it up as greedily as an ogre—an ogre, though, who holds sacred all women that happened to journey across history.

Barthes comes out victorious in the end. Reading Michelet's work, he *imposes a pattern upon Michelet's existence.* Against Barthes's will (although one never can tell, since Barthes does not always do as he says). The *paper being* comes to life. The blood running in his veins may appear to gush from the heart of the work, yet, after all, it might just as well spring from the critical text written upon the reading of this work. The brilliance and profundity of this *metalanguage* (literary criticism) wake up the books from their sleep, and, in the process, a memorable being is born.

Barthes's *Michelet par lui-meme* is an example of structural biography. The words *"par lui-meme"* are inappropriate here. Like Pico della Mirandola's achiever, Barthes will be second to none.[1] His Michelet is a do-it-yourself job, an image to his liking and in his likeness, supported by those texts that accord with Barthes's intention, texts ordered by the critic in view of a particular conclusion. The verb that best characterizes this biographical approach is *to signify.* Its subject is an *I* who deals with a *he,* until the former ends by securing, replacing, and depriving the latter of his meanings. The *he* is dispossessed or, rather, compelled to take over the meanings of the *I.* Elsewhere Barthes describes this subject as an *epic I* by means of which the critic makes room for himself in criticism.

Roland Barthes by Roland Barthes is an example of structural autobiography. Things seem to go here the other way around. *He,* the hero under discussion, does his best to undertake all the functions of an *I* who refuses to be the subject of his own story. The reversal is made possible by Barthes's determination to avoid retelling his life, by his intention to select images meant to introduce the readers to the world of his imagination. It is an *ergography* supported by various discourses— the discourse of childhood, the maternal discourse, the absence of the paternal discourse, etc. The first images are photographic. Barthes transposes them into a written discourse. Such is the image of Bayonne, the town where the *primordial imaginary world of childhood* was born.

Bayonne, Bayonne, the perfect city; riverain, fluvial, aerated with sonorous suburbs (Mouserolles, Marrac, Lachepaillet, Beyris), yet immured, fictive: Proust, Balzac, Plassans. Primordial image-board of childhood: the province-as-spectacle, History-as odor, the bourgeoisie-as-discourse. (Roland Barthes, 6)

Barthes adds the municipal gardens, the nurse, the two grandfathers without a *discourse*, the two grandmothers who have the last word in the family. In these two great families all discourse belongs to the women. Having died in the war, the father (like Sartre's father) has no discourse of his own. Below a childhood photo, Barthes writes, *"might boredom be my form of hysteria?"* (*Roland Barthes*, 24). A photo from adolescence bears on it the statement *"to become thin is the naïve act of the will-to-intelligence"* (30).

In conclusion, Barthes's intention is to convey the signs of a history, instead of the history itself, the traces left by a life *"condemned to the repertoire of its images"* (36). Barthes's autobiographical discourse consists of themes so varied that they cannot be joined within the same pattern, scenario, or line of existence. It is, if we may say so, a *discourse of the act of writing*, a life transposed into rhetorical figures, a life that, instead of being real, belongs to a man enclosed within language. Barthes is as good as his word: the narrator says nothing about himself, he speaks about a stranger, an *other*, a somewhat emphatic *he*. Here are a few instances: "what pleased him in Michelet is the foundation of an ethnology of France, the desire and the skill of questioning historically—i.e., *relatively*—those objects supposedly the most natural: face, food, clothes complexion. . . . Further, *he* [italics added] has always loved the great novelistic cosmogonies" (84). And elsewhere, *"he* tries to make up a discourse," "disappointment means to *him*."

Everyone knows the true identity of the *he* mentioned by the narrator. *I* and *he* are not really very far apart, because Barthes's style is possessive, irrepressibly self-referential. The undulating progress of thoughts from one paradox to another is the best clue as to their owner's identity. Wherever one looks, one is bound to find the same Barthes who fails to hide behind a distant *he* or a neuter *one*.

Author, narrator, and hero stand in an unusual relationship. In the opening pages, the author describes the joy of writing and, as has already been pointed out, he warns us that one cannot write a biography of the time previous to the composition of the work. A biography can only start when the Text has come into being, and this Text behaves like a Freudian father depriving the author of his narrative duration. It carries the author's *body* far away "toward a language devoid of memory." In short, the acquisitive Text is unable to narrate. The life of the man who writes is irreparably lost in the text. Irreparably? Well, until the reader turns up and starts decoding the signs in order to find out the pleasure of the text. The only confessions Barthes makes here are embedded with the *écriture* (he says so himself: "a new realm of imagination will be discovered, the one belonging to the *écriture*"). He steps aside from himself, as if striving to corroborate Rimbaud's famous words, "I is an other."

The question is whether this *I* actually manages to become an *other*. It is a question that involves many more names than Barthes's. We may safely admit that Barthes, for one, fails. He is lucky to fail. Barthes is always his own true, feline, challenging self, fond of infuriating assumptions that he eagerly withdraws, worshiping all along his fundamental theme—the pleasure of writing. Actual *life* only starts when the joy of writing has reached a certain intensity. Barthes's paper being is far from ascetic. An eroticized body moves inside the codes of this paper being. Elsewhere Barthes tells us that both writing and reading are erotic acts, and we might just as well take his word for it. The text chooses us and we choose the text out of an erotic impulse. Maybe Barthes uses other words to convey the idea of this *choice* of texts but, at any rate, his meaning is the same.

In the autobiographical discourse, written like a biographical one—as I said before—Barthes has an impersonal voice speak about a character (*he*) who is kept at arm's length. Then he compels the biography of the man who writes to hide within the *écriture*. The critic is not interested, though, in the history of the written text; he merely juxtaposes moments selected out of the imaginary world of the *écriture*. Barthes achieves thus an epic of the act of writing. The existential pattern, the hysteria, the *fading*, the pleasures of a man who claims that his own text deprives him of everything he has—all these survive in Barthes's achievement. The pattern is there, the man will not yield helplessly to his Text, and as a proof, his energy and imagination produce more texts; the critic repeatedly takes it all over again, with gusto, fascinated by the object of his own criticism, stirred up by a *Socratic demon*, determined to settle for no less than the realm of pure ambiguity.

A structuralist autobiography converts the pleasure of the narrative into the joy of writing. Author, narrator, hero all acquire the status of an equivocal grammatical person. A little effort on the reader's part dispels, however, the ambiguity of a text that obstinately claims to have nothing in common with the author's life. Whatever the text may claim, and in spite of it, the author cordially returns, welcomed by the solitude and the joy of reading.

21

An Array of Selves

*Any critic seriously concerned with a
man's work should be expected to know
something about the man's life.*

T. S. Eliot, *The Frontiers of Criticism*

Are we really expected to know something about the life of someone who has
written a book—shall we take Eliot's word for it? And suppose we were willing
to know, how much can we learn, after all? And, to quote an old joke, once we
know, does it really help? For one hundred and fifty years now, literary criticism has
groped for the right answer to this one and only question. Meanwhile, the critic
has been racing to and fro between work and author, author and environment,
author and nationality, nationality and work, work and author, then back, over
and over again. Sainte-Beuve can only pass judgment upon a book when he has
removed the masks covering the face of the person who wrote it. Consequently,
in the beginning was the author. The work comes second. Crossing the work, the
critic rediscovers the person. René Wellek is right to say that the power of the man
who created this method lies in his "sense of the individual," and he is right again
when he disapproves of the same man's inappropriate outlook: "the *depth* pertains
to the work, rather than to the man. . . ." Sainte-Beuve is not the only one to make
this error. It reveals the outlook of a century that worshiped the individual's truth
and power.

Taine also proceeds on his journey accompanied by the individual at first
("the man corporeal and visible who eats, walks, fights, and labors," 3), then changes
the individual for the *work*, the work for the *environment*, and the environment for
the "race".[1] Reflected in all these mirrors, the individual finally turns into a network
of phenomena resulting from general causes.

Lanson alters the course of this journey, but its aim stays the same. "While
[Sainte-Beuve] used a book in order to reach its author as a man, we mean to go
from man and author to the book . . ." (Lanson, 440). He means to use biography
as an explanation for the work. To this purpose, Lanson draws up a list of nine
questions aimed at the text (work) and warns us that four dangers lie in ambush

for any literary historian, one of them being the fact that this historian can never be acquainted with all the facts (Lanson, 31–56).

Literary criticism and the history of literature of our own century witness the same race to and fro as before, only this time each of the partners is in turn abandoned on the platform. The modern critic shares a compartment either with the work or with its author; the three are rarely seen together.

The question is whether the modern critical text actually needs this dialogue. Why can't we be cured once and for all of our wish to know something about the creator after all the striving to exorcise the author from the text? Gérard Genette, who tries to reconcile modern criticism to history, concludes that the work cannot be held responsible for everything, because it does not exhaust all possible relations:

> In its debate with the history of literature, modern criticism has endeavored for half a century to separate the two concepts of work and author, hoping to make them face each other, both being responsible for so many excesses and useless operations. We are now beginning to realize that the two concepts are related, that all forms of criticism are *necessarily influenced by this mutual relationship* [italics added]. It is now fairly obvious that, since the critical text has the status of a work as well, it will exhaust neither the reality nor the literariness of the literary text; even more than that, the condition of a work (its immanence) implies a large number of elements that transcend it. (*Figures III*, 10)

In this way, Genette justifies the union between literary criticism and poetics. However, he fails to explain the exact position of the two concepts "within their mutual relationship." He disapproves of Valéry's idea that the history of literature is a "huge hoax," yet he only allows this history a marginal place—and part—in the study of literature: "it can only examine marginal aspects (biography, sources, influences, genesis . . .)." Genette looks upon criticism as a fundamental approach to literature. Consequently, the critic steals into the "fascinating, deadly game of the act of writing." The critic redeems diachrony in a special way, *coming and going* between criticism and poetics—the critic penetrates into "the consciousness and the reality of their *complementarity*." Anyone would subscribe to the critical view. The *whirling act of writing* and the truths of poetics can hardly be ignored in our time.

Undoubtedly, literary criticism has changed immensely in the last fifty years. Its object, literature, has changed, as well as the concepts and ideas used by the theory of literature. The very idea of literature itself is different. A researcher, Albert Léonard, has written a book [*La crise du concept de littérature en France au XXᵉ siècle*] on the crisis of literature in our century that is, first of all, a crisis of its concepts. *Creator, work, character, reader*—all these concepts have acquired new meaning during our century. If the author experiences a state of crisis right now—which is most certainly the case—this crisis must be viewed in its general context. The author's crisis is paradoxically felt at a moment when, on the point of being crushed by civilization, the individual struggles mightily to come to the front. If life fails to be of help, art, at least those who write and meditate on the condition of art, ought to support the creator's force. They often fail to do so, and then we find intelligent people (*famous authors*) who do not give a damn about the person who writes, allowing the individual no place among the values of our contemporary world.

I wonder what started this periodical determination to alter the author's position vis-à-vis the work. Anyway, it must have been long ago, in ancient times, when, like Phemius, the creator claimed to receive inspiration from some god above. The creator has inside the "entrails of a god" (to use the image of the contemporary Romanian poet Nichita Stănescu),[2] which are infinitely more important than the skill acquired by an individual. The word *inspiration* that fortified ancient poets has been banished by contemporary rhetoricians. A poem owes its existence to patience and art rather than to inspiration. The creator harbors a text-writing machine, instead of a god. A thinker we have already quoted many times concludes that "a poem lies in its execution." Phemius begs of Ulysses to spare his life and promises he will use his god-sent inspiration to serve him. Modern poets would rather write a bad work than submit to inspiration in order to produce a masterpiece. They mistrust the *god above* (in other words, the metaphysical origins of poetry) and trust the rhetorical machinery inside them. These are the two faces of one and the same mythology, a mythology built around the origins of poetry.

It might be said that modern literature begins when the myth of the work is worshiped, while the creator's myth has no more audience. In 1848 when romanticism is at its highest, describing the way in which he wrote his poem ("The Philosophy of Composition"), Poe disparages the myth of poetic inspiration and belittles the myth of the genius. A work *shapes and arranges itself*, a poem is subject to mathematical rigor. The existence of the genius is out of the question. Poe says that

> most writers—poets in especial—prefer having it understood that they compose by a species of fine frenzy—an ecstatic intuition—and would positively shudder at letting the public take a peep behind the scenes, at the elaborate and vacillating crudities of thought. . . . It is my design to render it manifest that no one point in its composition is referable either to accident or intuition—that the work proceeded step by step, to its completion with the precision and rigid consequence of a mathematical problem. (Poe, 2:979)

Ecstasy, frenzy, inspiration are words that poetry and criticism still use, but, as this century draws to its end, they fade gradually, because of their imprecision. So the decline of the creator's myth begins the moment the works appear more important than the creator. After all, it is not the gods we need, but their acts. The gods may just as well be banished. The fate of this myth grows even worse when the creator claims to be an *other*, different from what we expect. The author who writes will have nothing to do with the person spied upon by curious contemporaries. *I am another, I am not the Stéphane you know, I am not what I seem to be . . .*

These sentences are more complicated than they appear at first sight. Their meaning can be explained (like others before us, we have already attempted it), but they conceal an enigma that is not easily dispelled. What does Stéphane mean by saying he feels he is not his own self when he writes—to what extent does he change, becoming an *other*, an impersonal voice? Modern stylistics pronounces all this to be impossible; the "withdrawals" from language point to a particular disposition, the digressions from the text are symptomatic. The man who writes undergoes a change, he is very keen on becoming an other, but his alteration leaves signs behind, signs whose "significance" is bound to be decoded. It goes without saying that the author of "The Azure," "Sea Breeze," "Hérodiade," "The Afternoon of a Faun" and the punctilious English teacher are not one and the same, but the function of criticism is to make this *Other* known to us, to estimate the distance between the two hypostases. How much impersonality can we detect in the voice who wrote the so very personal poems listed above?

In my opinion, Rimbaud's statement destroys one myth and invents another. Both myths are equally ambitious, the latter even more so, since it contemplates the creator inventing both the work and a personality. The creator molds a self in the shape of an *other*. This superficial denial could easily harbor a return to the myth of the creator, of the almighty genius. When one strives to depersonalize one's voice, one is sure to have great faith in one's force. It sounds like a provocation to announce that one's own work is being written by an *Other*. The creator alone is able to operate this mutation. In short, an *Other* is the creation of an I who, for some secret reason, wishes to be unknown.

The next question criticism must answer is to what extent *I* manages to turn into the *Other* (always capitalized), how far from the *I* the Other is able to travel. I must say that few of the studies I have read have been of any help to me in the matter. However, much of what I have read has made me think the other way round: namely, that the *I* fails to become an *Other*, and the *Other* finds it pretty difficult to leave the *I* behind. The writer does wear a mask, but, as Théophile Gautier used to say, the mask is a token of sincerity. Mallarmé's ideal impersonal voice is in fact a poetic voice specific to Mallarmé, which anyone would recognize amid a thousand others. While writing, Mallarmé fails to banish Stéphane, no matter how hard he may be trying. Therefore, these sentences must be considered with caution. Proud denials usually harbor the intense need to affirm.

The statement that follows distinguishes between the man who writes and the man who lives ("the work is created by some other I . . ."). Should we doubt it?

Not really, Proust is right. It is a commonsense idea that the author's deepest life is transferred to the work and that a work is, in its way, independent of the creator. First of all we read the book, afterward we inquire who wrote it, and then some may (or may not) wonder about its author's life. The *creative personality* is more complex than the *human personality*, and the truth was demonstrated sometime around 1894, before Proust, by the Romanian aesthetician Mihail Dragomirescu.[3] It is natural, then, that we should strive to identify this personality within the work, mistrusting anyone who claims to explain it by using details of everyday life (the author's life among other people). Bacovia's poetry and the overwhelmingly monotonous biography of the insignificant provincial employee can hardly be joined in view of explaining the work.[4] We may understand Rimbaud's poems quite well, yet never suspect that their author was involved for a while in the ignoble slave trade. I. L. Caragiale's works undoubtedly preserve some of the playwright's experiences as the employee of a tobacco company or owner of a Bucharest alehouse,[5] but explaining his remarkable plays and sketches by means of these occupations of Caragiale the man amounts to attempting an explanation of the flower by means of the dirt it is rooted in or (using a metaphor devised by the Romanian poet Marin Sorescu) to claiming that the song of the nightingale owes its existence to the tree on which the bird has happened to alight.[6] Valéry is certainly right to hold that a work owes its existence to much more than just its author's efforts.

A work is created by a complex spirit; all biographical information can at best point to the conditions under which the work was created—it will not explain the experience of writing. No information about the author's life (no *biographème*) is of any help whatever to the deeper understanding of a work, of the signs and myths concealed within its text and subtext. These signs and myths are often there without the author's being aware of them. A work exceeds or baffles its author's intentions (project) because of a paradox that occurs quite frequently. The writer means to convey one thing, while the work embodies another, more or less. Consequently, it is unwise to hitch a work to its author's views, which does not really mean that the author's views lack interest. Quite the reverse—these views outline a particular outlook on life and art, but, if transferred to the work, they acquire a new shape and a different aim. Balzac's case is well known.

The work is not mechanically engendered by some concrete biography, yet this *work* must have an author, after all, and one may wonder who this enigmatic hero is, a hero whom modern criticism forbids to trespass upon the boundaries of his or her own creation. Whose is the voice that claims that the deeper self has nothing to do with the social self? In spite of Proust's violent hatred of biographism, for half a century now biographers have been very busy searching the inside and the outside of his enigmatical existence.

The next question that arises is how an analysis is supposed to separate one self from the other. How can we tell the words of the deeper self ("the Proustian man") from the prattle of the superficial one ("the Beuveian man")? I should venture to suggest that hardly any critical analysis can make the distinction. It seems preposterous to attempt a separation between the hard-working self who writes and the other self, loafing about the nineteenth-century salons or the cafés of our own century. (Although great writers, such as Sartre, have actually written in cafés, I should be in no hurry to conclude from this that Sartre is more superficial than Michel Déon, for instance, although the latter even bought a Greek island in order to write there.[7] I might even be so bold as to suggest that Sartre writes better at Flore or Aux deux Magots, surrounded by the din of customers.)

Who is the true Proust, I wonder, the man who writes and encloses his life within a great book or maybe the man who claims that a writer's work has nothing to do with his life? The true Proust is in fact only one. He formulates the theory concerning the distinction of the two *selves*, and then he writes his great novel wherein his theory does not operate. What I mean is that we cannot split Proust into halves in order to identify the voice that talks and the voice that keeps silent. Even if his personality were actually a split one (and those outside were able to notice the fact), our interest in the biography of the *self*, the *deeper self* who writes, would not fade. What do existentialists mean by the *total self*, what does psychoanalytical criticism mean by *deeper self*, what does Valéry mean by the *pure self*, the rhetoricians by the *nonself*, and some others by the *mythic self*?[8]

The criticism of our century replaces Proust's Manicheism by various other Manichean positions; the author and the work seldom happen to share the same room in criticism (as it happens in Sartre's case). The person who writes (the author) is not regarded as a universe whose incoherences, discontinuities, and interruptions achieve a coherence of their own. As a matter of fact, modern criticism makes us see two kinds of distinctions, one between author and work, the other (beginning with Proust) between the two sides of the creator's inner life. The former contemplates the author as *scripteur*; the latter sees the complexes of the child still alive inside the mature creator. These *selves* disagree with each other, they part, then are reunited in accordance with ever-changing criteria, more and more alliances are concluded in a mad race for unity, coherence, oppressive wholeness, for an unsubstantial *whole*. How true, how useful are these *selves* to criticism? Can we really do without any of them, can we ever separate the deeper particles from the superficial ones?

22

Who Speaks in the Text?

*There is no possible connection
between my family, which is not a
noble one, and my works.*

I. L. Caragiale, fragment from a
letter to Horia-Petra Petrescu

The only answer to the question above is that the person who writes can be found only in the books. These books do not have much—if anything—in common with the writer's family, as Caragiale tells us with irritation. The books may find their way into the aristocracy of the spirit even if the author was born in a baker's family. If the books prove satisfactory, what is the use of rummaging through their author's biography? What could we expect to find there? The same I. L. Caragiale writes, "When your boots are both comfortable and cheap, wear them without inquiring into the shoemaker's birthplace or life, since these will not improve in any way the quality of your boots." I used to approve of Caragiale's views in this respect. Thinking twice now, I do not find them wholly true any more. As far as boots are concerned, Caragiale is right, of course. Good boots are supposed to be worn. One is not burning with curiosity to meet the shoemaker. In literature, however, things are somewhat different.

It goes without saying that the work has priority. It has both priority and autonomy. When one enjoys a work, all expectations external to it become unnecessary. They are unnecessary even if one does not enjoy the work. The value or the lack of value of a book can only be discussed in terms of the book itself. This is a victory won by twentieth-century criticism over biographical criticism. What an author writes may or may not originate in some private experience. Sometimes it does so (as in the case of Fyodor Dostoevsky's *Notes from the House of the Dead*), but it is risky and eventually useless to compare the private experience to the work in order to see how much truth there is in either. Truth? The truth of literature is somewhat peculiar, to say the least.

If, however, we do compare the two, more often than not we realize that the work has altered the meaning of experience. Eugène Ionesco confesses that in

Tueur sans gages he started from something experienced when he was seventeen or eighteen.

> I was in a provincial town. It was a noon in June. I was roaming along one of the streets of this extremely peaceful town. All of a sudden, I felt the world was going away from me, yet coming closer at the same time, or, rather, that it had gone away from me and I was in another world now, more congenial to me than the former, and infinitely brighter; I was passing by courtyards and dogs were barking, but their barks turned into soft music; . . . the sky had almost grown dense, light could be touched, the houses had an unparalleled, unusual, truly unusual brightness. A close description of the experience is impossible; I can only say that I was overwhelmed with unspeakable joy, I felt I had grasped a fundamental truth. . . . I told myself, "I am no longer afraid of death." It was an absolute, final truth. I realized that if I ever happened to feel sad or anxious from that moment on, I could find peace and joy by merely bringing this experience back to mind. . . . I do not recall the incident any longer; it is not utterly forgotten, of course, but it has turned into a kind of theoretical memory. . . . (Bonnefoy, 36–37)

The author's confession is certainly true. The play that has been cited is built around this revelation experienced by the writer in his adolescence (there is a certain theme of light, rather of *illumination* in Ionesco's theater), but I wonder how much of that old incident has really survived. One cannot know for sure, since the author made his confession some forty years later, when *Tueur sans gages* had already been written. He says so himself: *little is left of that memory*. He may have attached his meaning to the incident much later, when he wrote the play. Then again, the meaning may actually have dawned upon the author the moment he felt he had left the real world behind and was partaking of a world of light. One never can tell. We may know the origin of this play, because Ionesco confesses it to us, but, as far as his other writings are concerned, there is no palpable proof that he started from real incidents. As a matter of fact, even if we learned all the starting points, how could we tell what is true from what is not, and if we actually know the original truth, what if the work had altered that meaning completely?

It seems to me unwise and irrelevant to try to detect the points where the work and everyday life meet. The sources of a work are by far more complex, the source (in case it can be detected) and the finite work are far apart, and, in between, the writer's imagination alone is in control. Our reading and correct assessment of a book are unimpaired by our ignorance of its sources. It is only loyal, however, to consider in what way our being acquainted with the incident in which the book originated influences the value of that book. We know, for instance, that there is in Søren Kierkegaard's life a turning point, a secret incident that he never revealed. He found out something in connection with his father, seemingly. In his youth, his father appeared to have cursed God. Can this be the incident dcescribed by the philosopher as the "earthquake" of May 19, 1838? His whole life took another course subsequently. His work, too. I wonder whether his numberless interpreters have cleared up his secret. Probably not, but suppose they did, would that alter our response to *Diary of the Seducer?* I wonder whether, learning that secret, we should understand more of the writer's inner suffering, more of a possible complex that survived in the recesses of his being.

To show no interest in the philosopher's existence, claiming that his work is all we want, would be a proof of reprehensible superficiality on our part. We do want to know more because we are immensely interested in the fate of the most aggrieved nineteenth-century philosopher. Yet the work cannot be altered by any biographical revelation, that is certain. Both light and suffering are enclosed in the work. Light and suffering—to quote Mihail Dragomirescu again—are eternal too. The secret of the creator's existence died when the man died, but the work stayed and preserved it deep down in its core, altering it by means of factors no less important than the important secret of the writer's youth. We have a similar example in Romanian literature. In *Ion* (1920), the novelist Rebreanu started from the mystical gesture of a peasant kissing the earth, I think.[1] The scene may be sublime, yet it fails to account for the complexity of a novel that portrays peasants lacking the feeling of the sublime. They are all stodgy, stubborn, sly, even brutish peasants from Ardeal, but their gestures, acts, experiences are the proof of an extraordinary creative ability; their movements are incredibly true to life, the acts of these frighteningly elementary beings transcend their condition. The secret creation embodied in this transfiguration is more significant than the gesture of a peasant whom the novelist may have seen one fine day.

The same Rebreanu confesses that he started writing *Pădurea spînzuraților* [The Hanged Man's Forest] (1922) before he had learned about the tragedy of his brother Emil, hanged like the hero of his novel, during the First World War. Literary researchers later proved that it was true; the novelist's brother had been punished because, as an officer of the Austro-Hungarian army, he had refused to fight the Romanians, who were his own people. He was condemned to be hanged. We might have failed to understand this man's tragedy had not Rebreanu's novel lent it an exquisite intensity and meaning. If it had not been for the work, we should have ignored the tragedy of this young officer from Ardeal, just as we ignore so many others, and we should not be talking about it here. It becomes significant because of the work, because of an incident associated with the work. Literature abounds in tragic incidents that have nothing to do with the writers' lives, which can be traced to no incident known to us whatever. But all these things could have been true, and all the works prove it. Has there ever lived a man named Oedipus, who killed his father, married his own mother, and had children by her? Did the tragedies in Faulkner's novels originate in actual incidents? Maybe they did, but Romanian readers ignore them. Faulkner's narrative appears hallucinatingly true. It is as good as real—as a reader I am satisfied. I have no time to check everything, reading the books written by numberless specialists who have probably examined Faulkner's sources. I merely remark that the great American novelist illustrates an old Shakespearean idea: all is "sound and fury, a tale told by an idiot." *The Sound and the Fury*, in telling the story of the Compson family, conveys the feeling of the general tragedy of existence. What do I know, after all, about Hamlet, Prince of Sorrow? Some details here and there from old chronicles, information provided by Shake-speareans, very little, in all. And how much do I know about Shakespeare himself?

The facts go in two directions, making up two distinct patterns. Biographical criticism mixes them up, which is a mistake, undoubtedly, since they only meet deep down, at the core of the work. Their relationship is altered by creation (imagination, the *act of writing*), but we shall never know for certain in what way and to what extent.

However, I cannot say I approve of aestheticizing spirits, who are positive that a work comes from nowhere, that, quoting Blanchot, a work is "nobody's language, no writer's lines, the light of a selfless awareness" (Blanchot, 283). It cannot be denied that a work contains its author's project of existence. The author is or can be an *Other*, but this Other is more than just a paper being. The same Blanchot says, "The word conveys a being, but it empties it first" (283). There is ample room for doubt here. The word is uttered by the voice of some *being*, or we should not listen to it, it would not reach us. Of course, we ignore how much of the true being is preserved in this voice, but it certainly brings the "sound and the fury" of the world into the book.

Who speaks in a book then? Trying not to complicate something that is already complicated enough, we may formulate the following answer: an impersonal voice speaks about an indomitably personal one, a *deeper self* (a pure, all-embracing, mythical self) whose existence contains that of the superficial self as well. We hear the author who, writing about a self, cannot help writing about the person who lives, and who, one fine day, decides to live a life writing books. We hear a *nonself* (the paradox belongs to Blanchot) whose substance is replaced by language and whose being is gradually emptied in the process. The act of *emptying* is human in itself, since an act of thought and one of existence are necessary in order to give an idea of the void. The author's paradoxical metamorphosis into a linguistical being is impossible without the help of imagination. *The language of the person* belongs, in fact, to someone who claims that the writings represent nobody and have been written by no one. The individual has lost all priority. Yet the individual is the only one who can acknowledge this loss. We are repeatedly told that the work alone can convey a profound image of its author. This is the correct, yet fatuous remark of an author disgusted at superficial biographies and narrow, indiscreet biographical criticism: an author whose very name suggests a novelistic manner, a range of themes, an outlook on literature, even a way of life.

23

Eliot and Biography

When the poem has been made, something
new has happened, something that cannot
be wholly explained by anything that
went before.

T. S. Eliot

Can a poem be explained by its sources? T. S. Eliot, whom I have already quoted with a statement in favor of biography, tells us that "explanation may be a necessary preliminary to understanding" (17). He hastens to warn us, though, against a danger coming from the realm of biographical criticism, especially when the biographer "supplements his knowledge of external facts with psychological conjectures about inner experience" (12). Eliot differs here from Valéry and other great European spirits, who feel that no preliminary information is necessary to the understanding of a poem. He does not reject the method, he merely mistrusts its exaggerated use. Unlike Proust, Eliot feels that a critic is allowed to glance at the creator's life, on one condition, though—it must not be done while the person (creator) is still alive.

> I do not suggest that the personality and the private life of a dead poet constitute sacred ground on which the psychologist must not tread. The scientist must be at liberty to study such material as his curiosity leads him to investigate—so long as the victim is dead and the laws of libel cannot be invoked to stop him. Nor is there any reason why biographies of poets should not be written. Furthermore, the biographer of an author should possess some critical ability; he should be a man of taste and judgment, appreciative of the work of the man whose biography he undertakes. . . . But a critical biography of a writer is a delicate task in itself; and the critic or the biographer who, without being a trained and practicing psychologist, brings to bear on his subject such analytical skill as he has acquired by reading books written by psychologists, may confuse the issue still further. (Eliot, 12)

The traditional critical mind is likely to approve of such requirements. The author (the victim) must be dead lest the biographer should be accused of libel.

Besides, the biographer must also be a "man of taste" and appreciative of the author's work. Eliot adds that in such delicate matters the critic is supposed to consider each case individually and act accordingly. There is no general rule. Sometimes a biography or a study of sources is helpful; at other times it can divert the reader's attention from the substance of the poem. Eliot wonders whether our learning that William Wordsworth's best poems were written as a result of his affair with Annette Vallon makes any difference to our appreciation of those poems, as a researcher asserts. Need we really learn, from another biographer's scholarly study, that the same poems were inspired by the poet's sister, Dorothy, with whom Wordsworth was in love? These instances are preceded by a list of scholarly studies that attempt to trace Samuel Taylor Coleridge's reading in books of all kinds. Can they explain *The Rime of the Ancient Mariner*? T. S. Eliot's belief that biographical studies are of service to poetry falters.

> For myself, I can only say that a knowledge of the springs which released a poem is not necessarily a help towards understanding the poem: too much information about the origins of a poem may even break my contact with it. I feel no need for any light upon the Lucy poems beyond the radiance shed by the poems themselves.
>
> I am not maintaining that there is *no* context in which such information or conjecture as that of Sir Herbert Read and Mr. Bateson may be relevant. It is relevant if we want to understand Wordsworth; but it is not directly relevant to our understanding of his poetry. Or rather, it is not relevant to our understanding of the *poetry as poetry*. I am even prepared to suggest that there is, in all great poetry something which must remain unaccountable however complete might be our knowledge of the poet, and that is what matters most. When the poem has been made, something new has happened, something that cannot be wholly explained by *anything that went before*. (Eliot, 13)

All these distinctions were made by Eliot in 1956. He had already read I. A. Richards and the latter's pupil, William Empson, and he appreciated their efforts to judge a poem in itself, attaching no importance to its sources. He would not side with them, though, and called that new trend the "lemon-squeezer school of criticism." The new critics were experts at taking the poetic text to pieces, and Eliot was uneasy about the procedure; he complained that, when the machine had thus been disassembled, he (the reader) was left to reassemble its parts. The poet stuck to a few old principles, such as the importance of taste for any critic, no matter what method he might use ("To understand a poem comes to the same thing as to enjoy it for the right reasons").

Eliot is just as unhappy about impressionistic and explanatory criticism. By the latter he means both scholarly biographical criticism and textual criticism, two methods that aspire to becoming exact sciences. Nowadays, biographical and textual criticism are sworn enemies, but in 1956 they may very well have appeared to Eliot to be joining forces in an attack against poetry. Eliot's viewpoint is a commonsensical one, on the whole. He considers all possibilities, admits that biography may be useful (as the poet's *history*), and at the same time warns us that biographies are a menace to poetry because poetry is supposed to provide its own explanation:

> We must not identify biography with criticism; biography is ordinarily useful in providing explanation which may open the way to further understanding; but it may also, in directing our attention on the poet, lead us away from the poetry. We must not confuse knowledge—factual information—about a poet's period, the conditions of the society in which he lived, the ideas current in his time implicit in his writings, the state of the language in his period—with understanding his poetry. Such knowledge, as I have said, may be a necessary preparation for understanding the poetry; furthermore, it has a value of its own as history; but for the appreciation of the poetry, it can only lead us to the door; we must find our own way in. (Eliot, 18–19)

In other words, a biography is an individual's story, no more, while poetry is another thing; in order to understand poetry, one must be able to perceive its *entelechy*.

In my opinion, Eliot finds himself midway between traditional and modern criticism, treating all excesses with dignified aloofness. He is right, I should say. No poem can wholly be *explained by anything that went before*. Biography may find a way of access to the person who wrote the poem, but it will never reach the core of the poem itself. Historical information is useful, but it is no guide to our appreciation of poetry. *We must find our own way in*—here is a statement that allows us to hope that poetry has a long life and literary criticism is not a useless activity. Poetry has more than one meaning, more than one cause, so no critic can claim to own the only key to it. Each reader's education and sensibility elicits a peculiar meaning from the poem. The work is neither what the author conceived, nor what the reader interprets, Eliot finally tells us; the work exists between the two (writer and reader) in an ever changing nexus.

Eliot's standpoint is quite well founded, yet many of his statements are incomplete. How much freedom must one allow to the reader's interpretation of the poem, for instance? Why is scholarly criticism supposed to deal only with dead authors? How far is biography welcome and when does it yield to indiscretion or libel? Is the explanation of causes a really necessary preparation for the understanding of poetry? Obsessed with enthralling causal determinations, the modern critical spirit might raise a hundred objections. The heart of the matter, however, is that Eliot approves of biographies, studies of sources, comparatist researchers; in short, he approves of all scholars who strive hard to populate the void that stretches before the work. He forbids them to trespass on poetry proper, he mistrusts their scientific understanding of what cannot be understood in a poem. Once again, he is right. Are we not, though, entitled to wonder about the use of more studies that are denied access to the substance of poetry?

I will not question here the use of erudition. I must say, however, that to the history of literature erudition is useful insofar as it bears upon the "cultural codes" of a literary work (as Barthes puts it in *S/Z*), and it becomes futile, harmful even, if it is used by what Eugène Ionesco calls the *janitress spirit* ("the history of literature in its present state is a history made by and for janitresses" [Bonnefoy, 67]). Scholarly criticism may, at best, reveal the *voice of science* in a text, but there are four more voices (codes)—as counted by Barthes—that erudition, however profound, fails to perceive. We must manage on our own, go ahead alone . . .

Biographical erudition is of a different nature; it owes its existence to the creator's life, not to the work. Biography is unable to explain a work and, as has already been seen, it must not be required to do so. It can make us see (to use well-known terms) the coherence of a destiny, the pattern of a life. A written *life* is a work in itself, a discourse that operates according to its own laws. That discourse may be brilliant or unsuccessful, and it must be seen as such.

It may be a sign of hypocrisy or pathological incuriosity to say one is not interested in the life of the man who wrote *La légende des siècles*, *Les contemplations*, or *Les misérables*, works that have largely impressed the spirit of the century. I want to know Hugo's life, I am eager to learn whom he hated, whom he loved, whom he befriended, because all that reveals the inner nature of a great creator. I am greatly moved to learn from some book about Hugo's despair at the death of one of his daughters, the one he loved best. It is a true paternal drama, experienced by a creator whose poetry extols whatever is grandiose and sublime in the universe. I want to know how Hugo behaves when the sublime and the grandiose are of no avail.

One might reply of course that the artist's genius goes to the work, and only the talent goes to the life, that it is a waste of time to trace the reactions of the genius in everyday life. As Eugène Ionesco tells us, we can only learn there "trifling stories" told by an indiscreet, talkative janitress. It cannot be denied that some such narratives (biographies, memoirs, diaries) really describe the indigestions of a genius (as the Romanian essayist Zarifopol pointed out in Goethe's case),[1] the imposture and hypocrisy latent in him. One of our contemporaries did this to Goethe. These are odd attempts that must be taken for what they are. None of them is worth raving at. A pamphlet can hardly pull a status down. Literary criticism need not waste its time on such writings; its main concern must go toward those works that deal with the anxiety specific to the life of a writer of genius, if we are prepared to admit that the idea of genius has survived. A genius can only address us through the works, of course, but those works do not exhaust the reader's wish to know both the individual and the genius. It seems to me that the greater the creators, the stronger our desire to know their life. Their acts turn into models; their strange deeds (Baudelaire, Rimbaud, Verlaine) appear emblematic for a poet's existence in another age.

There is, for instance, a commonly accepted biography of the romantic genius that turns around the idea that the creator's myth is above the work, above common existence. A genius suffers from *incompletion* and demonism, has a Manichaean outlook on the world, cherishes a belief in singularity, and espouses an ethics of individualism, wherein the main law is that no law is acceptable. Byron, Hugo, Novalis, Eminescu are extremely different,[2] and yet in their works we can identify the common points mentioned above, which are also present in the works (documents) dealing with their lives. Byron is a restless nature; he is always in the heart of turmoil and ends as a hero, fighting for the cause of another country. From his exile, Hugo turns his eyes toward France, deploring the unbearable tyranny that stifles the country; his majestic exile is informed by a superb self-awareness, by his conviction that the poet is strong enough to resist a forceful political system all by himself. Eminescu prefers an inner exile: he finds refuge in an imaginary land, and in newspapers he attacks the superimposed social strata. He is not at home in his contemporary world, and the progress of his short existence evinces a chronic lack of stability, an intense desire for peace, and also an essential restlessness when confronted with stabilizing forces.

Consequently, art imposes upon life a certain manner of being, a common psychology. We may not always be able to tell whether art imitates the age or the age follows art in this respect, but, beyond all doubt, the way (model) of life is made known to us by art. The great literary modes (classicism, romanticism, symbolism) have produced particular *modes of life*, common to creators, no matter how unlike their lives may be, a mode of life visible in confessions, letters, biographies, memoirs. A biography is mainly interested in the individual side; it foreshadows an inimitable destiny by examining an ordinary existence.

It has been stated that only what an individual conceals is really significant; it has also been stated that an individual's personality can only be defined by the individual's acts. Of these two opinions, the latter belongs to Malraux, yet Malraux himself thinks twice and remarks in a manuscript that individuals can be found both in what they do and in what they do not do. Sartre's position is the same. The individual is everywhere, in superficial as well as in deeper acts (in case we adopt Proust's dichotomy). An existence is more than the mere sum of its acts; it is a meeting point of all the lines of force, a scenario foreshadowed by each act in its turn. This scenario encloses both great acts and failures, both sublime and inert moments; it may easily become the subject of a captivating book. In such a book, our interest is hardly likely to go to the common individual, to a frustrated or happy childhood, to restless adolescence, to love or lack of passions; we expect to find there the childhood, adolescence, and passions of the author who created the work. This person's existence was changed by the creation. The work turns the individual life into a symbol, a model, a way of life that must be up to the life of the work. I mean to say that the work forces upon us a certain view of its author's life, because this work turns author in its turn and starts fashioning an author to suit it.

24

Writing about the Author

"As an institution, the author is dead. . . ." Who knows? Anyway, as a person, the author should be reconsidered. The work is the best the author can give, yet the life must not lag far behind. Our appreciation of a work need not wait for its author to be forgotten; none of us wishes the author dead. I rather feel that the better we think of a work, the more we need to know about its author's life. It has often been stated that a mean person may write a great work. In that case, we shall wait for the work to make us forget the person (the Romanian critic G. Calinescu said so about the Romanian prose-writer Slavici).[1] The passage of time effaces the anger of the author's contemporaries, and (see Céline) the work wins its value back.[2] The process is rather tricky, quite intricate, especially when political views are involved. Repeatedly invoked by those who think that when a man's work is great his life may be mean, Villon himself has turned into a legendary figure whose life has been cleared of blame. Now that so many centuries have elapsed, the adventurous life of Villon the highwayman serves the cause of his poetry.

Verlaine, who frightens the moralists of literature as much as Villon, is much more than a man with *peculiar* tastes, a drunkard who used to scare old Charles (Sartre's grandfather); he is a poet who *sulks*, who resists everyday life and imitates the decadents. Was it "this" Verlaine who wrote those great poems? Why not? *This* Verlaine steals into the poems too, I cannot say how or how much, but he is definitely there; both his poetry and his life are a magnificent provocation. *The better Verlaine*, people say, has nothing to do with his getting drunk, his orgies, his "dirty tricks," as grandfather Charles used to say. It stands to reason that Verlaine's genius has nothing to do with these hateful doings, but these doings are part of his existence, they must be revealed (they *can be revealed*, rather than *must*), because they help us understand the author, even though they are useless to our appreciation of his work. It is not in our power to separate the time when Verlaine is in earnest and sets about writing from the time when he is superficial, goes from one Parisian bar to another, fights, fires his pistol at another poet. I cannot please Proust; I fail to separate the two sides however hard I may try. I am ready to believe that *the same* Verlaine first gets drunk then later sits down at his table to write; that something sublime is enclosed in his poems while the rest remains mere *literature*, as he used to say.

No writer is as saintly as readers would like; the writer merely sees things in a different way, leads another life than ours. Vices are not devoid of some meaning; such were Poe's dipsomania, Dostoevsky's addiction to games of chance, Hugo's promiscuity, Camus's fickleness, Malraux's selfishness and megalomania. All these belong to a whole and can only be judged as part of an existential pattern, which the creator embodies, whether aware of it or not.

The unavoidable question is, need the biographer really record Poe's fits of dipsomania, Goethe's indigestions, Rousseau's fits of insanity, Gide's acts of sodomy, Dostoevsky's epileptic seizures, etc.? I feel sure the biographer need not do so when dealing with an existence that has been turned into a great destiny, a myth, by the birth of the work. It is utterly uninteresting to read a catalogue of vices, to become acquainted with the trifling incidents recorded by the janitors and janitresses of literary history. I should even say it is very sad. When, in a book of confessions (*Propos secrets*), with incredible indecency, Roger Peyrefitte describes his own and other contemporary artists' homosexual experiences (Henry de Montherlant being one of them), the fact is irrelevant. Reading this indecent avowal, I reply, so what? What about it? Can the Montherlant who wrote *Malatesta* and *Pitié pour les femmes* be one and the same with the Montherlant who haunted railway stations and public lavatories in search of teenagers? If so, I must know in what way his odd sexual drive influenced his fate, how much of this fate was transferred to the work? Roger Peyrefitte says nothing of the kind; he just acquaints us, without the least sense of decency, with the fact that Montherlant's blindness was caused by a horrible fight aroused by his attempt to accost a young man, Montherlant being quite old at the time (Peyrefitte, 55).

Readers, do not inquire, pass by.

Many biographers have recorded an author's experiences, but few have been able to attach to them the meaning that made that life exemplary. Among modern writers, Gide has been the subject of such investigations that delight in the "heaps of everyday junk." Some literary historians waste their time trying to find parallelisms between the author's work and life. In the first volume of his *Life of André Gide* (1970), Pierre de Boisdeffre declares that the tender, ironical, and disapointing idyll in *La tentative amoureuse* originates "undoubtedly in Gide's own experience; unable to forget Madeleine, he strives once more to teach her a lesson and devises a number of characters to this purpose." "Undoubtedly," he says. Why *undoubtedly*, why is Boisdeffre so positive about the connection between the above-mentioned narrative and André Gide's affair with Madeleine Rondeaux, why does he assume that the transfer was only natural? This *undoubtedly* suggests that the work and the author's biography are fatally associated, that it is enough for the biographical critic to act as a good hound and trace the author's experiences in his works.

Obviously, such abusive interpretations are harmful to our image of the author's work and life. We have already seen why they are harmful to the work. Let us explain why the improper examination of an author's works may be harmful to that author's *life* (biography). Some biographers take the idea that the deeper self can be found in the work rather than in everyday life in its literal sense, and they hasten to attribute to the person the experiences recorded by the work. A disaster ensues. We are faced with a fabulous biography, consisting of the character's deeds. The moralists view it with a reproachful eye and scold the author for the hero's acts and thoughts. This procedure is the reverse of biographical criticism and I cannot say for certain which of the two is liable to make more errors. Writers are, of course, responsible for what they write, but their lives do not necessarily contain whatever incidents they record in their books. The work created by imagination will not reveal its secrets to a biographer; critical examination alone is able to contemplate it, and it does so in honor of the work, not of the author's life.

The *biographism* that rests upon the invented elements of a work appears to me to be as futile to literary criticism as traditional *biographism*, which resorts to the writer's life in order to pass judgment on the aesthetic value of the works. The *deeper self* cannot be traced in a work, since this self only exists within a lyrical or epic structure; its only body is the lyrical or epic form of expression. The critic who isolates this self in order to derive from it the creator's psychology and, ultimately, the creator's moral and spiritual biography takes on a great risk. Out of a writer's works we may, at best, infer a biography of the creative mind (a *figure of the spirit*, in the terms of more recent criticism), a biography that feeds primarily on the imagination and that offers some particular attitude toward the object of art. In this case, as Georges Poulet put it, the critic must strive to reach the *cogito* of the work, the brain concealed at the core of creation, the spirit that "makes a covenant with its own body, with other bodies as well, and adheres to the object in order to invent the subject" (Poulet, 10). Can the critic draw the diagram of this *pensive subject* who, while meditating, produces (writes) the text? The critic certainly can, even must, interpret the elements of this diagram in the light of several factors, which the *criticism of identification* (Poulet, among others) actually accomplishes. But to use such surveys in order to head for the author's social biography, thus absurdly overturning Proust's argument, is a grievous fault.

Ending this long digression, we must come back now to the relationship between the author and the work, which we have so far examined in several of the mirrors belonging to modern criticism. One last question arises: to what extent is a work answerable to the person who wrote it, what is the responsibility of the person who writes toward the work that carries this message into eternity, in case this work survives? To simplify things, we shall only say that, considering the incidents witnessed by the twentieth century, one can no longer afford to ignore the attitude of the person who writes toward history; one cannot disregard the position of the work itself in relation to history. However hard I might try to distinguish between things, however certain I may be (and I am, indeed) that eternity will harbor the supreme values of creation alone, since nothing else can resist the passage of time, I cannot and I will not accept that authors are free to do as they please. If, nevertheless, they do so, their works will have to pay for their deeds sometime.

Humankind has had so many unpleasant experiences in this most intelligent (yet not the wisest) century known to history that one can no longer disregard the moral status of an aesthetic consciousness. One is bound to consider a writer's public acts, as well as writings. A masterpiece is created in the narrow, utter solitude of a room, of course, but, surrounded by a world in which the mechanisms of history are on the point of crushing humankind, the moral *commitment* of the creator of masterpieces matters unspeakably much. To use the words of Tudor Arghezi,[3] we cannot behave like *swine* in everyday life and then pretend to be *angels* when we write. If this does happen—and it has in our century—the saint peeping at us from the pages of a book is very unlikely to continue this peaceful, pure life for very long.

I mean to say that the author's moral behavior can equally help or hinder the work. This will be true for a while, I think, in fact probably from now on. I once came across a story that should be remembered. One hundred and fifty years after the event, an insignificant researcher found a very sad document in the archives of the French police. It was a denunciation written by a mystical romantic poet against his revolutionary friends. Contemporary French intellectuals, well-known for their tolerance and radical liberalism, shuddered at the news. The poet in question cannot and must not be banished from the history of literature, of course, but the mystical poet who, on paper, was haunted by bright, ascensional symbols did something abominable that, to my mind, can never be excused. Not for a long time, anyway. The work will always have to defend the man whose private life was not up to his work.

In such cases, the work must fight time, which has the power to select and belittle, and also the idiosyncrasies aroused by a life that was unworthy of the work. A lasting legend must surround each work and the author's life must by no means delay or prevent it. The splendor of a work must rest upon a life that preserves its own splendor even when humiliated by history. If *splendor* is too ambiguous a word, it can be replaced by any other word denoting a proud responsibility of the person who lives as opposed to the person who writes.

II

The Author's Life of the Author

25

Sartre:
The Imposture of Childhood
and the Birth of Literature

The eagerness to write involves a
refusal to live.

The Words

In *The Words*, the issue of the *autobiographical pact* is exceedingly intricate. The opening lines of the book seem to belong to a perfectly realistic novel written during the last century. "Around 1850, in Alsace, a schoolteacher with more children than he could afford was willing to become a grocer" (9). Could one imagine a more commonplace *epic opening*? Readers may easily imagine they are confronted with a fictional work, and their inference is further supported by the extremely ambiguous title the author chose for his book. *The Words*—this label could hide anything, starting with a thriller and ending with a structuralist approach to language. The end of the text is more eloquent; there the author speaks in the first person: "What I like about my madness is that it has protected me from . . ." (255). Nevertheless, the change of person often fails to convince. So many books start in one manner and end in another. The reader has no choice, but must read the whole narrative in order to grasp its meaning.

There is hardly any clue in the text as to the common identity of the hero of the book and the author whose name is printed on the cover. Sartre's name is mentioned a few times, it is true, but everybody knows that there are novels, among them *Remembrance of Things Past*, that cover thousands of pages and within which the author's identity is slightly hinted at once or twice, if at all. As a matter of fact, the narrator's name ("Mon Marcel," "mon cher Marcel") and the author's first name are one and the same. How can the reader tell whether Sartre, the mystifying child whose life is narrated, is Jean-Paul Sartre himself? Narratologists place autobiographies such as Sartre's in a special category. In Sartre's case, the pact seems to rely upon the reader's uncommon perspicacity. The reader detects that *author-narrator-hero* are all one, although the author (deliberately) "forgets" to acquaint us with his narrative approach. Consequently, the autographical pact is never sealed.

The truth of the matter is that Sartre makes a point of parting with traditional autobiography. He comes incredibly close to fiction (the *novelistic pact*), but, at the very last, he is unwilling to stay away from the story of his own life. The ambiguity affects both reader and narrator. Speaking in the first person, the narrator extends so much the ability of this *I* that he is bound to make us doubt, if not the truth of the narrated facts, at least their actual place in the narrator's *history*. The reader is eager to yield to the flow of this narrative style, however, to the ability of this *I* to step aside from himself, to analyze himself as if he were somebody else, as if he were some imaginary hero. Both suspicion and naïveté are understandable on the reader's part. The *narrative* overpowers the *history*, the "I" who speaks secures and dominates the hero who admits several times that his name is Jean-Paul, imposing a new, almost novelistic, identity upon him.

The reader considers this identity in belief and disbelief at the same time. Belief springs from the fact that, in both text and subtext, the author confesses to his being narrator and main hero of the story at the same time. Disbelief—incomplete belief, rather—is caused by the fact that the author keeps talking about mystification, about the hero's extraordinary gift for imposture. What if this mystifying child simply posed as Jean-Paul Sartre? What if Sartre himself, while analyzing the mystification of childhood, mystified the analysis of this mystification?

In conclusion, when we read Sartre's book, we realize that out of the three unknown elements joined together (author-narrator-hero), only the first is certain. The status of the narrator and that of the hero are deliberately uncertain. It is an ambiguous status, placed at the point where reality and imagination meet, the point where the narrated world meets the narrator's world. Sartre makes us realize how difficult it is to enclose this area, claimed by both *narrative* and *history* in his autobiographical work.

In *The Words* Sartre describes his childhood. What is true in this narrative? If we are to find an answer, we must first remember that Sartre the philosopher esteems human acts according to their *authenticity*, rather than their *value*. The acts are neither good nor bad, they are either genuine or false. The attempt at narrating a biography is to be appraised according to its authenticity. Does authenticity side with the *history* or with the *story*? The answer to this question is somewhat simpler. It is the story that envelops history in an appearance of authenticity, all the more so when one deals with something as uncontrollable as the inner history of a life.

We often hear the absurd sentence *His life is a novel*. Sartre's life is not at all like a novel, but Sartre treats it as such. He begins by inventing his childhood, making up a myth, a hero, a history. The first to doubt the truth of the author's words is the narrator himself:

What I have just written is false. . . . Neither true nor false, like everything written about madmen, about men. I have reported the facts as accurately as my memory permitted me. But to what extent did I believe in my delirium? That's the basic question, and yet I can't tell. I realized later that we can know everything about our attachments except their force, that is, their sincerity. Acts themselves cannot serve as a measuring-rod unless one has proved that they are not gestures, which is not always easy. (*Words*, 69)

We have here an ambiguous statement concerning the deep ambiguity of a biographical discourse. The narrator is neither true nor untrue. The precision of facts depends on the relative precision of memory. Then too, how deeply does the hero (that remote *I* whom the passage of time has changed into an *other*) believe in what he is doing? Sartre doubts *sincerity* as well, although it is an essential concept in his system of values. One can know everything about one's moods, one's affections, except their force (i.e., their sincerity). But in that case what or whom is one supposed to trust? The only thing left is the authenticity of the narrative, which ought to be considered with the eyes of a child (as imagined by Sartre) who ends by believing that the comedy he is acting in is more real than reality.

When the story has a narrator, one must at once identify this narrator's attitude regarding his own experience. It is fairly obvious that in *The Words* Sartre adopts a willfully and essentially indeterminate attitude, since everything involved is highly uncertain. The very substance of *history* (the acts) is uncertain; everything depends upon the narrator's faltering memory. In his turn, the narrator calls up the past in the light of his *present* idea regarding his past acts (history). No hope for any certainty left. The uncertainty of all these facts is enhanced by the uncertainty of the theme itself, in Sartre's case, the theme of *childhood*. Talking about this golden age of a man's life, Sartre concludes that a child is some kind of monster brought to life by the regrets of adults. The grownups have created the myth of childhood that otherwise would not have been known. Sartre finds it positively repulsive. In *The Words* he is determined to debunk his theme. Whether he actually does so is an altogether different matter.

Jean-Paul Sartre does not actually tell us the tale of his life. He prefers analyzing it from the dawn of consciousness to the beginning of adolescence. To be more specific, the analysis of his life keeps pace with the *composition* of its story. Within Sartre's narrative, the analysis tends to overpower the history. The author means to destroy a myth created by the aged, a myth that lives on in literature first of all, and he ends by creating his own version for the same myth of childhood, *the myth of the child who mystifies his own image in order to please his elders.* If this is how things stand—and it is—the question arises whether the myth aimed at destroying an older myth, now generally accepted, is not in its turn just one more mystifying act.

Who can convince me that Sartre is right; why should I take the image created by him (at the age of almost sixty) to be more genuine than the other image that he angrily rejects? Sartre fails to avoid this sophism. He fails because literature merely creates myths that oppose false myths. The literary myths are pronounced false in their turn, then rejected, and the line is continued in this way endlessly.

There is only one way out of this paradox. The reader must take the *authenticity of the story* for granted, must entertain no doubt as to the ability of all literature to sacralize even the things it desacralizes, must realize that the *history* (the chronology of *acts* and *facts*) can be rendered credible by the force of an adjoining story, which assumes it and by whose *present* the former is inevitably mystified. There is, however, one point in this long line of mystifications (the time when the story is told) which is more genuine than the rest. It is at this very point that the myth meant to question all preexistent myths is born.

While most authors of biographies and memoirs are unaware of this complicity based on a double mystification, Sartre knows perfectly well what it is all about and will not have it simplified. This is where the complication of his thinking comes from. Whenever the confession grows open-hearted and the story comes close to perfect authenticity, the narrator makes a point of instantly dispelling our hopes. *I am not telling the truth, I wonder how much of what I am saying is actually true, sayings are neither true nor untrue.* Reading Sartre is not an easy thing to do. It is not easy at all. You must mind each of your steps because obstacles besiege your progress from all sides, and your watchfulness merely increases their number. All these obstacles seem to have been invented with devilish resourcefulness by an author who has no *area of safety* to offer his readers. Sartre's books are not in the least realms of delight or peacefulness. Abandon all hope, ye who enter, since it will be taken from you anyway. If the author himself has encouraged your expectations he is sure to baffle them soon. A book by Sartre leaves its reader a changed person, a man who is aware that the world is a monstrous relation of relations.

> *Someone's missing here. It's Sartre.*
>
> (*Words*, 114)

Can a life be pieced together out of this mess, can an existence come into shape in an absurd world? Sartre feels it can. An absurd world can harbor an existence that deems itself responsible for this world. Every person shapes his or her own being. The individual is doomed to be free and invent life at every step. Humans who *invent their lives*, humans, the only beings whose existence precedes their essence, have this supreme freedom, the freedom to force their life out of the hands of hazard. It is a unique life, too, a life that may become an existence aware of its own condition.

In *The Words* Sartre invents for himself a childhood very much unlike the usual childhood of a creator of literature. Few common elements can be traced.

Like François Mauriac, Barthes, and Ionesco, Sartre grew up fatherless. Like Gide and Malraux, he hates the family ("a trite graveyard"). Like Malraux, he imagines a child's life to be haunted by boredom, an immense boredom that borders on neurosis. In *The Family Idiot*, Sartre endeavors to demonstrate that Flaubert, both as a man and as a creator, was the outcome of a fundamental neurosis. In his own biography, Sartre detects a huge imposture. Life begins when one acquires the ability to mystify. The child strives to do what his elders expect from him. His elders are Charles Schweitzer (the grandfather, the patriarch, the great actor, the comic castrating *Parent*); Louise, the grandmother, who is mad at the world, skeptical, and mastered by her barren pride; Anne-Marie, the mother, afraid of life, bullied by everybody else, a widow two years after she married. There is one more character in the novel of this family: the father, Jean-Baptiste Sartre, officer of the navy, who died in 1906, one year after his *son* (Jean-Paul) was born. He is the absent hero, recaptured here and there by the narrative.

The narrative is focused upon the *child* (narrator and main character), such as the true narrator (Sartre the writer) invents him. This child is enveloped in a network of complexes, then dragged out to be confronted by the writer's present obsessions. To a certain extent, this bourgeois novel does not contradict the ordinary psychoanalytical pattern. The *son* abhors what he calls the institution of paternity: "There is no good father, that's the rule. Don't lay the blame on men but on the bond of paternity, which is rotten" (*Words*, 19). Sartre's *father* does him the favor of dying before his son can know him. It gives the son a great sense of freedom. Had the father survived, the son might have been crushed. But Sartre was not, like everybody else, compelled to act like Aeneas, who carried his father, Anchises, on his back. He is delighted at having been deprived of what a famous psychiatrist once called the *super-ego*.

> A father would have weighted me with a certain obstinacy. Making his moods my principles, his ignorance my knowledge, his disappointments my pride, his quirks my law, he would have inhabited me. That respectable tenant would have given me self-respect, and on that respect I would have based my right to live. My begetter would have determined my future. As a born graduate of the Ecole Polytechnique, I would have felt reassured forever. But if Jean-Baptiste Sartre had ever known my destination, he had taken the secret with him. My mother remembered only his saying, "My son won't go into the Navy." For want of more precise information, nobody, beginning with me, knew why the hell I had been born. Had he left me property, my childhood would have been changed. I would not be writing, since I would be someone else. (*Words*, 87)

In conclusion, the paternal discourse is absent from the narrative.

Grandfather Charles takes the place of the father, the latter having been gracious enough to vanish at the right moment, taking along with him an unforgivable guilt. Like Moses, grandfather Charles makes the whole family obey the law. A quaint Moses he makes, a droll patriarch who poses as Victor Hugo, a character who never stops acting his comic part. Next to him there is always a woman (grandmother Louise), who hardly believes a word of what her husband is saying. She is the lucid, skeptical side of the family, having a very clear image of the farce into which the patriarch has dragged them all. The child joins the two into one being: Karlémami. Such syntheses enable patriarchs to oppress more efficiently. This autobiography, mostly supported by the obsessions of the learned adult, touches upon the *theme of incest* as well, a theme that is essential to books belonging to psychoanalytical literature. The child longs to have a sister whom he can love. Anne-Marie is to him like an elder sister. Mother and son experience for each other a discreet feeling of incestuous love. This phantasm (the interdiction of lovemaking) is later transferred to fiction (*The Flies, The Condemned of Altona*). The analyst (narrator) does not fail to list it. Among others, this is one more illustration of the way in which the modern creator compels the biography to confirm a set of complexes.

Before discovering this psychoanalytical novel, however, we read a truly captivating novel, written in Sartre's own style. The novel begins, as shown above where the incidents are narrated in the third person, in a concise, energetic, authoritarian manner. The narrator has no identity, but waits outside the epic area. He is an impersonal voice, like the one heard in the classical realistic novel. The narrator acquires an identity only when his voice merges into that of the hero. The union takes place as soon as the father is no longer present. His absence symbolizes several things at once and is rendered more obvious by the change in the grammatical person. On a rhetorical level, the parent's death coincides with the birth of his son, who takes it upon himself to start the narrative, to continue their history, to find a meaning for individual lives. Here is a significant excerpt: "The death of Jean-Baptiste was the big event of my life: it sent my mother back to her chains and gave me freedom" (18). The freedom is both moral and rhetorical. The father dies just in time. His place is empty. Somebody must take into possession this deserted space: "Someone's missing here. It's Sartre" (114).

From now on, in the process of narrating himself, the *child* passes judgment on everybody else. Of course, we can hardly ignore either this child's ambiguity or the mind he disguises. Let us remember, moreover, that this child and narrator at the same time is called up by a writer who wastes no love on his childhood and no respect on his father. He is "nobody's son," he is his own cause, and in the absence of the true Moses he is brought up by a false Moses, his grandfather, the actor who reinforces the laws. The grandson turns this law *upside down* and declares it a huge, eternal hoax. The child's progress follows closely the image of this hoax. At a very tender age, he behaves like a second-rate actor because in this way he knows he can please his grandfather, his mother, his grownup friends. He feels at home in the family comedy and claims all its successful parts. He mimics wisdom, imitates his elders' gestures, produces memorable statements, is exuberant and melancholic by turns, sensing with precision what his spectators expect. Even his solitude is a show. He allows himself to be surprised in eloquent postures, withdraws to meditation, and professes immeasurable eagerness to acquire knowledge.

His first great imposture, his first part in this amusing mystification, is his determination to pose (act) as a *reader*. Jean-Paul "reads" before learning the letters. He reads the Larousse voraciously. He withdraws to his grandfather's library and sits book in hand for hours on end, following each line with his eyes. The whole thing, of course, is make-believe, but the grownups approve of it, are delighted, and praise the child highly. But the child is not fooled at all. His elders know the truth, play their own comic parts, are just like him, inveterate second-rate actors. So what? The comedy goes on. It breeds an immeasurable pride. The child is proud of his ability to take part in the show, to be the center of attention in a play skillfully staged by the grandfather and patriarch—the great, adorable imposter Charles.

The imposture ends happily when we least expect it; mimicking his elders, Jean-Paul finally and truly learns how to read. A first stage has come to an end; the child is cajoled by everyone, encouraged to lie. He experiences an adventure at the end of which he meets the *Book*. Henceforward, this object presides over the shaping of his being. Everything is vapid and hollow except books. The only clean space is the pure air of the library. As a matter of fact, the mystifying child is not so much in earnest. He merely realizes that such an attitude impresses, heightens his prestige, embellishes his reputation.

The trick is not devoid of a certain genuine joy. The *voices* discovered in grandfather Charles's books shape and rule the child's being. Sartre openly attacks here the old myth of humanity drinking at the fonts of nature. His spirit was shaped in the library, born out of books, straight out of the books the child pretended he was reading even before he had learned the alphabet; his grandfather's voice taught him how to listen to dried *voices* hidden within the covers neatly ordered on the shelves. The future creator begins his life in the dark of a library, surrounded by ceremonious words, first stolen from the grownups, later extracted from books with diligence that is really unusual for a child of his age. It was not nature, but literature (not even the best kind as we shall see) that taught him how to look upon life, how to know himself.

In vain would I seek within me the prickly memories and sweet unreason of a country childhood. I never tilled the soil or hunted for nests. I did not gather herbs or throw stones at birds. But books were my birds and my nests, my household pets, my barn and countryside. The library was the world caught in a mirror. It had the world's infinite thickness, its variety. (49)

Writing is the second imposture. It starts with the same Charles, the grandfather who cannot make up his mind whether he should take up the art of Victor Hugo or that of photography. During a holiday, the grandfather sends him a rhymed letter. The grandson studies prosody at once and by return post he sends a poem. This is the beginning of another great adventure. Considered a genius, the child is prompted to read Jean de La Fontaine's *Fables*. Fables? He dislikes them and tries his hand at rewriting them in Alexandrines. His literary calling is revealed. Mme. Picard concludes, "He'll be a writer! He's meant to be a writer" (154). Everyone in the family takes this for granted, so from now on the enthusiastic Sartre is said to "possess the gift of literature" as well. His grandfather does not object, apparently, but entertains the hidden hope of dissuading him.

> In short, he drove me into literature by the care he took to divert me from it, to such an extent that even now I sometimes wonder, when I am in a bad mood, whether I have not consumed so many days and nights, covered so many pages with ink, thrown on the market so many books that nobody wanted, solely in the mad hope of pleasing my grandfather. That would be a farce. At the age of more than fifty, I would find myself engaged, in order to carry out the will of a man long dead, in an undertaking which he would not have failed to repudiate. (161)

Charles Schweitzer mistrusts professional writers. In 1894 he caught sight of Verlaine in Saint-Jacques Street, entering a den "as drunk as a pig." His ambitions lie elsewhere—he means to have Jean-Paul graduate from the Normal School, in order to see him avenge martyred Alsace. The grandson does not object, but he also sticks to the imposture that was first forced upon him. He ultimately becomes a professional writer, rejecting any other job. For the time being, *writing* plays is a very concrete part in his life; it persuades his elders to let him be. Writing helps him find his own place within this vast comedy. He does not take to writing seriously yet, but he is eager to write books in order to escape the comedy he has been compelled to take part in.

> The craft of writing appeared to me as an adult activity, so ponderously serious, so trifling, and, at bottom, so lacking in interest that I didn't doubt for a moment that it was in store for me. I said to myself both "that's all it is" and "I am gifted." Like all dreamers, I confused disenchantment with truth. (159)

Escape, he says? Maybe, but not for good, or rather not yet. The comedy is still in full swing. It crosses the land of great expectations that is literature. Jean-Paul *writes*, and *writing* makes him feel absolutely free. He is determined to erect "cathedrals made of words." He must first choose between Corneille and Pardaillan.[1] As a matter of fact, he prefers Pardaillan, but, in order to reconcile both parties, he attempts to make Corneille look like Pardaillan. Endowed by Sartre with heroism and a sense of adventure, the former is turned into a knight. Sartre preserves part of Corneille's physical features (crooked legs, narrow chest, wan complexion), but absolves him from greediness and avarice. Can a great, rather sullen author be changed into a beaming hero? Why not? Clever little Jean-Paul finds the trick. He becomes aware of something essential: "as a result of discovering the world through language, for a long time I took language for the world" (182).

The world as language, language seen as a world, a structuralist intuition, one might say. Encouraged by the Machiavellism of the patriarch Charles, the child makes good use of this intuition. He encloses the world in a language, inventing amazing stories, adopting various styles (Zévaco is his favorite model; Sartre was faithful to him to the very end). He is enthusiastic about Courteline and, prompted by his grandfather once more, Jean-Paul writes to him, interspersing a lot of spelling mistakes in his letter, in hopes of making it seem as genuine as possible.[2] The letter ends peremptorily: "your future friend." Courteline fails to answer. Grandfather Charles is overwhelmed with indignation. As for Jean-Paul, he soon forgets all about it. He is very busy reading and writing. He goes indiscriminately from *Chantecler* to *Madame Bovary*. He rereads the last two pages of Flaubert's novel twenty times. He experiences his first disappointments: one fine day he realizes he is ugly. Having had his hair cut, he sees himself in the mirror and notices that he looks like a frog. He is already beginning to lose his right eye. But, to use grandmother Louise's diffident words, "Gently, mortals, be discreet" (255).

When the war breaks out, Jean-Paul's reaction is prompt. He writes stories on the subject, invents a kidnapping of the Kaiser and a brave character (soldier Perrin). Everybody is delighted at the exploits of this imaginative child, who thoroughly enjoys the struggle of his own imagination to protect him. Of course, he is not always at his best. Disappointments find him, he dreads insubstantiality, it seems to him he is not gifted in the least. "I was elected, branded, but without talent" (186), yet he persists with endless patience. Later, the creator of this ambitious child remarks that despair and determination are one. His anxiety is accompanied by a sense of responsibility. Jean-Paul is aware of his "nice little artfulness," he knows that, no matter what phantasmagoria he may devise, he still is no more than a "swot," but destined for fame as he hopes he is, he will not give in.

Meanwhile, he begins school. His grandfather warns the teacher that Jean-Paul is a child of genius, but the grandson's composition is the worst of his class. He catches up with the rest, though; he finds some of the things rather hard to grasp, yet, once he has managed, he masters them. He meets children and, after having lived exclusively among books, he discovers the joy of playing. He experiences an unknown, stern joy that "clears him of the family comedy." He learns about death but is not much impressed. One morning in 1917 in La Rochelle while waiting for his mates on his way to school, he disengages himself from God. "He doesn't exist, I said to myself with polite surprise, and I thought the matter was settled" (251). Thus Poulou (the endearment used for him by his family) banishes an unknown opponent from his existence, as a result of a brief judgment. He becomes an atheist. At a later date, he settles accounts with God for good: "If there is a God, then man is nought; if man exists. . . ." Elsewhere we find the same idea contained in a rougher, more worldly statement: "Why should I make love to you in the sight of God? Well, no, I hate the *barthusards*."

> *I am perfectly aware that I am no more*
> *than a machine for writing books.*
>
> Chateaubriand (quoted in *The Words*)

It must be obvious now that Jean-Paul Sartre's autobiography is in fact a pretext for meditation on the theme of childhood. The grownup author refuses to hide in the subtext; he is unwilling to take part in the comedy called objectivity. From the very beginning he settles down at the surface of the text, avoiding the illusion that he has *transposed* himself in time, that he means to ignore his existence as a grownup. He knows perfectly well that the voice in the text belongs to him all right. He is an almost sixty-year-old writer and also knows that the *past* can hardly expect to be more than a creation of the *present*. He wastes no love on his past or on his childhood at that. Whatever happened once is kept at arm's length.

> Adolescence, manhood, the year which has just rolled by, these will always be the Old Regime. The New is ushered in this very hour but is never instituted: tomorrow everything goes by the board. I've crossed out my early years in particular: when I began this book, it took me a long time to decipher them beneath the blots (239).

Can this nebulous, fading past be brought closer and examined? It can, at best, be recreated, pieced together from among corrections, compelled to meet the requirements of the *present*. This image of the past is the result of relentless analysis. A widely spread myth is pierced. The narrator warns his readers against romance. He states plainly that he hates his childhood, all the memories that have survived:

> Besides, the reader has realized that I loathe my childhood and whatever has survived of it. I wouldn't listen to my grandfather's voice, that recorded

voice which wakes me with a start and drives me to my table, if it were not my own, if, between the ages of eight and ten, I had not arrogantly assumed responsibility for the supposedly imperative mandate that I had received in all humility. (164–65)

We may as well take Sartre's words for granted. He actually means what he says; childhood is compliant, the child is fashioned by his elders, he constantly mystifies his own being in the process of mystifying others. From *The Words* we realize, however, that this absolute imposture ends by taking effect—it produces a writer. Sartre comes into literature (and he comes to stay) because he is *sick* of literature, prompted by a pride that is first feigned, but gradually grows more and more engrossing. Literature distorts his childhood, it drags him away from real life, and it ends by turning him into a professional writer. Sartre's great vocation began as an immense imposture. The *imposture of reading*, the *imposture of writing*, made a writer out of Sartre. We can believe him when he says, "Writing brought me to life." "The eagerness to write involves a refusal to live" (*Words*, 191), which might mean that he missed his childhood because he started mimicking literature at a very early age.

The mimicking yielded fruit though. Sartre did not miss literature. At the time he was writing his so very unusual confession, he had stopped believing in the redeeming powers of literature, however. His autobiography ends with a disturbing sense of failure.

For a long time, I took my pen for a sword; I now know we're powerless. No matter. I write and will keep writing books; they're needed; all the same, they do serve some purpose. Culture doesn't save anything or anyone, it doesn't justify. But it's a product of man: he projects himself into it, he recognizes himself in it; that critical mirror alone offers him his image. Moreover, that old crumbling structure, my imposture, is also my character: one gets rid of a neurosis, one doesn't get cured of one's self. Though they are worn out, blurred, humiliated, thrust aside, ignored, all of the child's traits are still to be found in the quinquagenarian. Most of the time they lie low, they bide their time; at the first moment of inattention, they rise up and emerge, disguised; I claim sincerely to be writing only for my time, but my present notoriety annoys me; it's not glory, since I'm alive, and yet that's enough to belie my old dreams; could it be that I still harbor them secretly? I have, I think, adapted them: since I've lost the chance of dying unknown, I sometimes flatter myself that I'm being misunderstood in my lifetime. Griselda's not dead. Pardaillan still inhabits me. So does Strogoff.[3] I'm answerable only to them, who are answerable only to God, and I don't believe in God. So try to figure it out. (253–54)

In spite of that, something has been preserved. It is Pardaillan's mood, the world of imagination, the world of subtle, largely fruitful imposture. Charles's cheap acting was inherited by his grandson, but the latter added to it the dilemmas of the crooked-legged Corneille, as well. The epic spirit (the spirit of Pardaillan, the mystifying spirit) is fettered to consciousness. The *epos* has been invaded by the anxious imaginings of a mind aware of its own anxiety. In our age, the epos is not, it can no longer be, idle, since we are all haunted by dilemmas belonging to Corneille or to some other name. What about *talent*, then? What about the eternal, thrilling mystery of a *writer's awareness in the act of writing?* Talent has never been explained. Sartre proves that talent is an assiduous imposture, a patient wait.

The one certain thing is that talent alone is no great matter unless it is well employed. It is fairly easy to open the gates of literature and step in; there are many writers who, though utterly talentless, persist and manage to fool a grandfather (Charles Schweitzer) and a mother (Anne-Marie). One must finally find someone to play the part of Corneille. It is the part of a knightly writer who becomes (*on his own*, though supported by other people's love, pretense, and ambitions) a *machinery* for writing books. Sartre quotes Chateaubriand in the second part of his narrative where he deals with the imposture of writing. I am just a machinery for writing books; his pretense intimates that *writing* is the sole aim of the writer's life. Sartre says so himself in *The Words*: "I existed only in order to to write" (153). Old age fails to change his mood, which is preserved in his autobiography as well. Sartre became and stayed a machinery for writing books, although—as we have seen—he lost his belief in the power of books to redeem the spirit.

In *The Words*, the author has no love to spare for his hero. He hates this character, he hates the first years of his own life. This disjunction between author and hero (though they are one and the same) is rather unusual in autobiographies. Sartre's hero is neither good nor bad; he is, as we have seen, true to imposture. Sartre treats him in the same way that grandmother Louise treats the sly Jean-Paul and his protector, Charles, the poor actor: he suspects him of falsehood. While molding his character, Sartre (the narrator) imitates those who molded him once (the adults who watched him grow, out of their own ambitions and disappointments). He does not abandon his initial idea: having become a grownup in his turn, Sartre takes it upon himself to recreate this phantasm (the child as he once was) to his own liking. In a way, he does so out of a sense of paternity, which is as tyrannical, as abusive, as culpable as can be. In the absence of real paternity, Sartre invents an (imaginary) son who is, in fact, the copy of his own uncertain past image.

What should we call this surprising and impure myth that grows out of powerlessness and pride, out of uncertainty and cheap acting, out of a great tragic lucidity? Maybe the myth of unpredictable creation, or the myth in which creation disowns its origins, or even the myth of the creator who, though struggling for freedom from all kinds of relationships, ends by dramatically experiencing each one in turn, under one disguise or another. In his childhood, people used to wonder whether, having read all the books before he had grown up, there would be anything left for him to do later, but the hypocritical Jean-Paul would reply, "I am going to live them all." There is much truth in this hasty, demonstrative answer: the creator sees literature as a comedy, he steps in and stays forever. He must invent a meaning, he must create its substance, his truths and doubts can only be voiced as part of this disgusting comedy. I wonder, does anything survive of the initial comedy? The ten-year-old child who thought himself famous and who affected a intimacy with the personalities of literature seems to have exceeded his own expectations. He has become precisely what he was sure he would never be. This is where the true comedy begins.

In Sartre's *The Words*, nobody is innocent, not even the narrator. He cheats although he claims he will never fool his readers. As a matter of fact, while pretending to narrate a *story*, to present the beginning and progress of a destiny (the child Jean-Paul), he takes hold of this imaginary child and simply bewilders him with his own obsessions, resentments, existential philosophy. The character is no more than a pretext, handled freely by this possessive narrative father. When least expected, he inserts his own discourse within the *discourse of childhood*: it is the *discourse of the authoritarian writer, of the man close to the last of his ages*.

I have the feeling that Sartre's autobiographical narrative is characterized by a kind of ravishment that is repeatedly reenacted: the world of cultured imagination bursts upon the creator's biography, the *story* ruthlessly gobbles up *history*. This story exists at several levels and its progress is prompted by a number of forces. The *author-narrator-character* alliance imagined by Sartre is not wholly loyal: the author and the narrator join hands in order to disgrace the character. Sartre does everything in his power to prevent his hero from becoming a likable fellow, a model for others, a novelistic image of childhood. The proof of this intention is Sartre's bantering determination to warn his readers that the hero of the story is a resourceful little quack. His alienating, grudging manner is quite unusual, if not unique, for autobiographies. Jean Starobinski is right: "A man's irony hints at the man's unwillingness to belong to his own past" (*Relation*, 98–99).

This violence is only partly successful. Sartre overlooks the fact that the reader is in a state of mystification as well. *Reading* is like a drug to the reader too. A text exposing imposture may sometimes arouse a deep love for imposture in the reader. All the more so when the imposture is exposed in a captivating book, by someone like Jean-Paul Sartre. The reader is in the position of a young countess described by the author. In a small Siberian station, she notices an old man with a large head, shabbily dressed, dirty, in a state of angered despair, and realizes that he is a well-known writer. She goes up to him and kisses his hand, saying, "'I no longer regard you as a man, but as the symbol of your work'" (*Words*, 192).

26

Malraux:
A Passion for Greatness,
a Religion of Fraternity

Malraux's autobiographical works are well worth considering. He attempts in them to view and explain the place of his destiny in this world and to generalize from his own fate to the fate of humankind in our contemporary civilization. These works include the *Anti-Memoirs*, *Felled Oaks*, and *Lazarus*, all of them direct or indirect confessions, closely related to Malraux's fiction, from which the theme of the author is never absent. Gaëtan Picon says that Malraux always wrote in the first person: "Out of his life, we know a number of memories and encounters . . . ; each new work was just another chapter of his *Memoirs*; he seems to have had no other theme besides his own life, so, before writing, he had to live first" (Picon, 13–14).

The statement is dangerously clear-cut. After Proust, writers are unlikely to admit that they merely record their experiences. Picon wrote his statement in 1961 and, on seeing the text before it went to press, Malraux acquiesced. One may infer from this that, as a rule, he expected literature to incorporate the creator's life (experience). Yet in *Anti-Memoirs* he disapproves of personal reports in literature. On various occasions, he also disapproves of *biography*; and this looks like a paradox at first sight, since, once one has stated that literature closely records the author's experiences, one can hardly deny the possibility and the use of a creator's biography.

The paradox is cleared as soon as Malraux produces his definition of a biography. In *Anti-Memoirs* he rejects traditional biography and the image of the human being it creates, an image very much like an *abject body of little secrets*. One of his characters says that a person's truth can be found in the things he or she conceals. The idea originates with Nietzsche: *the work expresses what its writer lacks, rather than what the writer has got.* Valéry slightly improves upon this idea: "Men differ by what they show, and have in common what they hide" (14:552). Malraux reshapes the statement. Picon, quoting, not quite accurately, from "The Walnut Trees of Altenburg," has Vincent Berger telling us, "Man is not really what he conceals; a man's true meaning lies in his acts" (Picon, 11). On rereading this sentence, the novelist writes, as a note among the illustrations on the facing page, "He [Vincent] is very explicit about it, yet this is not the whole truth: man may be more than just what he conceals, but anyway he is definitely more than his acts." In *Anti-Memoirs* again, Malraux writes, "Something eternal lives in man, in thinking man. Something that I would call his divine self: his capacity to call the world into a question" (28).

Once expressed, the idea that the modern individual is characterized by a sense of questioning accompanies Malraux everywhere. He is not alone in this, as has been seen. His *Anti-Memoirs* were meant to extend a fundamental question, "to reflect upon life—life in relation to death" (1), not to recollect the progress of a life (which is the aim of traditional memoirs, autobiographies, and biographies). In his notes to Picon's manuscript, Malraux discusses the style of a biography, "the style of a destiny exceeds the possibilities of the traditional biographical style, but I am not prepared to say that it defies analysis altogether" (Picon, 26). The older biographical style was inadequate because it dealt with human inessentials. Malraux views individuals in their greatness. His rejection of insignificant biographies amounts, essentially, to a rejection of mediocre destinies. That is why Malraux hates his childhood, the age when the being is small, both literally and figuratively. An individual must become aware of destiny before claiming a place in the universe. This awareness alone can turn human existence into a destiny and can support it in its struggle to become *anti-Destiny*.

Malraux's autobiography aims at confronting humankind with death, history, action, art, thus defying existence. It amounts to an inexhaustible questioning present in all important circumstances of the narrator's life. Malraux's reflections are intensely personal, yet totally irrelevant for the man's private biography, for the secret incidents of his life. Unlike the common memoirist, Malraux is indifferent to the possibility of creating a coherence for his past; he is eager to compare the style of his life to the *style of eternity* (the "style of a destiny"). His confessions reveal (to use Valéry's words) a true *religion of the personality*. Malraux converses with statues and follows the royal roads of history. One cannot fail to notice that the novelist's favorite place for meditation is the *museum*, that his sympathy goes to the *Leaders of History*, those Plutarchan heroes who achieved notable things in the world. He wants to see Jawaharlal Nehru in India, he talks to Mao Tse-tung and Chou En-lai in Beijing, he records his talks with de Gaulle in *Felled Oaks*. When the *Leaders of History* are absent, Malraux turns to works of art. The great personalities of history embody the grandeur of human action, while the works of art epitomize what is divine and eternal in humankind.

What does the narrator, who is at the same time author and character of the memoirs, do while all this is going on? He exists in the vicinity of greatness, stern and free of complexes, always ready to ask one of the decisive questions that bear on the fate of a civilization and on human condition. How very different, yet how similar are Malraux's *Anti-Memoirs* and Jean-Jacques Rousseau's *Confessions*. Rousseau turns his little misfortunes into a pattern of life for the man who can only find fulfillment in nature; two hundred years later, Malraux finds human greatness epitomized in art and the exemplary acts of history. Like Rousseau, Malraux believes in a religion of the personality. Rousseau's religion is centered on the human capacity for suffering, on the human ability to endure infamy. Equally proud, conceited, and uncompromising, Malraux turns this religion into an ethics of tragic heroism. His confession avoids the low inferno of the being, since to him, as has already been seen, life is human only at its highest. Malraux rejects intimacy, his narrator overlooks common situations, concentrating solely upon whatever borders on the meaningful and the sublime. If the memoirist happens to stumble upon a trifling incident, he is sure to hurl it into the sublime and the meaningful.

One might say that Malraux has no eyes for the incident, he records the history contained in it. He fails to notice the individual but identifies at once what is generally human. When recording his own life, he ignores his biography because he must grasp the destiny enclosed within an exemplary biography. When the biography is not up to the mark, the author improves upon it forcibly. In the process, he resorts to meditation rather than fiction. Roquentin, the hero of *Nausée*, remarks that the most trivial incident becomes an *adventure* once it is *retold*. With Malraux it is the other way around. The incident becomes an exemplary adventure as soon as *the author ponders over it*. Meditation confers the status of an issue on ordinary incidents. The ensuing pages always reveal that the issue is related to one or more fundamental themes of existence. Reading the *Anti-Memoirs*, one feels, above everything else, that the individual life is a point of intersection for the great roads of history, that all individual acts somehow reveal the human condition in the universe.

The author-narrator-character identity is flawless, but the absence of details encloses the author's biography within the abstract realm of ideas. The narrator is a philosopher of history, while his character aspires to be a "man of history." The "man of history," like the "man of art," will not be found in the suburbs of biography. "An artist's biography is his biography as an artist, the story of his converting ability." Should we be ignorant of the aim and resources of this converting ability, we might form a mistaken opinion of Malraux's memoirs.

The *Anti-Memoirs* fit into none of the categories suggested by Malraux for twentieth century memoirs. They are neither *records of events* nor *introspections*. They are related to both, of course. They do record the events, but Malraux's records, as we have seen, are dressed up in the clothes of meditation, and the events dealt with have already turned or are on the point of turning into history. Unlike Gide (the model in the matter), Malraux avoids sending his introspection toward the dark recesses of psychology. Malraux's introspection attempts to identify the encounter between a destiny and an idea that can rule it. "There are ideas the first encounter with which remains as immediate as if they were persons" (32); consequently one may write a confession about an author's encounter with the ideas that have shaped his existence. Malraux travels to Egypt, and that experience influences his reflections on art. The sarcophagi and statues reveal to him a face of death, but also another face of life. While writing his memoirs, Malraux attempts in fact to conceive of life and death in their relation to *Art*. In Malraux's ethics, the *humanistic heroism* (expressed in art) follows the *solitary heroism of adventure* and the *revolutionary collective heroism* (Picon, 103). Each one is a step climbed in the human progress toward eternity. Their force resides in humankind's determination to master its condition by growing aware of it rather than in its desire to overpower that condition. Kierkegaard tells us that humans pass from the *aesthetic* stage to a *religious* one, the latter enabling them to attain fulfillment. Malraux turns this image upside down, changing the nature of obstacles and advancing a morals based on courage, which mainly rests on the human ability to touch our share of eternity, as a result of our own deeds and intelligence. *Art* is a promise of eternity, more than other human acts. A work of art may not be eternal, but it always embodies the human longing for grandeur and immortality more intensely and for a wider span of time.

When Malraux makes up his mind to write a biography of his ideas and experiences, he feels that the heroism of art goes further, that a man of art is better qualified to face death. His confessions do not follow the chronology of childhood, youth, love, etc. (the traditional line of memoirs); they follow the order in which Malraux wrote his books. It is, after all, the order of his major experiences ("The Walnut Trees of Altenburg," *The Temptation of the West, The Royal Way, Man's Fate*). The narrator does not retrace his steps into the past in order to reconstitute a credible *story*; he examines the present, trying to find there signs of the experiences recorded by literature. The autobiographical narrative intimates that the works have not left history unaffected. The memoirist returns to China and North Africa, curious to see how many of his intuitions have been confirmed by history. He is not disappointed. Nor are we. History has not left the path traced by the restless youth back in the 1920s; even today, history follows the thoughts of this memoirist who is positive that he speaks in the name of humankind. This is the true reason his words are addressed to the great leaders of his time, to the makers of history, to temples moreover, to works of art, because they preserve the share of eternity of the human being always ambushed by time.

These memoirs can hardly be summarized, since the author is interested in meditating upon history, so the narrative does not deal with history proper. A very peculiar meditation it is, too: discontinuous, enlivened by memorable sentences, concerned with essential concepts and fundamental themes. In all places and at all times, Malraux is surrounded by vast concerns. His confession repeatedly returns to life, death, art, and their relation to humankind. The memoirist's main concern is to banish the *language of transience*. He is determined to identify the perennial and converse with essences; while narrating his life, Malraux always obeys this law of his own making. As a matter of fact, he does not narrate his biography; he appraises his existence, stepping aside and viewing it from a distance. His object is never close at hand, there is no question of identification; the object is contemplated from afar, compelled to make room for magnificent, exemplary symbols. In a strange way, the narrator's *self* is unfamiliar, impersonal, descending from some other tense than the present indicative. The voice heard in *Anti-Memoirs, Felled Oaks*, etc., seems determined to create its own grammatical tense and mood. It is a mood of absolute authority and a tense devoid of all chronology, a tense, a time of cathedrals, I should say, a style of duration and of the monumental, containing very few traceable self-referential elements. The reader who is eager to learn secrets stands no chance of finding out whom Malraux may have either loved or hated. In the text, Malraux invariably loves archetypes, looks into the heart of the matter, feeds on essentials and nothing else.

Owing to this, the meaning and progress of time cannot be judged by common standards. All *tenses* merge, they are joined together by the memoirist's meditation. In *Anti-Memoirs* Malraux heads chapters, "1934, Sheba/1965, Aden," "1913 Alsace." In another chapter, the dates are "1934/1950/1965." It is fairly obvious that Malraux considers all incidents according to a private chronology of his own. He finds a link between Queen Sebeth Fetish (a tree) and some moment of the Resistance Movement, between a temple in Egypt and the Long March of Chinese revolutionaries. Absurd links? Symbolical rather: the person of action and the meditating person (with whom Malraux identifies himself) harbor the symbols of humankind. Once more, *art* brings together things that would otherwise never merge. *Art* enables us to glance at eternity.

The first episode of *Anti-Memoirs* ("The Walnut Trees of Altenburg") is a conversation of imaginary characters (Walter, Mollberg, etc.), rendered in a conversation of symbols. From Egyptian sarcophagi to Hitler's room, from Pascal to Nietzsche, from museums to contemporary incidents. "Pointed-eared" Mollberg says that the soul was invented in Egypt, and somebody (the narrator) adds that serenity was invented in Egypt. Another remark: the world of art is not one of immortality, but of metamorphosis. One must deliberately slip some imperfection into one's creation, unless one means to anger the gods: "perfection is theirs alone." These are splendid statements, sentences with a promising future ahead of them. Among the writers of his generation, Malraux knows best how to coin such syntagms destined for celebrity. His novels teem with memorable sayings; his autobiographical works enlarge upon them, and produce new ones too, with the same constant eagerness to squeeze a truth into a few words that cannot fail to survive. Although we are not eternal, we can conceive of eternity, can phrase thoughts that render eternal whatever is limited, frail, and transitory in the human being.

Malraux narrates (generously, at last) an adventure of his younger days, his expedition to the queen of Sheba's land and the moment he "discovered" the biblical capital. He narrates with great earnestness, not in the least discomfited by his having mistaken some commonplace ruins for the remnants of the famous settlement. It is the adventure that matters; its failure cannot embarrass Malraux. The narrative peeps at eternity again, making use of metaphors of expanse and greatness that open up wide vistas to all incidents. The queen of Sheba and the oneiric land of North Africa are joined by the narrator to the *Resistance* and de Gaulle, in a spectacular leap over the ages of history. The style is not deterred, though. The same style describes the vegetal remnants and de Gaulle's peace of mind.

De Gaulle is the first "man of history" introduced by Malraux, the first Plutarchan hero who crosses the writer's path. "The historic chief" is enveloped in profound solitude and lives up to his myth. Malraux finds it natural to quote Caesar, Tamerlane, and Napoleon. He talks to Nehru about Hinduism and Buddhism, about the destiny of the Occident and the Orient. He is eager to learn a wise politician's opinion on the fate of politics. Culture is a vast resurrection; politics is action justified by its own grandeur and force. De Gaulle's minister shows no interest in petty politics at all. He would not have joined the cabinet unless *he had been summoned* by a historical leader. He does not work for a government but serves a "man of history." In this position, he goes to Guyana, to China, to India; all the travels of a man commissioned by history appear to him to be "Incarnations." The *Resistance*, in which Malraux takes part and which he describes in admirable pages, is an *initiation* as well, an initiation into heroic tragedy, a test that confers the feeling that, having passed it, one has become the *bearer of some kind of revelation*. Sentenced to death by the Gestapo, Colonel Berger (Malraux) reenacts the experiences of characters in *Man's Fate*. Like Dostoevsky, Gramat is brought in front of the firing squad and, faced with death, he gives no thought to his biography, he merely thinks of death. His drama is as magnificent as the incidents. Gramat's *execution* is burlesque, but that is of no consequence whatever. Against his will, the hero has been hurled into a predicament, and his intelligence watches him with eyes wide open. The writer experiences the incidents he once imagined in his work. Malraux does not always write about his experiences. He also experiences his own writings in order to be able to write another work, an autobiographical one this time. This is instance of where Malraux's life and work condition each other, that his existence and literature are handled by the same "templeless god"—Destiny.

Malraux's confessions intimate that the creator's existence either imitates art (as we have seen) or attempts to conform to the pattern of art, having previously grasped the directions of great history. The creator's biography is in fact a succession of relevations and historical meetings with "men of history" under circumstances so vividly rendered that they are perceived as true initiations. Malraux does not tell us in as many words, but we gather from his sentences that a creator's biography is the biography of a god who babbles the language of eternity. Consequently, an autobiography joins three myths: an *author* (creator) becomes a legend and is perfectly aware of the change, a *narrator* resorts to a syntax of the magnificent and tenses that point to fundamentals, a *character* acts as a *man of history* precisely because he is a *man of art*. Here is a beautiful alliance, a sacred family, a *narrative* that refuses to disobey *history*, and a *history* that hurries to reinforce the conceit and immense pride of the *narrative*. Instead of Malraux calling up his own image, we are faced with a figure created by Malraux's imagination.

In the first pages of *Felled Oaks* (excerpts from the second volume of *Anti-Memoirs*), Malraux advances a statement whose splendid arrogance may have escaped the writer's self-control: "we possess no dialogue between a man of history and a great artist" (*Oaks*, 7). He even lists a number of such unfortunate lacunae. We know nothing about the words exchanged by Pope Julius II and Michelangelo, by Alexander the Great and the philosophers, by Augustus and his contemporary poets, by Tamerlane and Ibn Khaldun. Voltaire never mentioned his conversations with Frederick II, Diderot did not write a single word about his talks with Catherine II. Napoleon's favorite pose, even when he is on Saint Helena, is the monologue. The "man of history" was often watched by innumerable witnesses but never conversed with the great creators. The moral of this introductory statement is fairly obvious. Malraux's imagination attempts to bring together the "man of history" and the "man of art." The writer feels positive that these two *leaders* can find thoughts of utmost importance to share. This magnificent possibility is embodied in *Felled Oaks*. Charles de Gaulle is the contemporary *man of history* (more than once, Malraux intimates that de Gaulle is the last great *leader* in the history of the Occident), while Malraux himself is the *man of art* who, at a crucial moment for France, joined forces with the former.

The book (which bears part of a line by Victor Hugo as a title) has a motto from Hegel, a sentence conveying a free person's worship of the great leader. This is the initial symbol in a long line of symbols pointing at magnificence. The dialogue took place on December 11, 1969. It is meant to present "a General de Gaulle within history and outside history" (*Oaks*, 9). But Malraux fails to carry out his intention. General de Gaulle is wrapped in history even when he no longer contributes to its progress. This seems to be the strongest impression produced by this highly unusual conversation. Maybe it looks unusual because one can hardly tell the voice who asks from the voice who answers. The statements join hands and finally merge. Who utters these memorable sentences? Without proper presence of mind, the reader fails to detect who speaks and who listens; all myths are at large in this text, whatever seems commonplace must first be apprenticed to magnificence. Among other things, the general says, "I had a contract with France" (*Oaks*, 16), but the words might have been uttered by Malraux just as well. Elsewhere he says as much: "France is my bride." The *man of art* is far from shy in the presence of the *man of history*. The fact is obvious from the first flawless sentences of the text, sentences that are carefully coined so as to be remembered by the generations to come. There is no question of substitution here; the author is not menaced. This is not an insignificant, ambitious individual eager to outshine the great model as so often happens in interviews. The solitude and magnificence of two equal personalities, two men who speak the language of the gods, come face to face.

It is not a complicated language, though. Malraux endeavors to coin a definition for the man who "eludes destiny." No *man of history* has a Christian name. We learn from Malraux that General de Gaulle's *Memoirs* never mention the name *Charles*. Malraux intimates that a strong personality, not unlike a myth, concentrates its essence into one unique, laconic, memorable word. No further explanation is necessary when one has uttered a word such as *Caesar* or *Napoleon*. Malraux, or maybe de Gaulle (we cannot know for certain), remarks that Napoleon actually become Napoleon when he stopped being Bonaparte, just as Michelangelo was no longer known as Buonarroti once he had become famous. On their way to glory, some leave behind their family name, others their first name. Malraux's hero, de Gaulle, is supposed to embody the spirit of a country (France) during a dramatic age, as well as the spirit of a civilization whose evolution has almost reached the end of one more cycle. Here are Malraux's own words, which we must hurry to quote before his voice merges with his hero's; in this dialogue utterly devoid of trifling private matters, de Gaulle "was expressing a destiny, and still expressed it when he proclaimed his divorce from destiny. Intimacy with him did not mean talking about himself, a tabooed subject, but about France (in a certain way), or about death" (*Oaks*, 22). These two, then, are the topics of the dialogue. They explain the relationship between narrator and his hero as well as explaining the role of the author. This author is expected to persuade the Sphinxes of history to talk, to help us understand the language of essences, to pave the way for the birth of a myth, to change *historical biography* into a *legendary* life. Why is Caesar a great figure of the West? Malraux replies: Caesar scored "a few victories, important but not fundamental; a great period of government like some others. But there was Plutarch. And Shakespeare" (*Oaks*, 66). It was literature that built a legend around an able leader. Malraux intimates that it must be the merit of the *man of art*.

While interviewing de Gaulle, Malraux contemplates these overwhelming models in his mind, and he feels positive that his hero's words and deeds are impregnated with stirrings of grandeur, that the general stands for history seen as a destiny. The dialogue is recorded with obvious concern for style and with surprising self-assurance. The style *reveals what is obvious* and *amazes by means of commonplace occurrences.* The style itself conveys the certainty of this glory. The narrative only records the most important incidents and attempts, as has already been pointed out, to produce an ethical definition of the "man of history." The definition is not easily summed up. Among other things, it implies that an agent of history assumes all great conflicts, since glory is never spared great controversies. Shakespeare says so, Malraux confirms it. De Gaulle is almost a religious leader, since he is not primarily concerned with his own person (like Napoleon), but with France, with its history, its civilization, its peculiar place in our world. When France parted with the general, the general continued on his own way until France came back to him. Do we know anything about death? "Our idea of death is only significant because of what it does to our ideas about life" (*Oaks*, 41–42). "Writing allows one to forget the crowd" (44). "Writing is also a powerful drug" (43). "The Revolution pushed France back into war and France has always been shaped by strokes of the sword" (58). Napoleon "had not time for the soul" (59).

Who is the author of all these memorable phrases? It is Malraux who records and writes them, but they belong to and are even phrased at times by de Gaulle himself, in his majestic solitude at Colombey. A few more excerpts from this lofty discourse are well worth being quoted. Malraux once hears de Gaulle state that the teachings of History (the word is always capitalized) have never been of any use at all. The general adds—unless the sequel belongs to Malraux himself—that the "man of history" is supposed to turn confusion into order. Then further: Napoleon *made France mad with ambition.* Napoleon was a *professor of ambition,* he opened the gates of aristocracy to the people at large (63). De Gaulle thinks (his words can hardly be mistaken for Malraux's this time) that "women are capable of the best and of the worst. Therefore they should never be shot" (70). Besides that, artists invent dreams, while women embody them. "The Eternal Feminine is a phenomenon of the Christian world" (71). I cannot tell for sure who the last sentence belongs to, de Gaulle or Malraux, his peer who gets involved in the *discourse* and adopts his interlocutor's ideas while recording them. At one point in the interview, Malraux inquires, "You like Greek sculpture, General" (72)? We may have few doubts as to whose voice inquires, but as far as the answer is concerned we are utterly in the dark. The style of this answer is obviously Malraux's. When is France great? "France was great only when she was great fo the world as a whole" (76). This is Malraux's idea, and de Gaulle confirms it: "There is a pact twenty centuries old between the grandeur of France and the liberty of others." The same Malraux feels that the incidents of May 1968 were the result of an alliance between the trade-unionists' revolt and the irrational revolt of the youth. A moral conclusion follows: "indignation is not a supreme value" (81). De Gaulle respects intellectuals, but he irritably advises them to place their causes in the service of France.

"Irresponsibility of the intellect" is short-lived (114). The really dramatic issue of the Occident is the condition of its youth, he states near the end of these interviews, which attempt in fact to create a pattern for participation to history as well as to find the morals of authority at the level of history. Both pattern and morals are embodied by de Gaulle. Where is Malraux, the author, in the meantime? Where else unless within these morals? It is Malraux who guides us toward understanding the "man of history," it is he again who makes up this little ethical treatise. He creates a mythical life out of a historical biography.

In conclusion, *Felled Oaks* makes us hear what the voices of history and of art have to say about the destiny of present civilization and about a relationship that, though not always fortunate, has always been necessary, the relationship (contract) between the stern, authoritarian, solitary, majestic de Gaulle and the fickle, inexhaustible France. The ceremonious dialogue intimates that there is another relationship, too, between the person who makes History (the political and spiritual leader) and the one who renders the former eternal (the creator of art). It is the creator who has the last word, who enables glory to survive.

In *Lazarus* Malraux writes:

Images do not make up a life story; nor do events. It is the narrative illusion, the biographical work, that creates the life story. What did Stendhal pin down, except a few moments of his? Each of us articulates his past for the benefit of an impalpable interlocutor: God, in the confessional; posterity, in literature. One has no life story except for others. (*Lazarus*, 74)

Then, on the next page, "And what is a past when it is not a life story?" Let us quote just one more sentence, uttered at the beginning of this confession: "Cornered, perhaps, by death, I take refuge in this account of one of the most enigmatic spasms of life" (*Lazarus*, 6).

Malraux was writing these words during the interval between two attacks that almost pushed him over the threshold of death. He can hardly be suspected of flirting with literature, of sporting (like most literary figures) with the idea of death. Death was prowling around him and, when cornered by death, all other meanings are lost. This is Malraux's mood at the time he brings up again the question of biography/autobiography for the eye of an unknown interlocutor, whom one can hardly afford to disregard, since this witness alone can make the story of a life look coherent and convincing. Further, he remarks that a narrative is a place of refuge. The true meaning of this idea becomes obvious if we join it to another idea, stated at another point of the same confession. The memory of the story entitled "The Walnut Trees of Altenburg" written thirty years earlier makes Malraux remark that "writing was then the only way to keep alive" (*Lazarus*, 54). The words of *Lazarus* almost intimate that Malraux hopes they can teach him how to die. Writing is his last effort to put off death. Though on the point of passing away, Malraux still claims that *being alive* is his true calling. Everything is conditioned, supported, conceived by means of the "passionate awareness of being alive—alive and nothing else." A superb consistency. To *be alive* up to the bitter end, to conjure up death with the spell of life, even when the mirror of this life is already veiled.

Lazarus is much more than the text of a last will. It is both a confession and a meditation. It is the meditation of a being who has already glanced at death ("this tourist trip through the archipelago of death," *Lazarus*, 79), who, like the biblical Lazarus, has come back to life and strives to hold the void in the arms of his mind. An arduous task. The vicinity of death blurs all *self*-awareness: "an 'I' without a self; a life without an identity" (84). Or "the proximity of the death throes of others drowns the question 'What am I,' makes it otiose" (79). It seems to me that Malraux proves the opposite, though. Anxiety does not affect his interrogative mood. Here is a sentence that confirms the fact: "Man was born when for the first time he murmured 'Why?' at the sight of a corpse" (79).

Such words restate Malraux's earlier conviction that, in the adventure of an existence, death goes hand in hand with life, that the human being is an animal who, by being aware of mortality, somehow rises above this miserable condition. Of course, the idea was not discovered by the author of *Man's Fate*, but it definitely ruled his life. In conclusion, then, having reached the point where a person learns to conceive the inconceivable, Malraux ponders *biography*, refusing to accept that a number of disparate images can make up such a biography, that a mere sequence of incidents can be mistaken for history. He mistrusts his own analysis of his life, and, which is worse, the proximity of death renders it futile. Yet the writer realizes that the only thing that will not be defeated by death is fraternity. *Lazarus* is another profound meditation on death, one more poem on fraternity. The author warns us that "the individual has no place in it" (6). He actually keeps his word: "the confession is not stained by any trifling incidents belonging to a previous private life." The refusal to write a biography is Malraux's own way of approximating the story of an exceptional existence. After all, only those who doubt their past can afford to ignore it. Those who have not got one (a significant past) always endeavor to invent it. Malraux entertains no doubts as to his past, so he is in no hurry to retrace his steps in his final confession. Others have done so or will do it sometime. He merely chooses two or three images (such as the firing squad commanded by Colonel Berger), which are supposed to reveal the way in which a person finds the *religion of fraternity*.

The pattern already described (including solitary heroism, collective rev-olutionary heroism, the humanism of art) acquires a new *stage*, that of *fraternity* ("fraternity, which fate does not obliterate," 116), a fraternity that is to be found at the other end of humiliation and death. A combatant once mentioned these words to Malraux in Spain. Malraux rediscovers their meaning while lying ill at Salpêtrière. Somebody's death rattle makes him write that "fellowship is often as powerful as death itself" (136), a mysterious relationship between death and fraternity. Here is the message of a great writer who scoured the world as a student of heroism, striving to find out in what way a life could be turned into a destiny. He reconsiders both his life and his books in the light of this truth:

> The most striking instance of fraternity I know, one that I thought up myself. . . . In a hotel in Peïra-Cava, I was writing the scene in *Man's Fate* in which the wounded Shanghai revolutionaries are about to be flung into the furnace of the locomotive. Katow has managed to hang on to his cyanide. During the night, his hand touches the hand of Kyo, who has been thrown in beside him and who grasps it. At that moment I realized that Katow was going to place the cyanide in the hand that has just clasped his. (119)

Malraux is mistaken, since he means Souen and not Kyo, but his mistake does not matter. What matters is that the novelist looks upon fraternity as a supreme value. It is a "holiday" for humankind. He writes: this value swallows all others and, on the threshold of death, it enables us to face bravely the whispering of our own end.

Lazarus (which could be entitled *meditations in the house of death*) contains even more dramatic sentences concerning suffering. When the narrator tells us that "this crisis was not so serious as the last. I realized I was going to let the pen drop," we can easily understand that all rhetoric has been renounced. The remark must have been recorded sometime after the crisis, but it fully conveys the confusion inflicted by the crisis upon the writer's spirit. The narrative seems to be placed outside grammatical tenses; the author forbids it to consider its incidents from a distance.

This could be interpreted in many ways. I shall choose an interpretation that fits into Malraux's biography. The narrative and its object are one (the object being more than an individual's existence, extending to the whole of human condition), and the meditation that orders the incidents enforces the values of this narrative. Malraux narrates (by *narrating* we mean that he records, questions, unveils the law that stirs all incidents, that he peers at everything with stubborn curiosity, determined to have his intellectual plans confirmed) only what can never be suspected of insignificance. He meditates on his own life only as far as it dwells in the realm of those "men of history," a realm wherein the language of myths is used. The last to enter this realm of significances is the myth of fraternity. Malraux rediscovers it in the antechamber of death, where he reviews his own existence for the last time.

27

Ionesco:
Childhood and Light,
Literature and the World on
the First Day of Creation

I think of myself: I am another.
The "I" is caught up in the "myself";
its root is myself. My
"self" is the soil that feeds the "I."

Fragments

Childhood and light are rejoined, become one in my
mind. . . . I write to recover this light and to test
the correspondence.

Antidotes

The existential condition is inadmissible.

Antidotes

Eugène Ionesco learns about death at the age of four and thus realizes that the world stays the same, with or without himself alive in it. He begins reading when he is five, and at the age of seven he experiences the original sin: looking at himself in the mirror, he notices he is unlike everybody else. A terrifying collapse ensues. He is haunted by the awareness of irreparable isolation, and he is condemned to abnormality. He already knows whatever there is to be known. Nothing more can he learn about life, death, or destiny from that point on, for the die is cast. The child finds out everything that his grownup self is to experience, namely, that "we were born, we are alive, we shall die, we ignore both the mystery of the being and that of the non-being." He has hardly turned nine when he makes up his mind to write his memoirs and actually begins recording his experiences and memories but finally abandons the copybook meant to enclose his revealing confessions.

Ionesco answers this question when he turns fifty.

> Talk about myself? I did not really love myself, not since I had glanced at myself, since I had understood my isolation, that cleft, the essential sin of being unlike others, unlike everybody else. That was in fact the reason I wanted to talk about myself, undoubtedly because I was different, abnormal, even monstrous. When three or four years had elapsed since I had had the first revelation of my particularity, I got used to the idea, more or less, that I was myself. Yet I could not accept it wholly. (*Découvertes*, 84, 88)

The explanation is typical of Ionesco; he hates talking about himself, and for that very reason he wants to make his confession just to let us know he hates confessions more than anything in the world. The author compels this dialectic to contradict itself, to come to terms with its own denial of itself.

These confessions, recording, when the author is sixty, his discoveries at the ages of four, five, seven, and ten, reveal something essential. For Eugène Ionesco, literature began with memoirs rather than with fairy tales or poetry. Unlike most children, he prefers confessions to fabulation. When he realizes that a heavy contrast separates him from the outer world, his first reaction is to bear testimony to this amazing revelation. In short, he means to write his autobiography. The pressing urge for confession drives him toward literature, although he cherishes no illusions as far as the power of literature is concerned: literature is powerless, it cannot cure him of the anxiety caused by his discovery of death; literature cannot make him come to terms with the outer world, and, what is worse, it fails to make him come to terms with himself as well. Whoever writes exposes this impossible relationship: *to conceive the inconceivable, retell what cannot be retold*, to state that *talking/writing is futile* and that the greatest victory of all is to learn how to keep silent. But one must write about the force of silence in order to let people know that silence is, indeed, a blessing.

Here is, then, an inevitable contradiction, an external sophism, a denial that breeds an uncompromising affirmation. Ionesco does not hesitate to enter the realm of impossible relationships. He invites them, his mind cannot separate the possible from the impossible, the front from the back view. Understanding begins at the point where whatever is possible, acceptable, and credible vanishes. Eugène Ionesco seems to judge the quality of a mind in accordance with the number of impossible relationships it can grasp. The drama of human intellect is caused by its clash with the absurd side of ordinary categories, and he conveys this drama in his plays. He outlines it in his *memoirs* too, that were written, of course, when he was much older than the almost ten-year old. In fact, the word *memoirs* hardly suits Ionesco. He does not want to be the witness of an age and refuses to lurk behind narrated incidents. Unlike most memoirists, he does not describe the famous people he is acquainted with and does not retell his life. While he may not retell it, he always finds some pretext to refer to it. In *The Colonel's Photograph* (the chapter "Spring 1939"), *Fragments of a Journal, Present Past, Past Present, Découvertes, Antidotes, Un homme en question*, in his numerous interviews, Ionesco's mind keeps "coining" its own image everywhere. In essays, in disparate memories, there is always a "je" [I] who will not part from the restless prolific "moi" [me]. This type of literary confession can hardly be said to belong to a particular narrative category. It is different both from Gide's diary and from Sartre's inventions in *The Words*. It has nothing to do with Malraux's *Anti-Memoirs* and, as a rule, Ionesco is not eager to write a treatise on life. Like Rousseau, he talks about himself but refuses to impart to us the story of his life. In *Fragments of a Journal* and *Découvertes* there are some purely biographical details, some memories and portraits, but their order and shape destroy the least trace of similarity with one model or another.

"Spring 1939"—the oldest fragment of a diary (actually the first to be published, in 1962)—bears as a subtitle "Fragmentary recollections: pages from a diary." The 1967 *Diary* is "in fragments." The terms are meaningful. We are confronted with *remnants, fragments* of a *story* (existence) that the *narrative* either will not or cannot piece together. Is there a past, a life, a chronology in these confessions, are there any incidents that can be said to make up a human destiny? History is true only insofar as it is experienced by the being who meditates on it; the past is never over, the chronological order of the incidents is changeable, a great number of facts come and go, while memory is unable to organize them. Memory always goes back to the beginnings, the *past* is open, all the fears and surprises experienced by the seven-year-old child are experienced over and over again by the sixty-year-old writer who records them.

Eugène Ionesco ignores the idea of a *contract* or *autobiographical agreement*; if such a thing exists in his works, it is utterly different from whatever we may imagine. First of all, the author says, *I am an other*, thus changing Rimbaud's famous statement. He compels the verb *to be* to agree with the pronoun.[1] Later on we realize that *I* is not an *other* at all, *I* is always one and the same, which the author himself states several sentences further, thus contradicting himself: *"Je c'est moi"* [I is me]. The strange thing about it is that none of these statements is false. Ionesco is always honest and right, even—or more so—when he happens to contradict himself. Since all these contradictions are his peculiar way of life, since he is unable to keep away from such accursed, unbearable relationships, he feels that he is called upon to make this statements. *I* is an *other*, of course, but this *other* is irrevocably, dramatically engulfed, overpowered, absorbed by the fecundity of an indomitable "moi." This is Ionesco's own image, out of which we can infer the place and power allowed to the author by the text. The first and most important certainty is that the *author* exists. There is no doubt about it; behind all masks, trapped in all kinds of incidents, bathing in the fresh light of childhood or in despairing confusion, we catch sight of the same Ionesco who *sees* himself in the guise of another but fails to be so, in fact, who, as we shall see, keeps retracing his steps into a remote past age, whence he returns with mere *fragments* and remnants, because he is unable to compel his *history* to yield more than that. Can he use these in order to build an image of his own life, to form a *view* of his past, like those other people who entertain no doubts as to their powers and history? Not really. The *fragments* refuse to form a whole, the repeated graspings are followed by no certainties.

As far as Ionesco is concerned, we can only be certain of one thing, namely, that, while considering his own history, past life, existence, and nature, he fails to find any certainty whatever. This paradox is not mine. One can find it at once in all the texts Ionesco has written. More often than not this is his way of turning impossibilities into possibilities, of making misanthropy look radiant. At this point, we become aware of the presence of Ionesco's *narrator*. This narrator is, beyond all doubt, unlike everybody else. Bewildered (the word is typical for Ionesco), this narrator describes the misfortunes and the blessings of the being. He is uncommonly eager to communicate what is incommunicable in an existence, to accept the irreparable, to venture into realms that common narrators are unwilling to approach, lands of shadows concealed within human beings. There is no end to his desire to be *bewildered* both by good and by evil, and his bewilderment is always accompanied by the force and innocence of a beginning. Ionesco's narrator is never exhausted by fatigue, and the most dreadful fears render him unbelievably loquacious, as if he were experiencing one revelation after another: the revelation of death, the revelation of Evil, the revelation of the outrageous human condition. Life is no feast, to be sure, but this artful narrator masters the art of the show; he can be firmly determined even when indecision and anxiety are at their highest. That is the reason not even a single page of this immense metaphysical diary (let us call it that for the time being) is either dull or prosaic. The narrator aims at other effects than those we might expect. The reader is bewildered in turn; here is a writer who describes the great misfortunes awaiting human destiny, yet whose sentences convey his intense delight in retelling all these misfortunes. In short, the unbearable history/existence is rendered bearable by the narrative.

It may prove interesting to consider the fate of the *character* in this text that allows the narrator to refute the author's premises systematically. This character escapes and returns to the narrative over and over again; he accepts his unacceptable condition and the victory in this battle is always his alone. But this victory merely enables him to begin everything all over again. The beginning is his favorite stage. Invariably waking up on the first morning of his affliction, one step away from his approaching unbearable condition, he sets out with fresh energy, firmly determined to cross the desert with his initial fears and hopes. For quite a while now, he has known, of course, what it is all about, what life consists of, yet he can bear no moment of dull rest; he harasses himself with unanswerable questions, he challenges those who claim to be wiser. *Why? How come? What am I? Who am I?*—such are the questions revolving within this autobiographical text, overwhelmed with both intense panic and the irresistible eagerness to speak out. The character escapes and returns to himself over and over again, bewildered, overwhelmed with despair, with the feeling that everything is irreparable, that life races death to some mad end. Nothing doing. Consequently, Ionesco's character accepts what is irreparable, but first of all he shows he is astonished that the irreparable should actually exist. Then he starts wailing about it, but he does so with such energy and resourcefulness that his lament comes out in the terms and colors of an incredible revelation. Ionesco "is an other" in a way, insofar as he "perverts" all concepts, moods, situations. Only this so-called *other* cannot go very far. He retraces his steps and, at the break of dawn, he once again finds himself on the doorstep of experience, willing to begin everything all over again, like the well-known mythical hero. He faces his destiny overwhelmed with amazement, indignation, and helplessness.

The meaning Eugène Ionesco attaches to *experience* is different from the one contemplated by Camus, Malraux, or Antonin Artaud. Experience has nothing to do with *adventure* and it does not end in tragic majesty. This experience takes place within the being. In Georges Bataille's words, it involves "putting the question (to the proof) in fever and in anguish of that which man knows is made of being." He goes on, "I call experience a journey to all that is possible in man" (321). It must be stressed that, to Ionesco's mind, experience is always accompanied by the impossible, the absurd, the inconceivable, the uncommunicable. Because they are all part and parcel of reality, a human being can only be understood in their company. The individual experiences an uninterrupted state of crisis and never stops wondering why. This is the main theme of the diary, the true explanation for what the above mentioned sentence called *I am*. When *considering himself or herself*, the creator is surrounded by all these concepts. Meditation does not help; the position will always be the same. The fact is recorded on one page after another. The *act of writing* may allow freedom to the spirit, but it will not exhaust its energy. "Le moi" keeps producing questions that are taken over by a "je" who carries them all over the place, staging them with inexhaustible gusto.

Consequently, in "Spring 1939," *Fragments of a Journal, Present Past, Past Present,* and *Découvertes*, we are faced with an *author* who makes no secret of his identity. The same person who gazes at us in bewilderment from the cover inhabits each and every page of the book; he is both the hero and the narrator of past and present incidents. He even warns us that he sometimes records things that have not come to pass: the presences, the epiphanies, as well as the absences, the occultations. This author takes everything upon himself, both victories and failures. He makes it very clear that his words cannot change his life. His is not an exemplary existence and he does not mean either to set a pattern or to introduce us to a likable character. On the contrary, he does his utmost to belittle his hero and dissuade the reader from imagining that a creator is bound to be sublime. The author is supposed to keep wondering about everything, to make an "issue" of existence (the French phrase cannot be translated). His calling is to treat the inevitable without the least sign of resignation. He knows he is mortal but he feels certain that he can at least ask his questions. He knows his condition is disgraceful, but he is determined at least to cry aloud that he finds his disgraceful condition disgraceful. The author is a playwright as well, and he confesses that his plays deal with his everyday life. We learn that life and literature share the same room within his mind. Only he does not say that the triumph and splendor of literature spring out of existential despairs and revelations. The readers are expected to guess at this guilty relationship.

By contrast, the *narrator* present in the text is unbelievably alert. He describes anxiety enthusiastically, his dramatic interrogations are recorded with such delight, in such a high-spirited manner, that the reader is perplexed. The narrator enjoys his glory, while the hero of so many misfortunes is caught like an insect in a net of contradictions. The narrator gambols, he makes all sorts of jokes while the author worries to death; the narrator's extremely resourceful and delightful imagination enjoys narrating the way in which the character is attacked by history and wounded by destiny. To put it briefly, Ionesco's autobiographical literature has three actors in its service: the *author*, who does the asking; the *narrator*, who is constantly *amazed*, unwilling to believe what he sees with his own eyes, and how redeeming force is remarkable; the *character* in question, who fails to find his place in a universe wherein initial innocence has been lost forever. Ionesco writes in order to protest against the universe being perverted. Moreover, he writes in order to bring back, to redeem the plenitude of a lost paradise.

There is a space and a time for beauty and delight in the world. There is somewhere a world of purity. It is the world, the time and space of childhood. Ionesco sees childhood as the paradise of human life. The only one there is, in fact. Unfortunately, too early and irrevocably, we are driven out of this paradise. Each of us reenacts the biblical fable in our own way. Ionesco did so at the age of four, when he realized that nothing and no one was everlasting. It was the end of innocence. The gates of paradise were closed behind him. Art alone can still enable him to go back to this realm wherein he is spared the awareness of his solitude.

The question is, can the solutions offered by art bring peace and satisfaction? The first pages of the diary ("Spring 1939") call up the "places of childhood." It is Ionesco's first return (the first one he records) to La Chapelle–Anthenaise, his paradise. His childhood was spent there, where there was a meaning to every life, to every object, where existence was always associated with joy. Ionesco, or rather the narrator (whoever that may be), remembers.

But already the past tense of the verb *to be* cautions us. "He was beautiful" when he was little, but what happened after that? Where is the beauty, where is the delight? Ionesco unravels the illusion early. The beauty and delight are behind, in a remote season, in a miraculous space where we try to re-enter. But we are never coming alone toward him. We are accompanied by a present that prevents us from reliving memories: *"Memories, mingled with present impressions, thronged to my mind, fragmentary and haphazard"* (*Photograph*, 127).

Malraux ignores childhood. Sartre hates it. Ionesco, pure and simple, adores it. His works of fiction and diaries are full of scenes of childhood, myths, and lights. Childhood and light are two essential themes in his works. They find themselves in a relationship of causality, and together they open toward a profound symbol: the symbol of salvation.

Fortunately, a place exists where a person who is alone and discouraged by existence can retreat again in the fullness of being and in the miracle of the universe.

It is the nest (the expression exists as such in the text) in which the spirit, tired from the harsh race against death, comes back to rebuild its forces. It is the primordial place, it is the space without fear, it is the time in which everything that exists has a justification and lives in harmony with itself. Ionesco's writing finds again its state of grace as soon as he comes near this sacred territory. A roar passes through the phrases, a new light falls on the words, the rhythm of the sentences accelerates. I don't have room to quote here the fragments in which the literature opens full of hopes toward the miracle of childhood

I choose a few. "Deep down in the heart of night there is a fresh spring, the light of childhood" (*Photograph*, 135). Then from the *Fragments of a Journal*:

There is a golden age: the age of childhood, of ignorance; as soon as one knows one is going to die, childhood is over. . . . Apart from childhood and forgetfulness there is only grace that can console one for existing or give one plenitude, heaven on earth and in one's heart. . . . How can we go on living without grace? And yet we do go on living. (20)

And further:

Childhood is a world of miracle and wonder: as if creation rose, bathed in light, out of darkness, utterly new and fresh and astonishing. The end of childhood is when things cease to astonish us. . . . The brave new world, the wonderland has grown trite and commonplace. That was our true Paradise, that was how the world was on the first day. Losing one's childhood means losing Paradise, becoming adult. You retain the memory, the longing for a present, a presentness, a plenitude that you try to recover by all possible means; to recover it or to compensate for it. (40)

In *Present Past, Past Present* the above quoted excerpt is repeated in full. In *Entretiens* he calls La Chapelle–Anthenaise "a place that heals anxiety" (13), which implies that childhood is the realm where he feels safe. In *Découvertes*, Ionesco confesses that the sole aim of his literature is "to describe that light, that amazement that is far stronger than anxiety" (60). Further on he states in the pathetic tone of utmost despair:

> How can I leave behind my beginning, my halo, my childhood, only to head for my end? I will not, I have no wish to do so, the rest is uninteresting. The beginning is what really matters. That is why I keep retracing my steps, trying to go back to where all beginnings start. . . . I feel that serenity has nothing to do with maturity. Serenity belongs to childhood alone. *The joyful acceptance of being and existence.* (78–79; italics added)

I will not continue the list. The same ideas are resumed in *Antidotes* and in *Un homme en question*. Mingled with all other symbols and themes, they bravely overcome anxiety. The theme of light and childhood is closely related to other themes of life and literature: the labyrinth of life, our inner hell, the disgraceful human condition, death, the theme of guilt, the theme of metamorphosis and that of the *engulfing mire*, the theme of history and the freedom it allows, the theme of science and of its powerlessness, and, once again, the theme of nightmarish existence and the escape from it.

The term *theme* has a particular meaning here. Ionesco is not so much interested in literature (not in these confessions, at least); he reviews the themes of literature while he *meditates upon himself*, his own existence. Caught in this complicated net of relationships, Proust's prudence and fears are alien to him. He does not make such a clear-cut distinction between existence and creation. He too dislikes biographers ("janitresses in the history of literature"), but, while narrating his life, he makes no secret of the fact that the source of his literature is the bustle of his own existence. We shall never know how faithfully this existence is recorded by these diaries (which are themselves *works of literature*, after all, *creations* first and foremost), but the diaries impress us as truly genuine.

Here, as in a number of other cases, Ionesco is unwilling to act like everybody else. Ionesco's autobiographical literature, like his other works, mirrors the author's determination to oppose whatever is constituted and threatens to affect the freedom of the mind. Like Flaubert, he firmly rejects all ready-made ideas. When innovating ideas tend to become prevalent, he uses the same firmness in rejecting them as well. As a rule, wherever everybody else may be going, Ionesco is not. He dismisses most ideas before they have had time to grow old. At a time when all French intellectuals were trying to humor their discontented youths, Ionesco wrote the proverbial sentence "The young people's revolt is ungrounded." It is hard to foretell what such an unpredictable author is likely to do next. At least, one expects him to be true to the condition of the creator, to speak his mind, to be brave enough to face us without a mask, and—as far as literature allows him—to deplore the human condition. By human condition Ionesco means our historical and, moreover, our metaphysical status.

Ionesco's articles and essays, whether they deal with a topical political issue or some trifling incident of early childhood, all lead to the idea of this condition; they start there and come back to the same point in the end. The natural order of *tenses* (i.e., times) and memories is disrupted. The moral and the spiritual biography are focused on several questions, there is no order in the narrative. Whoever means to draw up a chronology of the writer's life ends up in a sea of troubles. The author makes a point of effacing all directions. As we shall soon see, his *discourse* is actually meant to be an *antidiscourse*. The "janitress" of Ionesco's literature is undoubtedly in for very hard work. Her indiscretion costs her greatly. Where was this troublesome author born, in what family? There is no answer to this in the fragments from the diary, which were all shuffled like playing cards.

All incidents are gently led into analysis; as the author tells us somewhere, all memories are *broken to pieces*, invaded by a present much more vigorous than the past. Let us, however, try to capture a few moments from this *life* narrated by a writer who claims that his life will teach us nothing, that piecing it together is absolutely useless. First, we get the image of a moral, *reliable*, stable world—the world at Moulin, La Chapelle–Anthenaise. Its small deities are la mère Jeanette, le père Baptiste, Marie, le père Guene. The child is on his way to the confessional, the church bells peal, the sky is clear as if cleanly washed, the road is strewn with cobblestones, a brook babbles close by. The Mother is there too, for she is constantly present in Ionesco's confessions. The boy is determined to become a *saint* and hates anonymity. When he reads the life of Le Grand Condé,[2] he quickly makes up his mind to become a *general*. The *Father* is absent from this miraculous universe, at least for the time being. The fragments are reprinted almost identically by Ionesco in *Fragments of a Journal*. He adds several details, maybe. His mother comes to take him from the village, and he learns from her that they are going to move from the hotel. They have a flat in Paris, near aunt Sabine's house. That is all we are told. Another scene takes place in a kindergarten, not far from Paris. The child is repeatedly left there and feels intensely frustrated. His first intimation of death occurs when he is alone with his mother. "It was when I was with her that I thought about death, about her death, about my own. When I was alone, I mean without her, though with other people and children, I never, or hardly ever felt it" (22).

The *Father* turns up too, but in a different light. Ionesco provides us with all elements necessary to psychoanalysis. As a matter of fact, he psychoanalyzes himself, thus making an error that Freud had foreseen. It is the error of a man who psychoanalyzes himself, turns every incident into a proof in favor of a preconceived idea. Elsewhere—in *Parisian Diary* (Bucharest, 1977)—I have examined what meanings Ionesco attaches to the symbol of the Father. There I wondered whether someone who has already psychoanalyzed himself can be forced to lie down once more on the psychoanalyst's couch, to reveal what he was trying to hide when he tried to interpret his own complexes. I failed to notice an important detail at the time. I lit upon it while rereading *Present Past, Past Present*, Ionesco's harshest book. The author (narrator) warns us, "After all, one must not hide anything." As far as the Father is concerned, the author is as good as his word. He does not hide a thing, and his tone is invariably the same. There can be no doubt, Eugène Ionesco hates his father. It is his only resemblance to Jean-Paul Sartre. They have nothing else in common besides that. He does not deny that there may be good fathers in the world. The reason for this might be that at the time he was writing these diaries, Ionesco had become a father himself and, as can be inferred from the text, a very affectionate one at that. Montaigne claimed that his father had been "the best of all"; Rousseau, who complained about whatever there was in the world, did not speak ill of his father either. However, there seems to have been no love lost between Balzac and his mother, and if I am not mistaken Flaubert too is far from being fond of his father.

Ionesco is in a hurry to clear things up, he does not wait for interpretations in the matter. He writes a short psychoanalytical essay discussing the relationship between a resentful son (the phrase is his own) and a rude, ruthless father. Quite a number of significant images support the idea. *Present Past, Past Present* opens with the following sentence:

> I search in my memory for the first images of my father. I see *dark hallways* [italics added]. I was two years old, I think. In a train. My mother is next to me; her hair done up in a big bun. My father is across from me, next to the window. I don't see his face; I see shoulders and a suitcoat. Suddenly there's a tunnel. I cry out. (5)

Ionesco shows his skills as a stage manager here. Those who mean to spy a hostile relationship within these commonplace remarks are free to examine the order of words and their efforts need not go far beyond that. The author seems to remember his father and finds him in dark hallways. This is the first clue. *Next to me,* the mother. Another clue. *Across from me*—the father. The gradation is perfect, the strategy unequivocal. Son and Father *face each other* like true rivals. The mother is *on the son's side*. To make things even more obvious, the author adds that the son *does not see* his father's face. What follows is the *tunnel* and the *scream* of the frightened child. The order of these incidents is too logical, too meaningful. More images follow:

the father is bulky, tall, strong, and holds his son in his arms. But, once again, the son fails to see his face. While shopping, the father is dressed in a dark coat and the son is unable to see his countenance. A very short truce, a happy family scene (*"we are all joyous"*), with the father unexpectedly present. If I am not mistaken, this scene is the only one of its kind.

Very soon, the image is totally different, and for as long as we keep reading this second image is going to stay. A room: the mother and the daughter are out, father and son are alone at home. The father stands by the window—"in long underwear; he has already put on his black shoes. He is wearing garters. In his hand is an enormous razor" (*Present*, 9). Holding the huge shaving device in his hand, the father stands for the very image of paternal aggressivity, a typical symptom of the Oedipus complex. The father's (literary) body and the long underwear from now on are inseparable. Whenever the father steps into the text, he wears his disgusting long underwear. It is the emblem of vulgar, oppressive patriarchy. The above mentioned diary brings new evidence of that. In front of the hotel in Rue Blomet, the father is carrying a huge trunk. The son is four or five years old. Sometime later, in the early afternoon of a summer day, the father is lying on the bed, reading his paper. The tyrant's costume can easily be guessed: "he has long underwear, shoes, garters" (13). The son is playing with his sister nearby, and he happens to take away her toy. The father intereferes: on seeing that the dispute is not settled, he punishes the aggressor. The son is indignant and angry, but to his stupefaction, his mother fails to stand up for him. He masters his fury, but his revolt is fierce. He promises, "I will never be able to forget this humiliation" (13). At another time and place, the father is wearing a black overcoat, his figure dark. Semiotics may come in handy here. At home the father usually wears long drawers and garters. These are the signs of untidiness, triviality, and paternal cruelty. Outdoors, the father always wears dark clothes ("he wore none but a black overcoat"); he is solemn and "respectable." The opposition hints at an elementary Manichaeism. Ionesco makes no secret of that, hiding nothing of what he knows about the aggressive father, from ideology—which is usually favorable to history—to the long underwear that he wears at home.

What follows is the most meaningful detail, the worst proof of the accusation. The playwright feels his nature has been altered because of it. His confession is moving: "this memory . . . determined my outlook on life" (15) or "I owe everything to this initial fact; . . . I have the feeling that it is because of this memory that I hate authority, that it is the source of my anti-militarism" (16). The incident taking place in the house in Rue Blomet, is a marital quarrel that, seen from outside, does not seem terrifying at all. But the child who witnesses it sees it in a totally different light. The mother is weeping. After an altercation with her husband (the father), she grabs a bottle of iodine and takes it to her mouth. The father, "in his long white nightgown over his long underwear" (20), jumps out of bed and prevents her from continuing her desperate gesture. At this very moment, the son realizes the true face of the relationship between mother and father, between man and woman in general. The mother is "a puppet in my father's hands and the object of his persecution" (20). In his turn, since he himself is going to grow to be a man, the child feels guilty in advance. In 1947, when he records this atrocious incident, he is quite an experienced man, but he has not forgotten that feeling of guilt. "Being afraid of making women suffer, of persecuting them, I have allowed myself to be persecuted by them. It is they who have made me suffer" (21). Anyway, the above mentioned scene renders the son intensely unhappy. His relationship with his father is ruined for good.

> Come what may, he and I must be at odds until doomsday; before that, nothing can bring us together, our differences will not be forgotten. . . . Somehow, whatever I may have undertaken has been meant to prove I am not, I do not want to be, like him. . . .

Ionesco's father becomes a truly literary character. A negative one, some kind of mean demon. He is different from other, rigid, repugnant fathers in literature, because he is burlesque. The narrative systematically undermines his authority. When the father turns up, the light—blinding until then—leaves Ionesco's text. A sentence found at random in the 1968 diary: "A gray light, a yellow wall, the confused feeling of my father's presence." The meaning is obvious. Rhetoric uses no tricks in this paragraph. The father has all the shortcomings of the castrating father (in psychoanalytic literature), and all the vices of the social father. Ionesco depicts him as a *follower of history*, a man who cajoles history, an advocate of power. Very much like Sartre in a way ("the tyrants' advocate"), but devoid of the latter's philosophical existentialism. This means that the social father is essentially conformable, cowardly, and opportunist, a supporter of all parties and governments like the well-known Romanian playwright Caragiale's character Catavencu, who is the terror of his wife and children at home and switches from one party to another in public life, always claiming to be in the service of *history*. Ionesco's father prepares his doctor's degree in law in Paris, he studies reclining in bed, wearing *garters*, long underwear, and his immense nightshirt. He becomes a lawyer, a chief in the police force, joins the *right* before the war, then thinks twice and switches to the *left* to follow the major direction of history. This is only a meager summary of what Ionesco writes.

I cannot check the truth of these assertions, and it would be useless anyway. The Slatina lawyer may have been more than just a despicable *follower of history*. I hope that some day some bailiff of the history of literature may bring everything to light. A rather poor father, this tyrant in long underwear is, however, a perfect hero of fiction. In the same *extremist* manner, the author watches the man's civil and social life from afar. The father remarries, has more children, more quarrels, fights with his relatives. The witness (son) records everything and obviously enjoys narrating the life of this vaudeville father. Clearly, fathers are depicted as utterly devoid of glory by twentieth-century literature.

What about the *Son*? The son's biography abounds in gaps. The few facts we learn are enclosed in a meaningful mess. The truth of the matter is that the great playwright is not interested in the story of his acts. *Biographism* is of no use to the narrative of this *life* whose *epiphanies* are few. The diaries reveal few of the social events that shaped his destiny, in spite of the fact that in *Entretiens* he states that "one is altered by each new experience." The son once bullied by an absurd, comic father has become a writer in the meantime. This, at least, cannot be doubted. As a child, he felt that Paris was like a jail. He loved the village. He comes to Romania when he is thirteen, but does not feel at home here. He learns the language, graduates here, starts writing, publishes a book, but still "feels he is an exile." When he is seventeen or eighteen, he has a unique, decisive experience of a mystical nature. The experience has already been quoted. It implies the revelation of another world, another existence. He has archetypal, premonitory dreams; describing them, the resourceful man of letters invents, makes up *visions*, which he interprets himself using the help of specialists. Thus he creates oneiric literature of the best kind. I suspect that, just like I. L. Caragiale, Eugène Ionesco is superstitious. He may be, as will soon turn out, religious too. Let us examine his intellectual biography. He thinks that Romanian literature has not influenced him, that it has rather hindered his creative drive. I should say that this is not true, that Ionesco *is* indebted to Romanian literature, particularly to Caragiale, but that is another matter. Ionesco contradicts himself. Disgusted at the frivolity of western intellectuals, he says, "I hope I still have in me that Danube peasant I once was." He means that morally, I suppose.

What books have influenced him? Byzantine texts, Dionysius the Areopagite, Philokalia, Alain Fournier ("the model of my literary, dreamy adolescence").[3] He dislikes Gide's rhetoric. He owes his discovery of literature to Flaubert. His memories from Bucharest are blurred and oppressive. The playwright remembers with irritation, mentioning several names, however (Lovinescu, Vinea, Tudor Vianu, etc.).[4] I am sorry to say that his remarks on Balkan culture and sensibility are rather shallow. He even writes an absurd sentence: "The word *nation* ought to disappear from the dictionary" (181). Well, it has not, as we can all see. Ionesco's *bête noire* is Sartre. We have had enough evidence so far. We can bring more. One essay calls Sartre a small revolutionary conformist, another sees him as a superior rhinoceros, a subject of history, craving for power. In *Antidotes* Ionesco reproaches Sartre for "having counterfeited French intelligence too long" (10). Has Sartre left no fruitful landmark behind him, I wonder? I am afraid Eugène Ionesco exaggerates his reproaches, overdoing it, after all. He rejects all systems. I wonder whether he has ever happened to read Nietzsche's observation (*accepting a system—no matter which—denotes a lack of loyalty*), but it applies to him, anyway. Of course, the idea is debatable. Sometimes, unwillingly, we come to accept a system and obey certain norms. Whoever produces thoughts belongs to some system, after all, and has accepted a hierarchy of values. Even those who, like Ionesco, systematically reject all ideological systems, every method or morality, end by inevitably adopting one. As far as this charming nihilist called Ionesco is concerned, his is a system that denies all systematic coercion, a morality that rejects those already constituted.

Ideology breeds a particularly firm idiosyncrasy in the playwright. In *Antidotes* he states: "It is a titanic undertaking to expose the language of ideology and politics" (59). He mistrusts politics and is against all kinds of society "because they are all bad." He believes we are an easy prey to disorder and evil. His courage overpowers discouragement itself, but in spite of that he nourishes no hope as to the future of humankind (*Un homme en question*).

In the field of literature, Ionesco resorts to the same attractive nihilism. He is not prepared to be faithful to an idea forever. He is no fanatic, his opinions change as often as his moods. A fundamental sense of guilt presides over all intellectual activities. The writer who judges others in his diary is no exception. Ionesco avoids hypocrisy: "We are all mystified and we can all detect mystification" (*Découvertes*, 59). He is against arrogance and megalomania in criticism. He prompts all judges to look out for mystification ("one must never undertake a demystification of the demystifier," *Découvertes*). Lovers of methodology cannot depend upon Ionesco. In *Découvertes* he protests against the pedantry of *la nouvelle critique*: "a more conceited and more self-satisfied pedantry than that previously harbored by universities and older criticism" (11). We must admit that Ionesco is not always wrong. His faith in literature has its ups and downs. Elsewhere he says, "Literature is the only thing I am fit for. I was made for it" (73). Then he changes his mind and talks about his aversion to literature. This is all very natural. Most creators know what it feels like to hate what you are doing. Ionesco suspects that he is "chaotic and punctilious" at the same time. He adds, "Very often I am somewhere else." Does he travel much? Not really. He seldom makes up his mind to leave, and, when he does so, his only aim is to return to a *primordial condition*. Mircea Eliade ought to be invited to have his say here. An interest in *sources*, in *beginnings*, arises now. The ironical, the misanthropic, fearful Ionesco follows the ways of initiation. Incredible, isn't it? And yet, credible enough. Ionesco is a complex spirit, and, as he tells us himself, the comic outlook is in fact the outlook that allows more reality to tragedy. He firmly concludes that this comic outlook is the *starting point of the tragic*. Irony is one way of detecting and experiencing the absurd side of life.

There is nothing uncommon about the creator's biography if we take such a general, factual view of it. In order to penetrate the depths of his outlook on life, in order to understand his nature, one must examine his views upon two essential issues: *how must existence be considered* and *how must one write*. These issues seem to me to be the core of these diaries which abound in contradictory or repeated statements, whose moments of clarity and obscurity are dictated by reasons we shall never know.

The first issue has already been briefly considered. It must be added that, since Ionesco mistrusts all systems, he offers no definition for *existence*. He will not allow himself to get involved in philosophy, either his own or anybody else's. Existentialism looks suspicious to him. In spite of that, his texts provide the verb "to exist" with numberless connotations. Where should one start, I wonder? With a concluding statement, perhaps. Eugène Ionesco is a prophetic spirit, and his diaries often display accents of biblical despair. Why not try to read his books against the grain? In *Un homme en question* he writes, "We are all descended from Job" (213). And further:

> We ought to get together and protest against the creator. . . . There is a discontinuity between this world and the world beyond. That is what I feel. A discontinuity. We fail to understand the logic of it and consequently we are dissatisfied. Here is the first thing with which we could reproach the Creator: why are we denied the power of understanding? Why are we compelled to accept this game? (19)

Ionesco's fierce irony is here unsettled by metaphysical questions. Not only here, I should say; Ionesco's questions reach that level of the atmosphere where they can breathe the icy air of nothingness. Malraux states that, while considering death, Europeans are in fact highly concerned with the presence of life. It seems to me that Ionesco inverts their order. His thoughts of existence are in fact thoughts of death alone. Each new gesture pushes one closer to nothingness. This great comic spirit is "intensely vexed" by death. He sees the tragedy enclosed within the history of the human condition. It is a miracle that an individual stays alive, is able to survive: "Every morning I feel astonished I am still here. How come I am still alive?" (*Un homme*, 109). He adds then, "I have seen everything, everything has deteriorated" (113). Satan has become master of the world, God has withdrawn. "Good God waves to us from time to time. Only he is so far away" (114). The truth is that an individual is all alone.

Ionesco's plays hint at this despair. In these confessions, he takes everything upon himself. He is just as peremptory as before: "wrapped in our existence, we are all mastered by a fundamental ignorance. A major, capital, essential ignorance. A supreme misunderstanding" (142–43). Ionesco is not having fun, we can see that. Anyway, even when he seems to be having fun (as he does in *Exit the King*), he hints at things that are far from being funny at all. His literature reveals a deep sense of tragedy, a profound and very sad understanding. We are surprised, though, to see that these confessions have chosen the first person in order to speak of the same intense tragedy. The ideas do not change in *Entretiens*. "We are constantly in a state of crisis" (181). In *Fragments of a Journal*, "the thought of the end fills me with anguish and fury" (19). The existential uneasiness" is his permanent theme, his haunting obsession. It is always present in Ionesco's autobiographical writings, in his essays and political articles. What a curse, the writer exclaims, "because I am not sure of being once I have ceased to exist. Existence is the only mode of being I know, I cling to this existence, for I cannot, alas, imagine any mode of being apart from existence" (19). It may look like a clever pun, but these skillful sentences conceal deep sadness and despair.

It is obvious that Eugène Ionesco experiences (I cannot make up my mind to say conceives) existence as a forbidden joy rather than a burden. He feels that a person could be happy but is not, because the thought of death mars life. That is why he sometimes wishes he were outside of everything, while at other times he is more confident and believes that he might understand what *has not yet been conceived*. In *Fragments of a Journal* he writes, "The world is an epiphany, a splendid manifestation of divinity" (71). Further on we are blinded by the light of a suspicious rationalism: "It is absurd to say that the world is absurd" (83). Is it really? Ionesco must not be taken at his word. The next sentence wastes no time, it immediately sets about contradicting the statement that denies the absurd. There is not mysticism about Ionesco but, as has been seen, he does have a certain sensibility or rather intuition for signs from the world *beyond*. He actually uses words such as *manifestation, grace, trans-history*, but does not go into details. He is a religious spirit who has been denied a religion. At times he even waits for a Messiah, whom he sees standing behind the gate (*Present Past, Past Present*). He is not very hopeful, though, since we are presently told, "I have not altogether cut off the bridges to God" (40). Anyone knows that God will not come unless called for.

Ionesco's fright (a fundamental one, which determines his inner structure) is of an existential nature. He cannot distinguish *life* from absolute anxiety. "Fear" has been his companion since early childhood, he is certain that existence is an aggression. In *Present Past, Past Present* we find an image that tries to explain our past and present condition, which examines our behavior, the extent of our knowledge, our means of salvation. The image is far from cheerful, of course, "like a man going about with a lantern in the shadows, lighting only a tiny space around him as he advances. The luminous circle moves along with him and all the rest is in the deepest night or goes back into it again" (28). This is how the ironist looks upon life, then. *Did I really manage to reach the age of thirty, thirty-five?* he wonders in 1968. He has, by now, reached the age of seventy and is just as amazed at his having been able to bear this unbearable existence. Well, the human being is an animal that can come to terms with almost anything, the unbearable included.

"Torn to pieces between the horror of living and the horror of dying" (*Antidotes*, 81), he lives within *history* and wishes he could leave it. He advances an amazing idea: "to be free [is] to be out of history" (*Past*, 51). Is that possible? At least the playwright does his best to get out and anyway he is against the stream as often as he can be. Examining literature, he finds several famous people who were against the prevailing belief of their time, people like Poe and Baudelaire. In his latest books (*Antidotes, Un homme en question*), Ionesco violently attacks *History* and its heroes, Sartre first of all. Unavoidably, the writer's revolt against history is just another particular face of history. Those who wish to stay *out of history* finally realize that they inhabit one of its compartments all the same.

Ionesco warns us, though, that the reason for all this is hidden further away than we can imagine. His confession draws near metaphysics once again. This is one more occasion for him to distinguish himself from Sartre, whose hell was "other people." In the line of Byzantine mystics (the line of so many others, whether mystics or laypersons), Ionesco says, evil does not come from outside. It exists within us; hell is not elsewhere, hell is right here, "it is ourselves" (*Antidotes*, 326). Is there any way out of it, is there any hope left for humankind? As we have already seen, Ionesco advances no solutions, he is no more than an observer. He does not sound encouraging when he says that "the illness is inherent in the human condition. . . . Creation is a bust." We must not lose heart, though. He adds that "we are metaphysically alienated" and "the world may just as well be a huge hoax played by God upon man" (323–34). This last sentence reminds one of the famous Shakespearean line. Ionesco himself quotes it in one of his books, adding that it contains all the metaphysical wisdom of the English playwright. What about his own metaphysics? It is scattered here and there in these remarkable confessions, in his exaltation of *childhood*, of *primordial light*, of *beginnings*, in his biblical despair, in his horror of nothingness, in the violence of his protest against a destiny that forces mortality upon us. The most meaningful definition to be found in Ionesco's reflections is *humankind is being dedicated to death*.

Creation, the act of writing, must not be forgotten, though. Writing may be a way of life, even a way out for some. What does writing really mean to Ionesco, the man who questions everything? His statements in this respect are not always identical. It must be said from the very beginning that this man, who constantly *considers* himself with the eyes of his mind, never lets literature out of his sight. The verb *to write* never fails to follow the verb *to exist*. In "Spring 1939" the author claims he is fed up with writing: "I am busily writing, writing, writing. I have been writing all my life. I have never been able to do anything else" (*Photograph*, 135). That is not news. A lot of people believe that they are doomed to write and that literature is their only calling. Ionesco, however, adds another idea that undermines the former.

There is nothing wrong with writing, but can it achieve anything, has literature got any power at all?

"Literature is powerless," Ionesco concludes. "I can communicate this catastrophe to no one, not even to my wife. This unendurable thing dwells within us, shut in. Our dead remain with us" (146). We could add that they are ours, indeed, but they also belong to the text (*écriture*), since the author who claims in this diary he can convey his thoughts to no one is, in fact, communicating the incommunicable. This paradox is not new. Ionesco himself makes use of it more than once. It even breeds a theme in his diary: *the futility of keeping a diary*. This theme is to be found in "Spring 1939" as well:

> And why am I writing this journal? What am I hoping for? Whom can these pages interest? Is my unhappiness, my distress communicable? Who would take on that burden? It can have no significance for anyone. Nobody knows me. If I were a writer, a public figure, it might perhaps assume some interest. . . . And yet surely I am like everyone else. Anybody can therefore recognize himself in me. (148)

There is a very sophisticated rhetoric in all this. Its effect is enhanced by the drama of Ionesco's thought, which breaks in the middle of the sentence and takes the opposite course. And yet it looks like more than a mere rhetorical game. The broken idea conveys the insecurity of the mind. To use Ionesco's own words, this amounts to being certain about the uncertain. At times, within the space of several sentences, the mind climbs up and down both sides of an idea, as is evident in the excerpt above. The author argues both for and against keeping a diary—and writing in general.

In *Entretiens* he again advances an idea that brings him close to Sartre, closer than he might have wished. Sartre repeatedly said that *writing* originates in some kind of neurosis. In one of his interviews in *Le Monde* (May 14, 1971) he explained that *The Words* was written in order to reveal "the origins of my insanity, my neurosis." In his incisive, determined manner, Ionesco meets Sartre at this point. "I think literature is a form of neurosis. Where there is no neurosis, there is no literature either . . ." (Bonnefoy, 42).

To me he appears to be both right and wrong at the same time. Sometimes I have the feeling that Ionesco behaves toward himself in the manner of those medical students who imagine that they suffer from all the illnesses they read about. In *Fragments of a Journal* the author himself wonders: "I put too much faith in the myth of psychoanalysis" (80). Let us return to the *act of writing* now. In *Entretiens* Ionesco confesses to Claude Bonnefoy an idea that is characteristic of him. "Why did I write my first play unless it was to prove that nothing really mattered, nobody was really alive, whether literature or theatre, life, or values" (Bonnefoy, 63). We are not surprised, we already know the author's technique. It always ends in affirming a negation or denying an affirmation, which amounts to one and the same thing. I mean to say that it ends in a demonstration of intelligent speculation. There is nobody like Ionesco in this respect. His favorite position is the *opposition*. At a time when writing comes of itself—as somebody put it—Ionesco claims that "all literature renders, records what I see, what I think" (Bonnefoy, 73). Recovering from an illness, he writes *Exit the King*. All works spring from a nightmare. He only writes as a consequence of some *odd mental metabolism*, when something *abnormal* has taken place within himself ("some deteriorated or secondary impulse"). I understand from all this that he does not write because he is satisfied and happy to be alive; he only writes when his inner hell compels him to do so.

The act of writing induces a certain confusion, which may be exhausting at times. In *Fragments of a Journal* we find: "Oh, how I hate that verb *to write*" (24). Or even worse: "Today the thought that I've got to write fills me with sheer horror. Today, when I begin to write there stirs within me an even keener and more intolerable awareness of the tragedy, the danger, the universal anguish" (28). This amounts to saying that writing fails to bring peace of mind; it breeds horror instead. Literature arouses universal happiness. It is a frightening experience. And yet Ionesco does not reject it; he even records the thought of his spirit being so fiercely challenged. He continues writing, in spite of his conviction that "art brings no light at all."

To a certain extent, *Découvertes* is Eugène Ionesco's *ars poetica*. We find here most of his ideas on literature and even the act of writing. Whoever expects an orderly list of clear, immovable aesthetic principles will be greatly disappointed. Ionesco will never allow himself to be pinned down to one section of aesthetics or another. His principles are governed by his existential moods, by his unpredictable humors. His moods and ideas can, however, be classified and explained, if necessary. We can attach to each of them at least one out of the huge mass of contradictory meanings. The *work*, for instance, is for Ionesco an opportunity to ask, not to answer. That is no news. Still, Ionesco writes in order to alleviate his fundamental anxiety and return to the light of childhood. We know that too, but we are glad to find it stated here with surprising clarity. "All along, I have been writing books in order to talk about this light, about this astonishment that is stronger than anxiety, this overwhelming anxiety of mine" (*Découvertes*, 60). In the act of writing, the author "returns to and recreates the past." The writer adds a moving confession, which obliterates the idea that literature is a futile torture:

> The great surprise, the intense joy of literature comes from the fact that the writer is amazed to discover his own image in the process of contemplating the worlds, or the world, as if he himself had become the mirror. This image of himself is not horribly disgraceful any more; he sees himself integrated in and supported by a rich, immense, universal context. (91–92)

These sentences convey calm joy; the creator finds himself at peace with himself and the outside world. Ionesco's intense anxiety is rarely visited by such privileged moments. Literature is almost a renewal of life. Literature "redeems the unuttered" (96). Wonderful words. Ionesco follows the road of light now. What is the experience of literature? "Forgetting the world in order to be able to go back, or, rather, to reach it" (107), which implies reaching the plenitude of the world, the primordial wholeness, the light that preceded disorder, confusion, and despair. All this is beautiful, indeed. When writing, one reinvents everything there is, one reinvents the words themselves, whose existence only becomes real when they are uttered or written. The light of childhood seen as an everlasting morning pervades this text: "Everything must be reinvented, word by word. Nothing is ever repeated. Everything must be started anew, since it appears for the first time." Whoever reads these confessions catches a glimpse of that pride the creators have known from of old, namely, that they actually bring about and make known the beginning of the universe. This conceited thought brushes Ionesco's shoulder too. He feels that literature must help us step aside from *history* in order to go back to the origins, to the primordial state, to that world that was unaware of the existence of death.

This reverie is appealing, it promises a short escape from the clutches of absurd relationships. Ionesco does not indulge in it for long, though. It is present again in *Antidotes*: "I am in search of a world marked by initial purity, of the heavenly light of childhood, of the glory that presided over the first day of the world" (316). Soon, the tone changes: "One writes in order to stay at least partly alive." This hope cherished by the creator is not new, it has traveled a long way since ancient times. It sounds incredibly (desperately) genuine in this diary.

But then what meaning can be attached to the *act of writing*? Eugène Ionesco feels that the act of writing encloses everything, good and evil, horror and relief from it. Is *l'écriture* a means of redemption? Maybe, though only insofar as it can stir anxiety. It is a source of light, if it is able to redeem the miracle of childhood. But, in order to redeem this miracle, literature must cross the space of an existence afflicted with the idea of death. To put it more clearly, in the act of writing Ionesco experiences (records) a fundamental anxiety, which he means to preserve, in spite of the fact that his being is overwhelmed with it. The act of writing cannot relieve, it fills and refills. Literature may be an escape from existence, but it is also a challenge to shrink from no experience. It may be an attempt to step aside from history, but, at the same time, it pits this history against destiny. The creator's joy and grief come simultaneously from both ends of the awareness that one belongs to two worlds at once: the proximity of both life and death, the proximity of both history and an eternity by which history is repelled. Ionesco's remarkable art turns this fundamental Manicheism of his mind into an impressive performance. The roots of this Manicheism can be detected, though to a very little extent, in the diaries. Ionesco's spectacular art, by contrast, scatters it and surrounds it with multiple meanings. One must not forget, after all, that all confessions turn into literature, they can only exist as literary texts. All our screams, whether caused by suffering or by joy, are bound to pass through the gates of rhetoric.

I shall return now to an idea recorded at the beginning of this essay. Ionesco's art alters the *discourse*, turning his confessions into literature. This is as much as to say that the creator's *life* becomes a source of literature and harbors the alterations of whatever can acquire a literary nature. The ideas must undergo this *perversity* of the act of writing: "any act of writing is a perversity, a (special) sort of activity that means to shatter the subject, to smash and scatter it all over the page" (Barthes, *Sur la littérature*, 16–17). The effects of this are many. An essential one is the fact that *experiences* are loaded with literary connotations; recorded on paper, an existence is unavoidably looked upon as a literary work. The quality of expression confers upon autobiographies, diaries, and memoirs a *literary quality* that must be analyzed in itself. Under such circumstances, what is a literary critic supposed to do? I should hardly say this job is an easy one. The critic is in the position of one who is expected to read a literary text while being fully aware that its substance has very little to do with "literature." Is the critic supposed to use here the standards analysis resorts to when examining a work of fiction? Ambiguity and indecision still haunt this critic when finally leaving the precincts of this essay. Here is Ionesco's case, for instance. He is determined to tell us everything about himself, but his *everything* is enclosed within language and filtered by an *écriture* that, as far as Ionesco is concerned, is always full of surprises. *I am an other*, he tells us. Later, however, we realize that this—inevitably literary—discourse invests the *I* with implications that the author himself could hardly foretell. Why should his readers be expected to foretell them?

Let us examine more closely this discourse, which is usually more than just autobiographical, which observes no obvious chronology, and which takes place on several narrative levels at once. First of all, Ionesco's diary, unlike most writers' diaries, is not meant to supply information. The author is very much in a hurry to express his doubts as to the use of keeping a diary.[5] As a matter of fact, he even promises that the page *he has just written will never be printed at all. The promise is fortunately forgotten. Denials are part of his strategy. Ionesco's autobiographical discourse—as I have already pointed out—is a kind of antidiscourse*, a defiance of all norms, a stubborn attempt at escape from literature. We see here the failure of Ionesco's attempted escape: literature soon takes hold of this confession that protests against the private life being tampered with by literature. In his own, inimitable manner, Ionesco sees in all this a true drama, a fantastic performance.

It can hardly be denied that Ionesco's text is, indeed, subtly perverse. Let us examine, for instance, the way in which the discourse is repeatedly interrupted. The effect is that life appears as a heap of broken images, a sequence of disconnected incidents, moods, memories that fail to form a "whole"; the author's awareness makes a tragic attempt at piecing everything together, failing to enclose the whole in its airy embrace. This image of *existence* cannot be conveyed by means of a coherent, orderly discourse. When brought together, these fragments outline the image of a stupefied, irritated awareness, which is absolutely determined to make head or tail of a destiny that obeys nothing and no one at all. There is no orderly *history* within a destiny, and the narrative enjoys emphasizing its discontinuities.

This inability of the discourse to come into being is viewed with despair, and yet jubilation pervades the racing sentences, their easy flow. Ionesco's sentences are short and striking; there is room enough for each word to breathe. The idea is always moving, it races with a young man's enthusiasm toward its absurd goal, then comes back as if enlightened by a discovery that fails to overcome it. Very soon we see this idea bouncing again, on its way to another obstacle; it is as energetic, as innocent, as eager to find plenitude as before. In a confession we read, "It is the sadness of my mother, it is the revelation of death, it is the solitude again of my mother." Near the end of *Découvertes* we read:

> I see myself wishing to grasp the world. The more I am interested in this grasping, the more it escapes me. It is never enough. I am insatiably greedy. At such point I am exhausted by desires and feasts, and from being so replete, empty and full all at once, that I sink, I break. . . . From fleeting shadows or, perhaps from heavy impenetrable masses, a passion, a devouring rage devours me: me, the greedy one, who is no more than me. I no longer see beings. I no longer see being. (124)

The confession is undoubtedly tragic, yet the repetitions clothe this grief in lively colors and accelerate the pace of ideas.

The alertness of Ionesco's language is a sign of the extraordinary vitality of a spirit threatened by an overwhelming anxiety. The *act of writing* fails to dispel this anxiety, but at least it renders it bearable. Those who read Ionesco's intensely sad confessions are never sad themselves; something (the uncommon art) prevents them from despairing when they read about the despair of life. This realm of desolation is not utterly dark: in there, the light of creation, the force of words, enables us to consider our metaphysical destiny, as viewed by a writer who starts by complaining that he knows nothing, that he is amazed at what he sees, at what he experiences. His manner of saying all this is far more important than the statements themselves. I am not the first to notice that Ionesco enjoys trifling with earnest ideas. He does so, beyond doubt, but as a reader of his confessions, I cannot say I felt cheated. His texts reveal a fundamental innocence, an appealing modesty. Unlike Malraux, Ionesco is repelled by grandeur. He is not eager to be in the company of mythical individuals; scared and humiliated, he converses with himself and refuses to build a pattern for life out of his own nightmare and insolence. He prefers building an antimodel, but the force of his creation ends by making a model of it, all the same. Ionesco declares: there is the world on the one hand, and I on the other hand, "caught in the world." "I am being robbed by whatever there is. I am never my own home. . . . As a matter of fact, *I* is a *moi*." Is the ultimate sentence ("I am an other") very far from this one? The latter seems to add to the former a certain awareness of solidarity among *the others*, the feeling that the human species is doomed to solitude.

Ionesco's beings experience a continuous "disarray," an immense "bewilderment," they are scared to death by the destiny that is theirs and that they are hardly able (if at all) to understand. I seem to see these beings walking backward, heading for the future (a future which means nothingness), their eyes riveted on the light of lost childhood.

28

Barthes:
The Return of the Author to the Text

Camera Lucida

C*amera Lucida* was published shortly before Roland Barthes's death. Having, in fact, been written for other purposes, this essay acquires the value of a testament, in spite of its author's wishes. Whenever an important cultural figure leaves this life, we try to detect premonitions in his last work. One thing is certain: Roland Barthes was taken unawares by death. *Camera Lucida* is the feast of a spirit that has shaken off all constraints. After *The Empire of Signs*, this is the most impressionistic work written by the semiologist Barthes. He ventures into a land unknown to him (that of *photography*), just as he had earlier ventured into the Japanese world of signs. He had discovered there a vast, intricate *ideogram*. He decoded it (or at least he tried to) and, in the process, he experienced an inner tempest. The *texts* he had read until then, the *meanings* he had acquired, suddenly became meaningless: "Japan has starred him with any number of flashes" (4).

To a certain extent, photography is a small *empire of signs*, a concentrated ideogram. In what way should it be analyzed and decoded? What attitude should we adopt before this "emanation of the referent," inevitably placed in the past? Faced with such questions, Barthes rediscovers the joy of confessions. The semiologist goes all the way back to the old, despised, ridiculed art of impressionism, whose method is to do without a method. Analysis turns into confession, the author reappears in the text. In *The Pleasure of the Text*, I remember Barthes saying that the text had struggled free from the author's "formidable paternity." *Camera Lucida*, on the contrary, reveals to us the presence of the author within the text; the reader is attracted by the essayist's easygoing, self-indulgent analysis in which subject and object are all mixed up. Barthes broaches the subject of photography, soon changes his mind and talks about himself and his family, about death, then goes back again to his own moods in the presence of certain images. In this new, brilliant type of analysis, Barthes manages to redeem the analyst's right to be present. The analyst is no longer a stern, impersonal figure posted in the margin of the text. We find

191

him involved in his analysis, willing to take possession of his subject in his own particular critical manner. The essayist talks here in the first person: "I like bells, church clocks, . . . I like certain biographical traits in a writer's life, I find them as delightful as certain photographs, . . . there are times when I positively hate photographs . . . ." *To like, to hate, to enjoy,* these are essential verbs in the texts of Anatole France and Jules Lemaître.[1] Roland Barthes renounces impersonal moods, in favor of others that are now intensely personal. He switches from *they say* to *I say,* from *on* to *je.*

Another surprise: Barthes's analysis acquaints us with his own biography. The essayist had tried to do so in *A Lover's Discourse.* In both cases he focuses upon the image of his mother. To a certain extent, the essay on photography is a meditation on death, its tone openly melancholy. The paradox, so much cherished by Barthes, is still present but is gradually replaced by a vague need to grasp and convey essences. There is more to criticism than the pleasure of wit; one can go deeper than the mere ability of overturning the obvious. Great criticism must aim at being more than a spiritual challenge; it must be pervaded by the determination to convince.

During his uninterrupted progress Barthes rediscovers several standards belonging to traditional criticism. He adapts them to his views, even changing them, but they are not overlooked. Gérard Genette and some others do their best to join *la nouvelle critique* to *history* (diachrony). Barthes does even more: he forces analysis back into the first person of the present indicative, his critical approach has a more *human* air of *subjectivity,* and, most importantly, in spite of the change, the critic manages to preserve his original theoretical standpoint. He mistrusts the "local imperialisms" of semiotics. Consequently, he has to *adjust* his method. That is why he allows free play to subjectivity and imagination, placing the object of his analysis in an area of "intimacy." His aim is no longer or not only to *challenge,* to overturn commonly accepted truths, compelling the spirit to trust possibilities and verisimilitude. He seems to have abandoned *preterition,* too, which once enabled him to convey his ideas while apparently denying them. Barthes sounds more direct here; the plays upon ideas seem to appeal to him less. The analyst is haunted by one and only one idea: the overwhelming obsession with death. And death is not to be trifled with.

On the one hand, Barthes's manner looks simpler here; on the other hand, it becomes rather complicated, too, since it professes to be sincere—it is a confession—while, as a matter of fact, sincerity is often absent and sometimes confessions fail to reveal anything. Here he is, for instance, commenting on a photograph: his mother's image, at the time of her childhood, in the *Winter Gardens.* His remarks are subtle, elegiac, intensely melancholy. We hear the *son's* voice uttering thoughts undoubtedly sincere and genuine. Nevertheless, the semiologist is trying to catch us in a trap. He refuses to print the image (out of slyness? shyness? superstition?).

We find in his book all the photographs he is talking about, except this one. The analyst hides it from us, refusing to expose it to view and avoiding both our approval and disapproval. He seems to be protecting the intimacy of a relationship. When the confession looks hardly rhetorical at all, the author consciously or not suddenly comes up with a rhetorical device. He resorts to the need for propriety or protection, which results in driving the object out of the text. Barthes acts like a jealous painter who, at the last moment, decides to expel from the exhibition the portrait of the woman he loves, afraid it might be soiled by defiling eyes.

And yet, more than a confession, *Camera Lucida* is a study dealing with an indefinite topic: the "highly uncertain art" of *photography*, as Barthes puts it. Furthermore, this art is utterly unknown to the analyst, and he makes no secret of his ignorance: "I am not a photographer not even an amateur photographer" (*Camera*, 9). Despite all that, he is an excellent *reader* of images, and a resourceful aesthetician of photography, too (he never says so himself, but I think we are entitled to grant him this ability). Or maybe it was reckless of me to use the word *aesthetician*. Barthes is far from being an aesthetician in the common, stern meaning of the word. His intellectual ability prevents him from becoming a legislator, a *Guelph* of art. His hobby is to pull down, he delights in defying all laws, even those issued by himself. A definition for Barthes ought to read: a spirit that struggles toward a method only in order to blow it up. Or maybe, a Ulysses of textual criticism, resorting to a number of tricks, he steals into each work as if it were a Troy that must open a door to approximation and verisimilitude.

Then let us forget the words "aesthetician of photography" and stick to the words "reader of photographic images," which seem more adequate. His particular way of reading is "polysemous," it advances and withdraws at the same time; it is first overwhelming and engrossing, then suddenly turns cold, gazing with *indifferent* eyes at an image that slips further and further away, as if it had been rejected.

Roland Barthes warns us that the life of an image relies upon three persons: the *photographer* (who takes the photo), the *spectator* (who reads the image), and the *referent* (who is photographed). Barthes claims to be a mere *spectator* but rejects detachment and indifference. He is a spectator who can read an ideogram and produce unexpected interpretations. One of his clues is that every photograph hides some horror—"the return of death," a *specter*. All images are signs of mourning, promises of death, in spite of the fact that a photograph is meant to elude time, to pin a memory down, to immortalize some gesture, a particular moment in life. A Photograph is, as Barthes tells us (in his text the word is capitalized), "never, in essence, a memory (whose grammatical expression would be the perfect tense, whereas the tense of the Photograph is the aorist), but it actually blocks memory, quickly becomes a counter-memory" (*Camera*, 91).

Consequently, a Photograph has nothing Proustian about it (it fails to recall the past): its melancholy air and its pathos are caused by the fact that it is "an image devoid of a code," deprived of the right to share the future. A photograph cannot convey things that have *ceased to be*, because it merely records *what was*, which means that it contains an irrevocably ended, lost incident. Barthes does not take his time in playing upon words here: *what has ceased to be* is a phrase suggestive of some movement, of some recent parting, of a certain relationship established between spectator and referent. Unfortunately, no photograph can comply with this face of the past. It merely offers the terrifying image of an end, the nothingness into which all things flow. There is nothing immovable and irreversible except *what was*.

We have here a peculiar way of reading. Unlike most of us, Barthes ignores the power of images to go on inhabiting our memory, thus defying time. In the triumphant capacity of a photograph to preserve life, Barthes detects death, not unlike Baudelaire, whose eye replaces the beauty of present youth by the worm-eaten corpse it is going to become. The difference between them is that Barthes examines (i.e., contemplates) the image at a time when death has already occurred. The contemplation of a photograph is, then, a kind of posthumous acknowledgment of its existence. Consequently, analysis obtains the effects—and peculiar delight—of an autopsy. Barthes refuses to see beyond that: "the photograph is like old age: even in its splendor, it disincarnates the face, manifests its genetic essence" (*Camera*, 105).

Though unaware of it, the essayist mainly focuses on the theme of death. When he had started writing about photography, the spirit was free to go anywhere it chose; before Barthes has had the time to find his bearings, his spirit makes him face the void. Looking at photograph after photograph, choosing and ordering images, he suddenly feels as if he were rearranging a churchyard. All beings are either dead or on the point of dying; the hand of death touched them at the very moment they allowed themselves to be photographed. What is to be done, then? The semiologist dispenses with the *studium*, *punctum*, *noeme*, *eidos* of photography and starts talking about his own future fate, about his premonition of death. Photographs are now considered in a mood of solitary meditation:

> It is because each photograph always contains this imperious sign of my future death that each one, however attached it seems to be to the excited world of the living, challenges each of us, one by one, outside of any generality (but not outside of any transcendence). Further, photographs, except for an embarrassed ceremonial of a few boring evenings, are looked at when one is alone. I am uncomfortable during the private projection of a film (not enough of a public, not enough anonymity), but I need to be alone with the photographs I am looking at. Toward the end of the Middle Ages, certain believers substituted for collective reading or collective prayer an under-the-breath prayer, interiorized and meditative (*devotio moderna*). Such, it seems to me is the regime of *spectatio*. The reading of public photographs

is always, at bottom, a private reading. This is obvious for old ("historical") photographs, in which I read a period contemporary with my youth or with my mother, or beyond, with my grandparents, and into which I project a troubling being, that of the lineage of which I am the final term. (*Camera*, 97–98)

The recurring image of these interpretations is that of the mother. This is not the first time we hear Roland Barthes talk about his childhood, about the tender affection he felt for his family. As a matter of fact, his family is his mother. I do not think Barthes ever mentioned his father in his writings. I have even suspected him—who knows, it might be true after all—of fashioning his biography to fit into a psychoanalytical pattern. In the same way, I suspect Eugène Ionesco's diaries of exaggerating certain facts concerning the father's presence (or absence) in order to compel his biography to conform to the Freudian pattern. His grudge against paternal authority is greatly exaggerated, its literary effects enhanced in quite a number of ways. Barthes is more discreet in these matters; his grudge, if it exists, can only be inferred from the father's total absence—from the text under discussion at least.[2] *Camera Lucida* is forbidden to focus upon photographs of the father. By contrast, the text, especially its second part, abounds in references to the mother. The twenty-fifth fragment of the forty-eight opens, "Now, one November evening shortly after my mother's death, I was going through some photographs. I had no hope of 'finding' her, I expected nothing . . ." (*Camera*, 63), and the confession continues by quoting first from Proust and then from Valéry.

This is the beginning of a retrospective text, which strives to redeem the lost happiness of the past in Proust's manner. The narrator Barthes pursues a heroine who will not reveal her identity. The author (narrator) is haunted by one essential question: "Did I *recognize* her?" Photographs are of very little help; masks (every photograph is a mask, after all) can only reveal little fragments. The reader fails to see the whole. He feels so disappointed by the powerlessness of the image. Yet, in the long run, the reader comes across the very old photograph of a little girl in a winter garden. The image enables Barthes to retrieve his mother, to identify her in the fixed appearances of supreme innocence. If one were to find a related symbol, one might say Orpheus ends by finding Eurydice in the world of shadows and brings her back to life for a short while. The essay that narrates all this steers into lyricism:

I studied the little girl and at last rediscovered my mother. The distinctness of her face, the naive attitude of her hands, the place she had docilely taken without either showing or hiding herself, and finally her expression, which distinguished her, like Good from Evil, from the hysterical little girl, from the simpering doll who plays at being a grownup—all this constituted the figure of a sovereign *innocence* (if you will take this word according to its etymology, which is: "I do no harm"), all this had transformed the photographic pose into that untenable paradox which she had nonetheless maintained all her life: the assertion of a gentleness. In this little girl's image I saw the kindness which had formed her being immediately and forever, without her having inherited it from anyone; how could this kindness have proceeded from the imperfect parents who had loved her so badly—in short: from a family? Her kindness was specifically *out-of-play*, it belonged to no system, or at least it was located at the limits of a morality (evangelical, for instance); I could not define it better than by this feature (among others): that during the whole of our life together, she never made a single "observation." This extreme and particular circumstance, so abstract in relation to an image, was nonetheless present in the face revealed in the photograph I had just discovered. "Not a just image, just an image," Godard says. But my grief wanted a just image, an image which would be both justice and accuracy—*justesse*: just an image but a just image. Such, for me, was the Winter Garden Photograph. (*Camera*, 69–70)

This is not the first time that Barthes lends himself to psychoanalysis. Let us take, for instance, the classical substitution: the son devotedly tends to his sick mother, who seems now to be once more the innocent little girl preserved by the photograph taken in the *Winter Gardens*. In other words, the *Son* replaces the *Parent* (the substitution is twofold, as a matter of fact):

At the end of her life, shortly before the moment when I looked through her pictures and discovered the Winter Garden Photograph my mother was weak, very weak. I lived in her weakness (it was impossible for me to participate in a world of strength, to go out in the evenings; all social life appalled me). During her illness I nursed her, held the bowl of tea, . . . she had become my little girl, uniting for me with that essential child she was in her first photograph. . . . Ultimately, I experienced her, strong as she had been, my inner law, as my feminine child. (*Camera*, 71–72)

Barthes warns us elsewhere that he intends in principle to forget two institutions, the *family* and the *mother*. Does he really? Obviously not, at least not in the texts discussed so far. His mother is his family: nothing else matters. She epitomizes whatever is irreducible and unspeakable in his life.

For what I have lost is not a Figure (the Mother), but a being; and not a being, but a *quality* (a soul): not the indispensable, but the irreplaceable. I could live without the Mother (as we all do, sooner or later); but what life remained would be absolutely and entirely *unqualifiable* (without quality). (*Camera*, 75)

I read a certain meaning of my own in this confession: while endeavoring to retrieve the mother's lost image, the text (*écriture*) acquires its *quality*, becomes irreducible, *irreplaceable*, and it can at last be *qualified*. The same rhetorical device was used by Barthes in *A Lover's Discourse*. While saying that the loss of his mother has rendered him unable to *qualify*, he proves the opposite; the very discourse that mourns for the loss of Barthes's ability to *qualify* manages to preserve it, after all. Barthes's text (like all essays) does two things at the same time: first it records an absence, then sets about retrieving it, in the process of suggestively formulating (expressing) the absence.

One thing is certain: Barthes the author becomes here identified with the narrator (essayist), and the essayist (narrator, author) takes active part in the progress of his analysis. Starting from the photographs taken by Alfred Stieglitz, Nadar [Felix Tournachon], Nicephore Niepce, Alexander Gardner, André Kertesz, he finds himself talking about the photo in the *Winter Gardens*, about himself, that is. There comes a time when Barthes the reader starts looking for himself in other people's images. Is this an old-fashioned way of reading? It looks more like a rediscovery of an old pleasurable act, a subjective way of reading, which brings back the old commerce between *author* and the *text*.

I cannot say that Barthes goes so far as to deny the autonomy of the text, but something seems to have gone wrong there: until now an exile, violently thrown out, past use, the author comes back—the author may not return as a ruler but is not powerless either, and that is a fact. In *Camera Lucida*, the author becomes identified with the *inner reader* (if we may use that term): a reader enclosed within the text, a reader who, to a certain extent, becomes identified with the author's name. This inner reader voices part of the truths that are supposed to reach the other, true reader (the *reader without*), the unknown reader who opens the book. The latter is expected to detect even what the former (the narrator) hides. The reader must unveil the latent message of the work.

All along, Photography as an art is being analyzed, too. Does Barthes resent its uncertainty? Not in the least. Several remarks have already been cited. There are others, as well. One of them explains how difficult it is to define the essence (*eidos*) of Photography, the paradox that it cannot or will not avoid: "On the one hand the desire to give a name to Photography's essence; . . . on the other the intractable feeling that Photography is essentially . . . only contingency, singularity, risk" (*Camera*, 20).

This means that nothing essential or final can be said about this art that changes its subject into an object, which turns the body into an image. We do learn some things about Photography, nevertheless. We read, for instance, that a photographic portrait is a "closed field of forces," that a photographer who wants to make one must strive hard in order to prevent the photograph from becoming an image of death (the meaning has already been enlarged upon).

One of Barthes's next distinctions is of utmost importance. It is concerned with the *act of reading* and the *essence* (nature) of Photography at the same time. Barthes explains that the relationship between the photographic image and its reader (interpreter) is governed by two things: *studium* and *punctum*. *Studium* implies more than just the act of studying; it suggests a wider range of interests, as well as application and the ability to view the image as a whole, to discern the background, the countenances and gestures, the acts recorded by a photograph. *Punctum* is a certain peculiarity of the photo, something that hurts, "pinches," "pricks" the reader's sight. The analyst's eye may be caught by some detail that can easily be overlooked at first sight: the necklace round a woman's neck, the gesture of a child in some remote corner of the photo, the disposition of furniture. *Punctum* leads toward the essence of the image, it is the *living* soul of a dead image, so to say. I feel this *punctum* could be replaced by a term first used by Gide, later inherited by the theory of *le nouveau roman*: "dropped into the abyss." It is the force (mirror) that focuses the strength of the image, only to make it outwardly visible, to foretell its future progress.

Do Roland Barthes's words reveal the essence of Photography? I wonder. He has managed to do more and yet less than that: with unprofessional mind and words, he has asked a number of questions concerning the essence of a photographic image. What is more (what is more important), he has placed himself in front of the camera. In this way, he has led the *author* back into the text. The author's "leave" has come to an end.

A Ghibelline among Guelphs

I am trying to place Roland Barthes somewhere, in a category of the spirit. Easier said than done. Most minds are *atopic*. Barthes's strong, disturbing, whimsical *personality* resists all classifications. Yet even the most rebellious minds belong to one common family: the family of those who resist classifications and designations. In *A Lover's Discourse*, imitating Michelet (who imitated Dante in his turn), Barthes claims to be a Ghibelline, not a Guelph. He means he worships pleasure above laws, he serves his body rather than the Code.

In a 1979 interview, talking about his *Ghibellism*, Barthes comes very close to creating a theory on the importance of "affectivity" in criticism:

But his should be carried even further, almost to the postulation of a theory of affect as the motive force of criticism. A few years ago, criticism was still a very analytical activity, very rational, subject to a superego of impartiality and objectivity, and I wanted to react against this approach. (*Grain*, 331)

One must remember, though, that Barthes was among the authors of the semiologist *Code*, that he lived among the Guelphs of recent rhetoric, and waged battles meant to enthrone the rule of *la nouvelle critique*. A *Ghibelline* he may have been, but one watched by disciplinarian Guelphs. He is the creator of a system within which he feels ill at ease, a spirit unable to comply with a law for too long. He will not play second fiddle, come what may.

I wonder, is Barthes a *refined spirit* or a *geometrical* one? Does he stare at us with hard, unflinching eyes, or could we apply to him Pascal's description: "In the eyes he saw down into the heart and by the movement without he knew that which passed within" (539)? Reading Barthes, one cannot fail to realize that his essential *esprit de finesse* longs to turn into a geometrical spirit, but dissatisfaction sets in as soon as his desire has been fulfilled. *Geometry* stifles him, the *Law* maims his personality. The *Code* restricts the freedom of his movements. In the long run, his refinement usurps the tyrannical spiritual geometry. No sooner is Barthes settled in one place than he is already somewhere else. He systematically perverts concepts. He feels the field into which he was ushered with great pomp and which cannot choose but obey his intellectual rule. He does not mind plotting in secret against the doctrine of his own making.

Is Barthes then a Byzantine spirit of nuances, a subtle usurper of his own dogmas? Let us take our time before passing judgment. With Barthes one can never be sure where one stands. He is fidgety, restless, he resists all those who expect to see him safely categorized. In his own words, he "belongs nowhere," he is atopic, alien to all classifications, always on his way to another stronghold. This uninterrupted pace reminds me of the Renaissance artists wandering from royal court to royal court, from one prince to another. I suddenly recall Barthes's remark on the delights of laziness, the pleasure of doing nothing at all. I leave aside the image of the intrepid Renaissance spirit, whose eyes were wide open to take in the whole. Barthes formulates the theory of the fragment and claims to be particularly prepared to perceive the fragment and detect the way it works. Nevertheless, he can afford to be philosophical—and is. During the last years of his life, the word *philosophy* often recurred in his confessions. In a 1978 interview he said:

I've participated in many types of intellectual activity: the theory of the meaning, literary and social criticism. . . . But if there is a word that would truly define what happens within me, and not within my writings, it would be the word "philosopher," which does not refer to a degree of competence, because I have had no philosophical training. What I do within myself is philosophize, reflect on my own experience. This reflection is a joy and a benefit to me, and when I'm unable to pursue this activity, I become unhappy, because I am deprived of something important to me. Philosophizing? It belongs more to the ethical order than to the metaphysical one. (*Grain*, 306–07)

Philosophizing is, then, the necessary joy of the Ghibelline spirit. A Guelph does not waste time on meditation, but is busy obeying—not questioning—the law. Such is the fate of quite a lot of Barthes's admirers, small Guelphs of semiology, seduced by this hypocritical Ghibelline who lays down a method, then betrays them all in his mind, when on the hundredth evening, he furtively steals away from the window of rhetoric, just like the mandarin he once described. For ninety-nine nights this mandarin had been patiently striving to win the love of a ruthless princess, but impatience overcame him on what might have been the last night of waiting. E. M. Cioran talks about spirits that are interested in the process, and others eager to see the result, spirits interested in the origins and the progress, spirits that focus on the final point.[3] The first category is characterized by amplitude, the second by the superstition of conciseness. Where does Barthes belong, I wonder? To "finalists," maybe. He does have a genius for the nuance, and the terseness of his sentences is remarkable. He likes moralists, he is a brilliant moralist himself, one surrounded by lexical codes. But he is equally interested in the process, he is eager to find out how a text works, his curiosity cannot be appeased by the mere result. He is not an encyclopedic mind, he is not "intoxicated with possibilities" (Cioran), indeed, but his sentences are all ambiguous, his concepts are slippery. In short, here is one more classification that Barthes skillfully eludes.

Let us make one more attempt—the last—starting from Michel Tournier this time (*The Wind Spirit: An Autobiography*). One more Manicheistic text that Barthes rejects. He is not in love with the past, he is not obsessed with the future, he is displeased with the present. In a way, he inherits Gide's position, only his sensibility and his interests are different. He confesses somewhere that he likes to "write captions" for photographs (*Grain*, 359); since these photographs are images of the past, one might see Barthes as a primary spirit that longs nostalgically to become secondary. Anyway, he leaves the secondary status in a hurry, disenchanted with its maze of underground galleries; he drastically opposes traditional criticism, which does not prevent him from stating that analysis relies on *affectivity*. My endeavors to classify the unclassifiable Roland Barthes must cease now; none of the sentences I devise can ever pinpoint him. I shall accept his suggestion that he is a transitional spirit, hostile to both intellectual and ideological fanaticism. He created a method and left it behind as soon as he realized that his method was on the point of becoming the tool of intellectual violence ("the small local imperialisms"). Barthes refused to officiate in a church, he did his best not to turn into a merely geometrical spirit; he was fundamentally unable to exercise or bear terror in the life of the spirit.

I strongly feel that Barthes viewed the human calling just like Pascal: "man is born to pleasure; . . . he obeys his true law when he indulges in pleasure" (Pascal, 540).

In conclusion, Barthes does not want the human being to be enslaved to Codes; we are equally meant for meditation and pleasure. *Writing* is the highest of all pleasures. It is sacralized joy ("I definitely sanctify the bliss of writing," *Grain*, 278). The fact is obvious in all his texts, even where the Guelph spirit is stronger (*Writing Degree Zero, S/Z*). When Barthes writes, he is aware he distorts; analysis makes one lose the object of analysis among the nuances of possible interpretations. The sternest of demonstrations is partly a game, a pleasurable show. More than a *mathesis* ("a complete field of knowledge"), more than just an imitation (*mimesis*), literature is a vast system of signs, staging symbols (*semiosis*). The performance has not got very much to do with the substance; it relies heavily upon detours, returns, and joys of a symbolical nature (*Grain*, 239).

Well then, what about criticism, that secondary discourse? I reread the thick book including Roland Barthes's interviews between 1962 and 1980, hoping to detect in these confessions something of the semiologist's *personality*. The book is a document, an admirable text. In an oral, parallel discourse, Barthes retraces the steps of his works, with an air of intimacy and an affectionate irony that make readers feel flattered. Barthes is not eager to talk, so an interview is an intrusion, an aggression that is finally put up with. Semiology is a science focused on the act of writing; talking about it is of no avail. Barthes's joys flock around this act of writing. Talking about that requires a huge effort and inevitably brings about a sense of treason. Barthes manages to change the treason contained within the act of writing into a peculiar joy. On finishing *The Grain of the Voice*, I feel that, as an orator, Barthes is quite close to the *scripteur* in him. I find the same ambiguity of style, the same pleasure of the understatement, the same superior playfulness of the mind—the discourse is equally theatrical in both. Something elusive flits by, tenderness is there all along, and, once again, the ideas are ever so cleverly staged.

The strange thing about Barthes's oral discourse is that both questions and detours survive in it. The idea reaches the reader more easily, maybe, but a meaning never comes alone. The initial thought is clouded by some nuance that diverts us by means of the unexpected turn of a phrase, by repetitions or parentheses (which, in Barthes's case, instead of explaining, rather amplify and distort). I read Barthes's statement that "form and content cannot be separated" followed by "clarity does not mean very much" (*Grain*, 322) and I think I see what he means to say. But the semiotician wastes no time, he confuses me there and then by adding to the ambiguity of the *signifiants* an endless line of details and nuances; at the end of a paragraph, the aforesaid ambiguity is totally, hopelessly ambiguous.

Let us go back to Barthes's theory concerning the pleasure of the text, which turns up again, although the writer has already written an admirable book about it. I shall quote a breath-taking sentence: "There is probably nothing more cultural, and thus more social than pleasure" (*Grain*, 176). And further on: "An erotics of reading? Yes, on the condition that perversion—and I would almost say: fear—is never erased" (*Grain*, 176). We already know that Barthes sees the reader meeting the text in a kind of love encounter. He now adds perversity and, more dimly, a suggestion of fear. The act of reading is not innocent; no encounter with a book can be an innocent one. I am not going to devise an explanation for this sentence. Barthes himself does not do so. He feels called upon rather to state than to justify.

In these delightful "interviews" I am trying to find Barthes the man (the man whose mind is focused upon the act of *writing* and the act of *reading*); the man is now supposed to talk about these delicate matters in a manner different from that of his texts, where he can resort to multiple meanings and endless digressions. Several *biographèmes* look to me very interesting. The semiologist is unable to write in a hotel room. It is not because of the unfamiliar atmosphere; he fails to detect a meaningful order in the surrounding space (*Grain*, 180). This means that the structuralist needs a proper structure for the room he works in. He starts writing at 9:30 and stops at one in the afternoon. This discipline is essential to the quality of the text. He sleeps and works in the same room. His house has a corner for music, another for painting. He plays the piano every afternoon at 2:30, and once a week, often on Sundays, he paints. His country house is structured in the same way. His writing table must be wooden by all means ("I might say that I am on good terms with wood," *Grain*, 180). By its side, there is another table for books and papers. Although he does not require them all in the act of writing, they must be somewhere close by. Barthes dislikes libraries and is not very fond of erudition (*Grain*, 181). He is not even an exemplary reader. Like all of us, he reads with a certain purpose in mind, he takes out quotations, jots down his thoughts, and, as soon as his own plan has come into shape, he sets himself to writing. According to the reader's purpose (and position), there seem to be two kinds of books. Barthes reads some of them in bed, in the evening (linguistical or classical books), while he reads others seated at his writing table, in the morning. Here is the moralist's own interpretation of such habits: "the bed is the locus of irresponsibility. The table, that of responsibility" (*Grain*, 181).

If I am not mistaken, the semiologist reads the important books in an area of irresponsibility, while the less earnest books are read in the area of responsibility. There must be some compensation here that Barthes is unwilling to explain. He prefers to confess how pleased he is when he can cut off or correct a word, "temper some fit of elation or a figure of speech," find out a neologism—all these make Barthes experience "a gourmand savor of language, truly novelistic pleasure" (*Grain*, 182). I understand the subtlety and promptly check on my own the habits of this Alexandrine spirit. He experiences the act of writing as intensely as the moment of lovemaking, it is to him almost rapture, when he writes he is like someone gradually falling in love. Barthes's above-quoted description of the way he corrects or edits parts of a text involves an irrepressible tenderness, an irrepressible desire to "forge" the style, to clothe ideas in a mantle that, although not exquisite, must by all means be meaningful. The act of writing is usually associated with a long line of obstacles. Barthes turns these obstacles into pleasures, he devises the delight of writing. He exclaims: "I love writing" (*Grain*, 193). What would be the use of a rough bodiless text, from which the desire and the tenderness of the spirit are absent? Barthes seems to shrug his shoulders at this question and avert his eyes.

The act of reading is discussed too. In *The Grain of the Voice* and *Prétexte* (1978), Barthes talks more about the *act of reading* than the *act of writing*. He even makes up a little theory concerning "*l'écriture* of the act of reading." He dealt in turns with the relationship between *author* and *work*, with the act of *writing*, and finally with the *act of reading* and the *reader* (*Prétexte*, 152). I am more interested in Barthes as a reader than in his theories concerning the act of reading. I am suddenly disappointed when I read, "I read very little, and rather casually" (*Grain*, 199). Then further, "I am a casual reader, casual in the sense that I very quickly take the measure of my own pleasure" (*Grain*, 220). His pleasure comes first. Barthes provides now an explanation that was long due: he finds perversion in the act of reading, he describes the reader as a *cruiser*. He says that "perversion is the search for a pleasure that is not made profitable by a social end" (*Grain*, 232). All right, but what about the cruiser's approach to a book? Barthes provides further information about his own laziness and perversities as a reader. He can read a book in three different manners. First, he gazes at it. By merely looking, he establishes a link that, though flitting and shallow, is important nonetheless. His second manner of reading is programmatic. It envisages a new book by Barthes himself; the writer reads in order to start himself writing. In this particular case, Barthes is an earnest reader, seated at his table, always in the morning. His last manner of reading belongs to the evenings spent reclining in bed. This is how he reads classical authors (*Grain*, 273–74). Contemporary writers do not usually go beyond the first of these manners. Barthes merely gazes at their books. Few are those (like Sollers) whose inner code is examined by Barthes. Sollers is a fairly important contemporary, anyway. He is a first class theoretician who also writes novels. His theories on the novel become subject matter for the novels he writes. Like Ricardou, he sees literature as a commerce of *écritures*. With Sollers, Barthes feels at home: he can still indulge in his own interests and joys, which feed upon his meditations on concepts.

I cannot help noticing that, as a reader, Barthes is not at all original. His reading habits are rather commonplace. The quality of his reading can only be seen in his own texts, however. We shall never know whether he read Racine while he was reclining in bed in the evening, in a *space of irresponsibility*, or in the morning, programmatically seated at his writing table. *On Racine* is utterly devoid of laziness, anyway. It is an incisive, intensely coherent book, whose intellectual force is remarkably penetrating. Barthes was younger at the time he wrote it and had not discovered the charm of "la paresse [idleness]" yet. His texts had not yet "fallen in love," the classical authors' books were still safely deposited on his writing table: they had not been transferred to the sleeping room and had not yet become part of the night rituals.

In his late fifties, Barthes starts complaining that Paris has forgotten laziness (*Grain*, 339). The cafe no longer shelters idleness (reverie): "an idleness, but with refreshments." This writer in love with style is saddened by the passage of time, by his inability to find surroundings suited to slow reading and, moreover, to philosophizing—which is another face of the act of reading: while philosophizing, his mind reads an imaginary text and converses with the reader, this reader being Barthes himself. As a reader, Barthes seems to have experienced real happiness when he traveled to Japan. As he did not know the language at all, he found everywhere only the signs of an immense photograph. He was that reader who would not go beyond gazing. The result was a delightfully impressionistic book, which, I feel, is not devoid of a code. At last the Ghibelline gets the better of the Guelph; not for long, though. Once seated at his writing table, he is once more the law-giver, the maniac of ambiguity, the scribe. The Guelph devises codes within which to enclose the Ghibelline's joys.

Notes

Introduction

1. Andrei Codrescu, in *The Hole in the Flag* (New York: William Morrow, 1991), his post-Ceauşescu account of Romania, describes how only the writers kept their integrity during the recent bleak years in the country. He singles out Eugen Simion as one of the two critics these writers now defer to.

1. Proust on Sainte-Beuve's Method

1. Paul Bourget (1852–1935) was a critic, novelist, and friend of Henry James.

2. Proust is quoting here from Sainte-Beuve's "On Sainte-Beuve's Method," where the critic set out his principles of criticism (*Sainte-Beuve: Selected*, 281–92).

3. Pierre Bayle (1647–1706), a lexicographer, was the subject of some gossip included in the multivolume history of French literature written by Antoine Gachet d'Artigny (1704–78).

4. Emmanuel-Nicholas Viollet-le-Duc (1781–1857), not the nineteenth-century architect, was speaking of Jacques-Henri Bernardin de Saint-Pierre (1737–1814), a travel writer who wrote a biography of Rousseau.

5. Sainte-Beuve published a group of academic lectures about the Vicomte de Chateaubriand.

6. From 1849 to 1869 Sainte-Beuve's biographical criticism appeared as the *Causeries du lundis* [Monday Essays] in weekly pieces, mostly in *Le constitutionnel*. Sainte-Beuve's career had begun with pieces on literature in the *Globe* in the 1820s.

2. Proust on Sainte-Beuve on Baudelaire

1. Comte Daru (1767–1829) and Comte d'Alton Shée (1810–74) were very minor writers, the former perhaps more remembered for having been a cousin of Stendhal, the latter as having been a cousin of Sainte-Beuve.

2. In 1857 Baudelaire was fined for publishing in *Fleurs du mal* [Flowers of Evil] six poems the court considered immoral. Proust objected, as seen here, to Sainte-Beuve's reluctance to support Baudelaire openly.

3. Kamchatka, being at the eastern extreme of Siberia, represents the margins of the world.

3. Balzac's "Vulgar Genius"

1. Jean Santeuil is Proust's title character in a posthumous novel, considered to contain much that influenced what later became *Remembrance of Things Past*.

2. Of course, I am not the first to notice this contradiction. Bernard de Fallois, in his quoted "Preface" (33), makes it very clear: "Proust hopes to find in Sainte-Beuve's character an explanation for the inadequacy of his method." Others have taken up the suggestion: J. Belaval, "L'homme et l'oeuvre," *Nouvelle revue française* (February–March 1966); Dominique Fernandez, *L'Arbre jusqu'aux racines*. [Author's note]

4. Sainte-Beuve: The Critic Who Was Never Right

1. In his notice on the life of Sainte-Beuve at the beginning of the two-volume *Oeuvres*, Maxime Leroy cites these assessments of the French romantics from the *Memoir* of Comte d'Alton-Shée (1:25). Sainte-Beuve had an affair with Victor Hugo's wife, Adèle. George Sand (1804–76) was prolific in her writings and in her lovers. Juliette Drouet (1806–83) was an actress who, as Hugo's mistress, joined him—and his family—in exile. Mme. Biard was another actress with whom Hugo had an affair. Madame Delessert had a long affair with Alfred de Musset (1810–57), who was engaged in a long and stormy liaison with George Sand, who also had been a lover of Franz Liszt (1811–86), the Hungarian composer and pianist.

2. Alfred de Vigny (1797–1863) was a poet and novelist; Louis-Mathieu Molé (1781–1855) a statesman who wrote of his experiences; Victor Jacquemont (1801–32) a naturalist and friend of Stendhal and Mérimée; Jean-Jacques Ampère (1800–1864) the son of the great physicist and friend of various French romantic writers.

3. Pierre-Paul Royer-Collard (1763–1845) was professor of the history of philosophy at the Sorbonne. Pierre-Jean de Béranger (1780–1857) was a popular poet of his day.

4. Ernest Feydeau (1821–73) was the author of the popular *Fanny*.

5. Louise de Boigne (1781–1866) and Albertine de Broglie (1797–1838), Madame de Staël's daughter, both presided over salons.

6. Albert Thibaudet (1874–1936) was a renowned literary critic.

7. The Goncourt brothers, Edmond (1822–96) and Jules (1830–70), were novelists and men of letters. Edmond's bequest is responsible for the Goncourt prize for prose.

8. Nerval (1808–55), as Proust indicates, left a large body of work, most notably his poetry.

9. Alfred-August Cuvillier Fleury (1802–77) was a literary critic and contemporary of Sainte-Beuve.

10. Jean de La Bruyère (1645–96), like Virgil, of course, represents the classic as model.

11. Theodore Barrière (1823–77) was a dramatist; Alexandre Dumas *fils* (1824–95) a dramatist credited by some with reviving the French stage; Eugène Sue (1804–57) a popular and somewhat exuberant novelist; Frédéric Soulié (1800–1847) a journalistic fiction writer; Charles Monselet (1825–88) a journalistic critic; and Jean-Emile-Horace Vernet (1789–1863) a minor painter.

5. Proust against the Deeper Self

1. Villeparisis is a character in *Remembrance of Things Past*.

2. Champlâtreux, where people of fashion and talent gathered, was one of the country estates of Comte Molé, the July Monarchy's foreign minister.

3. In chapter 5 of *Contre Sainte-Beuve*, entitled "The Article in *Le Figaro*," Proust describes at length relishing and prolonging the experience of first seeing his work in print. Cf. *Art*, 70–82.

6. Proust's Biographism

1. Madame Michelet was the wife of Jules Michelet (1798–1874), the greatest French historian of the nineteenth century.

2. Not to be confused with the eighteenth-century political philosopher Charles Montesquieu, comte Robert de Montesquiou (1855–1921), aesthete and minor writer, was an intimate of Proust's and served as something of a model for Charlus in *Remembrance of Things Past*.

3. Georges Rodenbach (1855–98) was a Belgian symbolist poet.

4. Robert de Flers (1872–1927) was a minor French dramatist.

7. The *I* Is an Other

1. Critics associated with *Tel Quel*, the journal edited by Philippe Sollers, who were known for taking poststructuralist positions to their limits. Best known among this group is Julia Kristeva.

2. *Le livre, instrument spirituel* (1895). I quote from *Oeuvres complètes*, introduction, bibliography, illustrations, and notes by Henri Mondor and G. Jean-Aubry (Paris: Editions Gallimard, 1945), 378. The same idea had been voiced by Mallarmé four years earlier, in his answer to Jules Huret's inquiry. The answer was published in *L'Echo de Paris* (1891), then reprinted in another volume, issued during the same year. Mallarmé says, "Au fond le monde est fait pour aboutir à un beau livre [at bottom, the world is made to result in a beautiful book]." [Author's note] Huret (1864–1915) was a journalist who chronicled the transition from naturalism to symbolism.

3. Philippe-Auguste Villiers de l'Isle-Adam (1838–89), novelist and dramatist, is considered one of the early symbolists.

8. Valéry as Precursor

1. All of these are works by Valéry. "Monsieur Teste" is a fictional character created by Valéry in 1896.

2. Constantin Noica (1908–87), Romanian Heideggerian existentialist, was an associate of Mircea Eliade in the 1930s.

9. Valéry as Biographer

1. Gustave Lanson (1857–1934) was a critic and literary historian whose positivistic principles formed the basis for an unrealized project to gather all facts and information about literary figures into one source to provide the data for an assessment of the authors.

12. Probing the Unconscious

1. Genetic criticism is a name given to forms of psychocriticism.

2. Charles Mauron (1899–1966), translator and aesthetic formalist, was also a psychological critic.

3. The designation *Geneva critic* (here applied to Starobinski, later to Georges Poulet and Jean-Pierre Richard) refers to those thinkers connected with the University of Geneva who wrote from a phenomenological base and who sometimes were interested in psychobiography. The thrust of their thought was invariably antiformalist.

13. Sartre, the Writer, and the Reader

1. The Constance school of criticism, centered in the University of Constance, put forth the *Rezeptionstheorie*, a concentration on the role of the reader in the

engagement with literary texts. Its most notable figures are Hans Robert Jauss and Wolfgang Iser.

16. Critical Methods and Literature

1. G. Calinescu (1899–1965) was a Romanian critic and literary historian.

17. Starobinski and Method

1. Leo Spitzer (1887–1960) gives his name to a stylistic approach to literary criticism invoking a linguistic analysis of style distinct from scientific linguistics.

18. Barthes and the Author

1. Lucien Goldmann (1913–70), a sociological critic, played a large role in genetic structuralism.

2. Barthes used the concept of *university criticism* several times (in *Critical Essays*) when he talked about the old positivist spirit, which, indeed, was born and bred at the Sorbonne. Meanwhile, *la nouvelle critique* had taken hold in the university. A few years before his death, Barthes himself, once a heretic, had been accepted by Collège de France. What we today term *university criticism* is, in fact, *immanent criticism*, the *criticism of significances*, i.e., *la nouvelle critique*. [Author's note]

3. It was said that Racine wrote *Andromaque* for the marquise du Parc (?1633–68), his mistress at the time. Nero and Burrhus appear in Racine's *Britannicus*. Nicholas Vitart provided for Racine a link between the Jansenists of Port Royal and the royal court.

20. Barthes as Biographer

1. Giovanni Pico della Mirandola was a fourteenth-century Florentine humanist.

21. An Array of Selves

1. Taine uses "race" in the sense of "nation," as one might have spoken of "the English race."

2. Nichita Stănescu (1933–82) was a noted Romanian poet.

3. Mihail Dragomirescu (1868–1942) was a Romanian academic critic.

4. George Bacovia (1881–1957) was a Romanian poet.

5. I. L. Cargiale (1852–1912) was Romania's preeminent dramatist.

6. Marin Sorescu (1933–   ), Romanian poet and parodist, was Romanian minister of culture after 1989.

7. Michel Déon is a French novelist.

8. Boris de Schloezer speaks about a " mythic self" in Bach's music "as real as the *self* of Bach the man" (97). [Author's note]

22. Who Speaks in the Text?

1. Liviu Rebreanu (1885–1944) is one of the fathers of the modern Romanian novel.

23. Eliot and Biography

1. Paul Zarifopol (1874–1934) was a critic and essayist noted for his sarcasm.

2. Mihai Eminescu (1850–1889) was the great national poet of Romania.

24. Writing about the Author

1. Ioan Slavici (1848–1925) was a poet and writer.

2. Louis-Ferdinand Céline (1894–1961) was a French novelist whose work engendered controversy and hostility.

3. Tudor Arghezi (1880–1967) was a major Romanian poet.

25. Sartre: The Imposture of Childhood and the Birth of Literature

1. Pardaillan is the heroic character in a work by Michel Zévaco (1860–1910), published in *Le matin*.

2. Georges Courteline (1861–1929) was a turn-of-the-century French humorist.

3. The title character in *Michael Strogoff, a Courier of the Czar* by Jules Verne (1876).

27. Ionesco: Childhood and Light, Literature and the World on the First Day of Creation

1. Rimbaud's *car je est un autre* is changed in Ionesco's writing to the technically correct *je suis un autre*, changing *is* to *am*.

2. Le Grand Condé (1621–86) was a correspondent and, under Louis XIV, a successful military commander.

3. Philokalia are Eastern Orthodox Christian spiritual writings designed to lead to mastery of physical states, analogous in some respects to Sufi texts. Alain

Fournier (1886–1914), author of the well-received novel *Le Grand Meaulnes*, was killed in World War I.

4. Horia Lovinescu (1917–   ), Ion Vinea (1895–1964), and Tudor Vianu (1897–1964) are leading Romanian dramatists.

5. Mircea Eliade writes in his journal (October 4, 1945): "I spent the afternoon with Eugène Ionesco. We had a long conversation. For the last few years he has been writing several hundred pages which will be added to his diary, only he wonders whether this can be of any interest to anyone. In Romania there lives now a new generation. Our own has come to an end. I reply that a diary is interesting at any time; it is a document and a testimony" (Eliade, 10). [Author's note]

28. Barthes: The Return of the Author to the Text

1. Jules Lemaître (1853–1914), a drama critic, was given to strong critical opinions.

2. In *Roland Barthes by Roland Barthes* the father's photo is accompanied by the following words: "The father, dead very early (in the war), was lodged in no memorial or sacrificial discourse. By maternal intermediary his memory—never an oppressive one—merely touched the surface of childhood with an almost silent bounty" (15). This is as much as to say that the father is absent from the discourse of remembrances. He is absent from the discourse of childhood as well. The *son* is guided toward his father's image by his *mother*. Barthes's image of paternity amounts to its total absence from the text. [Author's note]

3. E. M. Cioran (1911–95) was a Romanian philosopher of a pessimistic bent who, like Ionesco, spent most of his life in France.

Works Cited

Allemand, André. *Nouvelle critique, nouvelle perspective*. Neuchâtel: La Baconnière, 1967.

Barthes, Roland. *Camera Lucida*. Trans. Richard Howard. New York: Hill and Wang, 1981.

———. *Critical Essays*. Trans. Richard Howard. Evanston: Northwestern University Press, 1972.

———. *Criticism and Truth*. Trans. Katrine Pilcher Keuneman. Minneapolis: University of Minnesota Press, 1987.

———. *The Empire of Signs*. Trans. Richard Howard. New York: Hill and Wang, 1982.

———. *The Fashion System*. Trans. Matthew Ward and Richard Howard. New York: Hill and Wang, 1983.

———. *The Grain of the Voice: Interviews 1962–1980*. Trans. Linda Coverdale. New York: Hill and Wang, 1985.

———. *A Lover's Discourse: Fragments*. Trans. Richard Howard. Hammondsworth: Penguin, 1990.

———. *Michelet par lui-même*. Paris: Editions du Seuil, 1965.

———. *On Racine*. Trans. Richard Howard. New York: Hill and Wang, 1964.

———. *The Pleasure of the Text*. Trans. Richard Miller. New York: Hill and Wang, 1975.

———. *Prétexte*. Paris: Union Générale d'Editions, 1978.

———. *Roland Barthes by Roland Barthes*. Trans. Richard Howard. New York: Hill and Wang, 1977.

———. *Sade, Fourier, Loyola*. Trans. Richard Miller. New York: Hill and Wang, 1976.

———. *Sur la littérature*. Grenoble: Presses Universitaires de Grenoble, 1980.

———. *S/Z*. Trans. Richard Miller. New York: Hill and Wang, 1974.

Bataille, Georges. *L'Expérience intérieure*. Paris: Gallimard, 1943.

Belaval, J. "L'homme et l'oeuvre." *Nouvelle revue française* (Feb.–Mar. 1966): 238–48, 421–42.

Blanchot, Maurice. *Le livre à venir*. Paris: Gallimard, 1959.

Boisdeffre, Pierre. *Vie de André Gide*. Paris: Hachette, 1970.

Bonnefoy, Claude. *Entretiens avec Eugène Ionesco*. Paris: Editions Pierre Belfond, 1966.

Doubrovsky, Serge. *Corneille et la dialectique du héros*. Paris: Gallimard, 1963.

————. "Critique et existence." In *Les Chemins actuels de la critique*. Paris: Union Générale d'Editions, 1968.

————. *Pourquoi la nouvelle critique?* Paris: Mercure de France, 1967.

Eliade, Mircea. *Fragments d'un journal*. Paris: Gallimard, 1977.

Eliot, T. S. *The Frontiers of Criticism*. Minneapolis: University of Minnesota, 1956.

Fallois, Bernard de. "Préface." In *Contre Sainte-Beuve* by Marcel Proust, 7–53. Paris: Gallimard, 1954.

Fernandez, Dominique. *L'Arbre jusqu'aux racines*. Paris: Editions Bernard Gasset, 1972.

Freud, Sigmund. *The Standard Edition of the Complete Psychological Works of Sigmund Freud*. London: Hogarth Press, 1974.

Genette, Gérard. *Figures I*. Paris: Editions du Seuil, 1966.

————. *Figures II*. Paris: Editions du Seuil, 1966.

————. *Figures III*. Paris: Editions du Seuil, 1972.

Ionesco, Eugène. *Antidotes*. Paris: Gallimard, 1977.

————. *The Colonel's Photograph*. Trans. Jean Stewart. New York: Grove Press, 1969.

————. *Découvertes*. Geneva: Albert Skira, 1969.

————. *Fragments of a Journal*. Trans. Jean Stewart. New York: Grove Press, 1968.

————. *Un homme en question*. Paris: Gallimard, 1979.

————. *Present Past, Past Present*. New York: Grove Press, 1971.

Jauss, Hans Robert. *Toward an Aesthetics of Reception*. Trans. Timothy Bahti. Minneapolis: University of Minnesota Press, 1982.

Jean, Raymond. "Une situation critique." In *Les chemins actuels de la critique*, ed. Serge Doubrovsky, 101–7. Paris: Union Générale d'Editions, 1968.

Kristeva, Julia. "La sémiologie: Science critique et/ou critique de la science." In *Théorie d'ensemble*, ed. Philippe Sollers, 80–93. Paris: Editions du Seuil, 1968.

Lanson, Gustave. *Essais de méthode, de critique et d'histoire littéraire*. Ed. Henri Peyre. Paris: Hachette, 1965.

Léonard, Albert. *La crise du concept de littérature en France au XXᵉ siècle*. Paris: José Corti, 1974.

Mallarmé, Stéphane. *Oeuvres complètes*. Paris: Gallimard, 1945.

————. *Selected Poetry and Prose*. Ed. Mary Ann Caws. New York: New Directions, 1982.

Malraux, André. *Anti-Memoirs*. Trans. Terence Kilmartin. New York: Holt, Rinehart and Winston, 1968.

————. *Felled Oaks*. New York: Holt, Rinehart and Winston, 1972.

————. *Lazarus*. Trans. Terence Kilmartin. New York: Holt, Rinehart and Winston, 1977.

Mauron, Charles. *Introduction to the Psychoanalysis of Mallarmé*. Trans. Archibald Henderson, Jr., and Will L. McLendon. Berkeley: University of California Press, 1963.

Pascal, Blaise. "Discourse sur les passions de l'amour." In *Oeuvres complètes*. Paris: Gallimard, 1954.

Peyrefitte, Roger. *Propos secrets*. Paris: Albin Michel, 1971.

Picon, Gaëtan. *Malraux par lui-même*. Paris: Editions du Seuil, 1953.

Poe, Edgar Allan. *The Complete Poems and Stories of Edgar Allan Poe*. Vol. 2. New York: Knopf, 1951.

Poulet, Georges. "Préface" to *Littérature et sensation* by Jean-Pierre Richard. Paris: Editions du Seuil, 1954.

Proust, Marcel. *Contre Sainte-Beuve précédé de Pastiches et mélanges et suivi de Essais et articles*. Ed. Pierre Clarac. Paris: Gallimard, 1971.

————. *On Art and Literature, 1896–1919*. Trans. Sylvia Townsend Warner. New York: Meridian Books, 1958.

————. *Pleasures and Days*. Trans. Louise Varese, Gerard Hopkins, and Barbara Dupee. New York: Howard Fertig, 1978.

————. *Sur Baudelaire, Flaubert, et Morand*. Ed. Antoine Campagnon. Brussels: Editions Complexe, 1987.

Raymond, Marcel. *Paul Valéry et la tentation de l'esprit*. Neuchâtel: Editions de la Baconnière, 1964.

Ricardou, Jean. *Nouveau roman: Hier, aujourd'hui*. Vol. 1. Paris: Union Générale d'Editions, 1972.

————. *Pour une théorie du nouveau roman*. Paris: Editions du Seuil, 1971.

Rimbaud, Arthur. *Complete Works, Selected Letters*. Trans. Wallace Fowlie. Chicago: University of Chicago Press, 1966.

Ruskin, John. *Sésame et le lys*. Translation, notes, and preface by Marcel Proust. Paris: Mercure de France, 1906.

Sainte-Beuve, Charles Augustin. *Oeuvres*. 2 vols. Paris: Gallimard, 1956.

Sartre, Jean-Paul. *Baudelaire*. Trans. Martin Turnell. Norfolk, Conn.: New Directions, 1950.

————. *Being and Nothingness*. Trans. Hazel E. Barnes. New York: Philosophical Library, 1956.

————. *The Family Idiot*. Trans. Carol Cosman. Chicago: University of Chicago Press, 1981.

————. *Saint Genet: Actor and Martyr*. Trans. Bernard Frechtman. New York: Georg Braziller, 1963.

————. *Search for a Method*. Trans. Hazel E. Barnes. New York: Knopf, 1963.

————. *Situations VIII*. Paris: Gallimard, 1972.

————. *Situations IX*. Paris: Gallimard, 1972.

————. *What Is Literature?* Trans. Bernard Frechtman. New York: Harper and Row, 1965.

————. *The Words*. Trans. Bernard Frechtman. New York: George Braziller, 1964.

Schloezer, Boris de. "L'Oeuvre, l'auteur, et l'homme." In *Les chemins actuels de la critique*. Paris: Union Générale d'Editions, 1968.

Simion, Eugen. *Timpul trăirii, timpul mărturisirii, Jurnal parizian*. Bucharest: Cartea Romaneasca, 1977.

Sollers, Philippe. "Ecriture et révolution." In *Théorie d'ensemble*, ed. Philippe Sollers, 67–79. Paris: Editions du Seuil, 1968.

———. *Logiques*. Paris: Editions du Seuil, 1968.

Starobinski, Jean. *Jean-Jacques Rousseau: Transparency and Obstruction*. Trans. Arthur Goldhammer. Chicago: University of Chicago Press, 1988.

———. *La relation critique*. Paris: Gallimard, 1970.

Taine, H. A. *History of English Literature*. Trans. H. Van Laun. New York: Henry Holt and Company, 1879.

Todorov, Tzvetan. "Poïétique et poétique selon Lessing." In *Recherches poïétiques I*, 25–41. Paris: Editions Klincksieck, 1975.

Tournier, Michel. *The Wind Spirit: An Autobiography*. Boston: Beacon Press, 1988.

Valéry, Paul. *The Collected Works of Paul Valéry*. Vol. 1. Trans. David Paul. Princeton: Princeton University Press, 1971.

———. *The Collected Works of Paul Valéry*. Vol. 2. Trans. Hilary Corke. Princeton: Princeton University Press, 1969.

———. *The Collected Works of Paul Valéry*. Vol. 3. Trans. David Paul and Robert Fitzgerald. Princeton: Princeton University Press, 1960.

———. *The Collected Works of Paul Valéry*. Vol. 4. Trans. William McCausland Stewart. Princeton: Princeton University Press, 1956.

———. *The Collected Works of Paul Valéry*. Vol. 6. Trans. Jackson Matthews. Princeton: Princeton University Press, 1973.

———. *The Collected Works of Paul Valéry*. Vol. 7. Trans. Denise Folliot. Princeton: Princeton University Press, 1958.

———. *The Collected Works of Paul Valéry*. Vol. 8. Trans. Malcolm Cowley and James R. Lawler. Princeton: Princeton University Press, 1972.

———. *The Collected Works of Paul Valéry*. Vol. 9. Trans. Martin Turnell. Princeton: Princeton University Press, 1968.

———. *The Collected Works of Paul Valéry*. Vol. 10. Trans. Denise Folliot and Jackson Matthews. Princeton: Princeton University Press, 1962.

———. *The Collected Works of Paul Valéry*. Vol. 13. Trans. Ralph Manheim. Princeton: Princeton University Press, 1964.

———. *The Collected Works of Paul Valéry*. Vol. 14. Trans. Stuart Gilbert. Princeton: Princeton University Press, 1970.

———. *The Collected Works of Paul Valéry*. Vol. 15. Trans. Marthiel Matthews and Jackson Matthews. Princeton: Princeton University Press, 1975.

———. *Oeuvres*. Vol. 2. Paris: Gallimard, 1960.

Index